JOSEPH

FRUITFUL IN AFFLICTION

DON ANDERSON

LOIZEAUX BROTHERS
Neptune, New Jersey

JOSEPH: FRUITFUL IN AFFLICTION
First Edition, September 1988

Printed in the United States of America. A publication of Loizeaux Brothers, Inc., a nonprofit organization devoted to the Lord's work and to the spread of his truth.

Library of Congress Cataloging-in-Publication Data

Anderson, Don, 1933-
Joseph: fruitful in affliction.

Bibliography: p.
1. Joseph (Son of Jacob) 2. Bible. O.T.—Biography. 3. Bible. O.T. Genesis XXXVII-L—Criticism, interpretation, etc. I. Title.
BS580.J6A7 1988 222'.110924 88-9476
ISBN 0-87213-004-5

The author wishes to acknowledge the editorial assistance of Jane Rodgers.

Dedication

To my daughter Becky, who has been fruitful in affliction. It was she who wrote the following:

Dear Dad,

I remember the Christmas I gave you the plaque you now keep on your desk that says, "It is well with my soul." As time goes on, I realize how much more important it is that it is well with my soul than for it to be well with my physical body.

I recall that when I was on dialysis and my eyesight was getting worse, I expressed to Ray my fears of being blind. I'll never forget his words. "Honey, I know that would be hard on you," he said, "but all it would mean to me is that I'd get to walk a little closer to you." This not only reminds me of God's unconditional love, but it also reminds me of the way suffering lets us "walk a little closer" to God.

When I was younger, I prayed often to be healed of my illness. I always got the same answer as the apostle Paul: God's grace would be sufficient for me. Now I understand how wonderful God's grace is. The Lord healed me emotionally by doing a miracle and bringing Ray into my life. God has given me more love and happiness during my marriage than most people experience in a lifetime.

When I am tempted to fear death, I remind myself that it is God's love flowing through Ray to me that brings me so much joy in this life. I also think of how wonderful it will be when I do get to heaven and experience Christ's pure love.

Dad, it is seeing God in the lives of others, like you, Mom, and Ray, that strengthens my faith and keeps me strong. Thanks, Dad.

I love you,
Becky

אֲנִ֤י לְדוֹדִי֙ וְדוֹדִ֣י לִ֔י

I am my beloved's, and my beloved is mine
Song of Solomon 6:3

πάυτα χαὶ έυ πᾶσιυ Χφιστόζ

Christ is all and in all
Colossians 3:11

Contents

Foreword 11

How to Survive . . . and Soar 13

PART ONE
The Training

1. Dreamer in the Pit
Genesis 37 27

2. Just Say No
Genesis 39 53

3. On Hold
Genesis 40 86

4. In His Time
Genesis 41 109

PART TWO
The Testing

5. The Dreams Unfold
Genesis 42 *139*

6. Sovereign Stress
Genesis 43 *167*

7. Passing the Test
Genesis 44 *193*

PART THREE
The Triumph and Transition

8. Freedom of Forgiveness
Genesis 45 *217*

9. Trust and Obey
Genesis 46 and 47 *243*

10. Nearing the Finish Line
Genesis 48 *273*

11. Going Out a Winner
Genesis 49 *300*

12. Rites of Passage
Genesis 50 *326*

Reflections 346

Suggested Readings 352

Acknowledgments 354

Foreword

It was early October of 1986; the year had been a financial disaster for Texas and for me. My income is derived from oil, farming, and real estate. Since January, the price of oil had dropped from $23 to $11 per barrel. Our wheat crop had the lowest yield in the fourteen years that I had owned our farms. The Dallas real estate market was the worst I'd seen in the twenty-two years I had been in business. I was clearly in a financial crisis!

Not only were my finances a shambles, but my dad had died suddenly just sixty days earlier. Although I had the assurance that he had gone to be with the Lord, I missed him very much and this added to the pressure.

During this time, my wife Becky and I were attending one of Don Anderson's Bible study series. After class one night, Don handed me a set of tapes and said, "I want you to meet my friend, Joseph." The gray cover read, "Discover How to Face the Trials, Tests, Traumas and Temptations of Life Triumphantly." Was this great timing!

Over the next few weeks I spent twelve hours listening to those tapes, and developing a respect for and closeness with a man who clearly had many more problems than I faced—and who had responded to his circumstances with clear principles, resulting in clear victory. It was especially comforting to know that when his dad died Joseph experienced the same feelings of loss that I did. As I look back on those hours spent in my first serious study of the man who has become *my* friend—Joseph—I still recall the excitement of the picture of God's plan as it unfolded. I now feel excitement for you as you begin this same study, for the fourteen chapters of Genesis that record Joseph's experiences present a beautiful road map for successful living.

Joseph taught me that God does not always remove the pressure, but is always with us in the pressure. He wants only our best, and uses those pressures to bring about the "perfect result, that [we] may be perfect and complete, lacking in nothing" (James 1:4 NASB).

My study of Joseph and the accompanying hours of prayer and reflection gave me a new outlook on life. It is my prayer that through the pages of this book, God will reveal to you what your true needs are, and that you will come to appreciate, as I have, the wisdom of *our* friend, Joseph.

DICK CREWS, PARTNER
CREWS-LORIMER AND ASSOCIATES
DALLAS, TEXAS

How to Survive . . . and Soar

Composer Irving Berlin once said, "Life is ten percent what you make it and ninety percent how you take it"—insightful words from the man who displayed eternal optimism by lyricizing that he was dreaming of a white Christmas with every Christmas card he wrote. It isn't always easy to have such a positive outlook.

In fact, let's be honest; life is tough. We're asked to take a lot as we plod along. And what is perhaps most difficult about living our threescore and ten is that somewhere along the way we are forced to acknowledge the fact that most of life is beyond our control. While undergoing a tremendous crisis of meaning in his own life, King Solomon realized this truth. He wrote in Ecclesiastes 8:7-8:

> Since no man knows the future,
> who can tell him what is to come?
> No man has power over the wind to contain it;
> so no one has power over the day of his death.

This honest admission of human helplessness should not be surprising, until one recalls that Solomon was the wealthiest, most powerful man alive at the time he penned those words—an ancient Hughes, Rockefeller, or Getty, if ever there was one. He possessed huge silver and gold reserves and vast landholdings; he ordered and financed the construction of architectural wonders; legions of soldiers, servants, and women fulfilled his slightest whim. If even a man as important and powerful as Solomon could not control his destiny, then who can? The plain truth is that most of life is beyond the command of those who must live it.

Just ask Paul and Silas, if you don't agree. The apostle and his companion followed Paul's vision to travel to Europe in Acts 16, then while teaching the gospel in the city of Philippi in the region of Macedonia found themselves dragged before the local justices of the peace, beaten, and imprisoned (Acts 16:14ff). Paul and Silas couldn't control a tough situation, but they could control their responses to it. And God used their circumstances greatly to his glory. Acts 16:25 reveals that, chained deep inside the Philippian prison, they prayed and sang hymns of praise to God instead of bellyaching about the treatment they'd received. Suddenly, a tremendous earthquake shook the jail, the locked doors flew open, the prisoners' shackles dropped off, yet Paul and Silas did not do the natural thing and attempt to escape. They controlled their responses by staying put, and because of their obedience a frightened jailer and his family came to know Jesus Christ as Lord (Acts 16:25-34).

Learning the Hard Way

1986 proved to be the year in which the entire state of Texas was force-fed the lesson that life is beyond our control. Deemed "The Year That Went Belly-Up" by *Texas Monthly* magazine, 1986 was doomed to begin and conclude on a long, drawn-out, sour note, thanks largely to the machinations of Sheik Ahmed Zaki Yamani, then oil minister of Saudi Arabia. With Yamani's policy of increasing his country's oil production, oil prices fell drastically worldwide, and a Texas economy, which for years had boomed with the climbing price of crude, suddenly went bust. In April of '86, the price of a barrel of oil dropped below $10, and by July there were fewer than 650 rigs pumping what once was called black gold.

With the collapse of the oil industry came a severe downturn in commercial and residential real estate in Texas. Seventy-two high-rise office buildings stood empty in the city of Houston. Multimillion-dollar houses in Dallas couldn't be unloaded for half their hefty pricetags. Corporations laid off huge numbers of workers and pulled out of major cities. Borrowers defaulted on oil- and real estate-related loans to the point where savings institutions and banks were foundering. Things got so out of hand that, as a friend of mine put it, "Most of my pals started pawning their Rolexes and buying alarm clocks!" We usually self-confident Texans found ourselves powerless to stop the economic disintegration. And frankly, 1987 wasn't a whole lot better. Recent events on Wall Street indicate our entire country is following suit, too. October of '87 ushered in the worst stock market downslide since the crash of '29. A buddy of mine told me that when the recent big drop took place in the market, he owned stocks in two industries: paper towels and revolving doors. The crash came, and he was wiped out before he could turn around!

Irving Berlin was right. In spite of our highly-touted American ingenuity, independence, and get-up-and-go, life is not so much what we make it but how we take it. Like Paul and Silas, we cannot control the circumstances; we can determine our responses to them. When digesting life, we can expect to swallow our share of suffering. As we've found in Texas, there will be lay-offs, shake-ups, and fold-ups. On more personal levels, we'll experience the deaths of loved ones, disappointments in our families, rough spots in our relationships with friends. We'll find ourselves unable to save a parent from the ravages of cancer, an adult son from making a foolish career decision, a best pal from leaving his wife for another woman. Try as we would, we won't be able to avoid the trials that God permits in our lives. But even in the midst of suffering we can learn to cope and even to praise the Lord who holds all events of our existence securely in his hand. A friend of mine put it this way: "We can't give in to forces, faces, farces, fences, frustrations, fantasies, fears, fatigues, faults, forecasts, fates, frenzies, or foes. We've got to just hang onto our faith."

Yes, dealing with the reality of circumstances beyond our control is a part of life that we must accept. Perhaps no biblical character does it more beautifully, more consistently, and more triumphantly than the patriarch Joseph. His life is like a fabulous drama. Each act of the play builds upon the other and, when the final curtain drops, we find ourselves singing the doxology in wonder and awe.

The Big Four

Who is this man Joseph? He is one of the "big four" in the history of Israel—the fourth in a line of Hebrew patriarchs which begins with Abraham, and continues with Isaac and Jacob.

Abraham: the Power of God

In Abraham's life we especially witness the power of God. Genesis chapters 11 and 12 tell us how the Lord called the obscure seventy-five-year-old sheepmaster forth from a pagan village and directed him to journey toward an unknown land. God promised Abraham (or Abram, as he was then known) that he would exalt Abraham's name and multiply his descendants. The Lord further pledged to bless the ones who blessed Abraham and his seed, and curse those who cursed him. Finally, God promised that through the line of Abraham all the peoples of the earth would be blessed (Genesis 12:1-3).

In these promises—which we know as the abrahamic covenant—God revealed that from Abraham's loins would spring forth a significant race of people, the Jews or Hebrews. Through this line would come a special descendant whose presence would be a blessing to the entire world, even the entire universe! This descendant is, of course, Jesus Christ, the God-man, the greatest earthly seed of Abraham and the divine son of God (Matthew 1:1-17; Romans 9:1-5).

There was a problem with all of this, though. At the time when Abraham received the call of God in his hometown, Ur of the Chaldees, he had no children. His wife Sarah (then called Sarai) was sixty-five and barren (Genesis 11:30). If they were ever to have a child it had to be the result of a miracle . . . and so it was. Twenty-five years later the awesome power of God displayed itself, as Sarah (then ninety years old) gave birth to the baby Isaac (Genesis 21:2). Through this much-loved boy, the issue of a womb long dead by human standards, the promises of God to Abraham continued.

Isaac: The Provision of God

While the power of God is especially made manifest in his father's life, Isaac's biography gives vivid testimony to the provision of God. Isaac himself was born into the world as a result of that provision; he was a truly amazing gift specially delivered to two geriatric parents.

When Isaac was a young man, his life was once again marked by the provision of God as he obediently accompanied his grieving yet faithful father to the top of Mount Moriah. There the boy submitted as his elderly father, following instructions from God (Genesis 22:2), bound him with cords and laid him upon a crude stone altar. The Bible records no hint of resistance on the part of Isaac as Abraham, preparing to sacrifice his son, lifted a knife-wielding hand into position for its awful downward thrust. And then marvelously—miraculously—the voice of the angel of the Lord rang forth from the heavens, stopping Abraham from his dreadful task. Abraham lifted his eyes to see that God had supplied another suitable sacrifice: a ram caught in a nearby thicket. Isaac was spared as God provided (Genesis 22).

As Isaac grew older, we see that the Lord gave him a beautiful wife, Rebekah (Genesis 24). When the pair could not conceive, Isaac prayed and God answered with the provision of twin boys (Genesis 25:19-26). Truly, from the moment of his own birth, the patriarch's life was characterized by the provision of his heavenly father. And through Isaac, the line of the promised seed continued.

Jacob: the Purpose of God

The twins born to Rebekah and Isaac were called Esau and Jacob. Perhaps never have two brothers been as completely different from each other as these. Esau, the elder, grew into a hairy, rough-and-tumble outdoorsman, a man who disdained responsibility, preferring the sensual to the spiritual. Jacob, though wily and scheming, was a man confronted with God's eternal purpose on numerous occasions, and in his latter years became an individual sensitive to his Lord.

In the life of Jacob we see God's purpose worked out as he selected the younger twin (Genesis 25:23). It was Jacob, not Esau, who was divinely chosen to receive the promises made long before to Abraham. From the line of Jacob, not Esau, would eventually spring forth the messiah, Jesus Christ.

Joseph: the Plan of God

Many assume that the line of the promised seed then continued with Joseph, Jacob's much-loved son and the fourth patriarch of the nation of Israel, but that was not the case. Instead, it was Judah, the fourth-born son of Jacob and his first wife, Leah, who inherited the messianic promises made to Abraham. It was Judah, not Joseph, who was the earthly ancestor of Jesus Christ. Yet this does not diminish Joseph's importance in scripture.

Through Joseph's life we witness the plan of God—a plan tailor-made for the education of an individual and the salvation of a budding nation. Decades earlier God had prophetically spoken to Abraham, promising him that his descendants would "be strangers in a land that is not theirs," where they would be "enslaved and oppressed four hundred years" (Genesis 15:13 NASB). According to God in Genesis 15:14, eventually the Israelites would emerge from this strange land, which we know as Egypt. As they made this mass exodus, they would be loaded with money and possessions, and the nation of Egypt would experience divine judgment.

Abraham's descendants would control the land of Canaan, but before their possession of the promised land they would spend four centuries in Egypt, first as guests of the Egyptians and later as virtual slaves. There the young Hebrew nation would grow and multiply in relative safety. Over 100,000 times the number of Jewish men, plus all the women and children, would one day emerge from Egypt as had entered the country originally. In God's divine plan, it was Moses who would lead this massive return to Canaan, known as the exodus (Exodus 12:33ff). But long before that, it was Joseph whom God would use to bring his chosen people onto Egyptian soil in the first place.

Walking without Growing Faint

Joseph is probably one of the most lovable characters in the Old Testament. He ranks up there with Moses, David, and Jesus Christ himself when it comes to biographical material within the pages of scripture. As we shall observe, only a couple of times in his long life does Joseph appear somewhat selfish or manipulative. His track record is phenomenal.

When I think of Joseph, I think of two verses: one in the Old Testament and one in the New. The first is Isaiah 40:31:

> But those who hope in the Lord
>   will renew their strength.
> They will soar on wings like eagles;
>   they will run and not grow weary,
>   they will walk and not be faint.

How well that verse describes the life of Joseph! Constantly he hopes in the Lord—communication with his creator is a way of life for him. With his triumphs and God-given successes, Joseph soars with the eagles and runs without growing weary of the race. More significant than either of these, he manages to walk without fainting—to keep on keeping on in the midst of agonizing adversity.

It is easy to soar when lifted upon the wings of God's favor. It is not difficult to run with the breeze at our backs. But the most trying discipline of all is to walk, to keep trudging along when the howling winds buffet and hurl us against the jagged rocks of crisis, when the bone-chilling blizzards of confusion blind us from the path and conceal our way, or when the drudgery of day-to-day life descends upon us like a thick fog, choking us with boredom. Yet that is exactly what Joseph does. He never throws in the towel, but walks without growing faint or surrendering his faith, through some of the toughest and most tedious situations we can imagine. In all and through all, Joseph proves to be as resilient as the apostle Paul, who boldly and bravely states in 2 Corinthians 4:8-9: "We are afflicted in every way, but not crushed; perplexed, but not despairing; persecuted, but not forsaken; struck down, but not destroyed" (NASB).

Along with Isaiah 40:31, a New Testament verse from Romans also aptly describes the life of Joseph: "And we know that God causes all things to work together for good to those who love God, to those who are called according to His purpose" (Romans 8:28 NASB). At seventeen years of age Joseph is tossed into a pit by jealous brothers, and sold into bondage in Egypt. From the pit he is forced to serve in the Egyptian Potiphar's house, until his master unjustly throws him into prison, where he stays until he reaches the age of thirty. He faces trials of the body, the soul, and the spirit, yet all occur within the framework of God's purpose. Ultimately, the education of the pit, the house of Potiphar, and the prison prepare Joseph for ascension to the palace. Against all odds he is transformed overnight from lowly prisoner to all-powerful prime minister. And he is ready for the responsibility of leadership in the land.

In Joseph's life, all things do work together for good — God's good, that is. He fully recognizes the truth expressed in Proverbs 16:9, where we read, "In his heart a man plans his course, but the Lord determines his steps." By becoming pharaoh's second-in-command, Joseph precedes his people into Egypt and prepares a place for them. This is God's intention. Eventually, every difficult trial becomes a dim memory as the amazing plan of the Lord unfolds in the young man's life.

When the Pieces Don't Fit

Joseph's life speaks eloquently to us today as we are pounded by the crashing waves of trial and tribulation. As our businesses fail, our kids rebel, our parents age ungracefully, our friends betray us, we need remember one simple yet powerful truth: God is at work in the midst of the adversity. As he was with Joseph—everywhere, in every situation—so God is at work in our bodies, souls, and spirits even when it seems that the pieces of our lives are cut crooked and the jagged edges don't connect.

The truth is that sometimes our lives look like pictures composed of ill-fitting pieces. I suppose the reality of hard times is difficult to swallow for a generation raised on the pablum of television. Problems on the small screen are designed to disappear; they are magically presented and resolved within spaces of twenty-three minutes. On TV father always knows best.

But not only does secular television offer up ample portions of instant solutions to life's dilemmas, Christian television also promises a host of trouble-free good times to the believer who trusts Jesus Christ. I do not mean to condemn Christian TV as a whole, but the truth is that some of the "joy boys" of the Christian media, sporting six-hundred dollar suits, Gucci loafers, and Rolex watches, preaching at us from the stages of multi-million dollar sets, often promise us the "abundant life" in exchange for a belief in Christ. To their way of thinking, the abundant life consists of health, wealth, and prosperity. If we would only place our faith in Jesus, these would be ours. Fortunately, it doesn't work that way.

In the foreword to Paul Powell's book on Job, *When the Hurt Won't Go Away*, Pastor John R. Bisagno puts it this way:

> In spite of the current deluge of "health-and-wealth theology," the fact of the matter is that Jesus promised His followers only three things in this life: they would always be in trouble, never alone, ever at peace. The Christian faith was never intended to be merely an absence of human suffering; it is, rather, comfort in the midst of the storm, God's working out His purposes, revealing His grace, blessing with His presence. We get sick, we get divorces, we lose our jobs, our kids go bad like everybody else's. But we don't have to blow our brains out or jump off tall buildings! We have a Saviour who has answers, help, a purpose, and a presence to reveal through it all (Powell 11).

God is not an all-powerful Santa Claus who showers us with microwaves, VCRS, yachts, swimming pools, summer homes, happy marriages, and healthy bodies whenever we ask. Instead, he permits us to face the tough times so that he can shape us and mold us into the types of people he wants us to be. He uses the trials to conform us to the image of his son, Jesus Christ (James 1:2-4; Philippians 1:6; 2 Corinthians 3:18).

Saving Us in Trouble

God doesn't desert us in our times of trial, either. He joins us in the midst of the adversity. He manages the misfortune, if we allow him. He becomes a participant—often a protective participant—in our problems. To paraphrase Paul Powell and others, the Lord does not save us *from* trouble; he saves us *in* trouble.

Sometimes he fully protects us from the blows of an enemy. Let me give you an example. When the armies of King Nebuchadnezzar of Babylon overran the land of Judah, the cream of Israeli youth—the well-bred, handsome sons of the nobility and royalty—were seized and taken in captivity to Babylon. There, every attempt was made to assimilate the youths into the Babylonian culture. As far as we know from scripture, only four resisted: Daniel, Hananiah, Mishael, and Azariah (Daniel 1).

Some time later, Nebuchadnezzar ordered that an immense golden image be erected on a plain. Most of the officials of the kingdom attended the dedication ceremonies and were instructed either to bow down before the image in worship or else be burned alive in a roaring furnace. Of those present, only Shadrach, Meshach, and Abednego (as Hananiah, Mishael, and Azariah were then known) refused to pay homage to the golden idol. For their obedience to God and their disobedience to the king, they were sentenced to the flames (Daniel 3:1-15). "O Nebuchadnezzar," cried the young men, "we do not need to defend ourselves before you in this matter. If we are thrown into the blazing furnace, the God we serve is able to save us from it, and he will rescue us from your hand, O king. But even if he does not, we want you to know, O king, that we will not serve your gods or worship the image of gold you have set up" (Daniel 3:16-18).

As the king's rage erupted against the three men, he ordered that the furnace be stoked until the flames burned with seven times the usual intensity. Tightly bound, the captives were led to the fire, which roared with such awesome heat that the guards who escorted them were consumed. Into the fiery furnace the three fell . . . off dropped the ropes that bound them, and then, miraculously, a fourth man appeared in the midst of the inferno. In such a way did God himself (either by sending his angel or through the presence of the preincarnate

Christ) conduct the three Hebrew men through their time of trial. Shadrach, Meshach, and Abednego emerged from the blazing furnace unscathed, their hair unsinged and their clothes without even a trace of smoky smell (Daniel 3:19-27). God had not saved them *from* the trial of the fiery furnace, but rather had rescued them *in* the midst of the trial.

Centuries later a man named Stephen, who had placed his trust in Jesus Christ, made an eloquent defense of his faith before the Jewish governing Sanhedrin and its high priest (Acts 7). Enraged at his statements, the Jewish leaders gnashed their teeth in anger, while Stephen gazed into "heaven and saw the glory of God, and Jesus standing at the right hand of God" (Acts 7:55 NASB). As Stephen announced his vision to his accusers, they fell upon him and drove him outside the city gates. There they stoned him unmercifully . . . but it did not matter. Stephen had caught a glimpse of the risen, glorified Christ as he underwent this trial. "Lord Jesus, receive my spirit" (Acts 7:59 NASB), the martyr cried as the stones crushed him. And into his savior's arms he peacefully went even as the multitude raged viciously on.

God did not spare Stephen from trouble, or even from physical death, but he delivered his loved one in the time of severest trial. His presence was a constant, comforting reality to his suffering servant. Indeed, as Paul proclaimed years later:

> For I am convinced that neither death, nor life, nor angels, nor principalities, nor things present, nor things to come, nor powers, nor height, nor depth, nor any other created thing, shall be able to separate us from the love of God, which is in Christ Jesus our Lord (Romans 8:38-39 NASB).

Four Fs

Nothing—not trial nor trouble nor tribulation nor even prosperity—separates Joseph from the love of God. God is with him in the pit, in the prison, and in the palace. The story of Joseph is the story of divine providence, the explanation of the presence of the children of Israel in the land of Egypt for so many years. It is also a story of personal character, the account of a man of quality who places his trust in the living God and is enabled by that God to withstand the pressures and disappointments of a life filled with both.

It can be said that four Fs—forgiveness, forgetfulness, fruitfulness, and figure—give us an accurate picture of Joseph. He forgives his enemies, even his brothers who treat him abominably; after he forgives, he does what is often even more difficult: he forgets the wrongs that others have done to him; he is a fruitful bough in the midst of a barren wasteland; and he is a figure of the Lord Jesus Christ. Over four hundred parallels can be drawn between Jesus and Joseph, and we'll examine some of them as we study the life of the patriarch.

It is such a comfort to know that all the tears, trials, and tragedies are the master carpenter's hammer, chisel, and file which he is using to make us more like Jesus. No wonder Joseph is so much like Christ! What an enriching experience it is to be in the presence of people who have weathered it all, and yet maintain radiant smiles and sweetness of character. When they are around, we feel like we're in the very presence of Christ.

Let's turn now to the book of Genesis, chapter 37, and meet this man who can teach us so much about living, loving, forgiving, forgetting, surviving, and soaring—all within the will of God.

PART ONE

The Training

1

Dreamer in the Pit

Genesis 37

As any honest parent will admit, sibling rivalry is very common. Conflicts, arguments, even fisticuffs erupt once in a while between otherwise loving brothers and sisters. Christian psychologist James Dobson writes, in *Dare to Discipline:*

> Conflict between siblings is as natural as eating and sleeping. In fact, it could almost be considered unnatural for them to coexist in constant harmony, although that does occur occasionally (Dobson 77).

But just because sibling rivalry is natural does not mean that it is necessarily always healthy. It can be dangerous—even deadly. The first murder in human history occurred when brother slew brother as Cain exploded in a jealous rage against Abel (Genesis 4).

Family infighting kept within acceptable bounds has its place in preparing children to deal with conflict as adults. While arguments often occur over infringements of personal rights (i.e. sister hogs the bathroom or brother eats the last piece of cherry pie), there are frequently more subtle, and more severe, causes of sibling conflict. Sometimes deep-rooted jealousies develop over time. If allowed to fester through the years, these jealousies will eventually boil up to the surface, potentially leaving a raw, gaping wound in the relationship.

Playing Favorites

There are many reasons why siblings envy one another. This chapter makes no pretense of being a psychological treatise on the subject. I have noticed in my own experience, however, that one cause of sibling jealousy is parental favoritism. When Mom or Dad plays favorites among the kids, then an unnatural environment of competition springs up as the favored child strives to hold onto his position, and the less-privileged ones vie for their parents' attention. It can be an emotionally devastating situation, particularly for the children who feel less loved and unimportant.

I have run across numerous families in which the oldest child is considered next to perfect, while the younger one never seems to measure up. Try as he will, every effort exerted by the younger sibling is treated as inferior. It's no wonder that soon the parents have an unmotivated rebel on their hands. With a self-image scarred beyond repair, the child simply quits trying.

It is nearly impossible for brothers and sisters who grow up in an unnatural environment of favoritism to develop close, loving relationships among themselves. How can a less-favored sibling do anything except resent the brother or sister on whom the family showers the lion's share of attention, praise, and affection? I think of Ishmael and Isaac in the Bible. For thirteen years, until the moment of Isaac's birth, Ishmael was the apple of his father Abraham's eye. Abraham and Sarah apparently believed that Ishmael, the child of the handmaid Hagar, was the son promised them years earlier by the Lord. They believed that Ishmael would inherit the promises of the abrahamic covenant, and he was raised accordingly, with every right and privilege of position. All that changed the day Isaac was born.

When the baby Isaac appeared on the scene, Ishmael's place as his father's favorite son was irrevocably lost. It had to be so, because Isaac was the child God had promised; he was the son whom the Lord intended to inherit the promises made to Abraham a quarter century before (Genesis 12:1-3). Of necessity, Isaac assumed privileged status in the family . . . and events inevitably came to a head within a few short years.

It was a feast day, a huge celebration thrown by Abraham in honor of Isaac's weaning. The teenaged Ishmael sulked during the festivities and then, as his resentment mounted, began mocking his little brother (Genesis 21:9). The elder boy quite naturally couldn't stand being second in his dad's life, and so there was no love lost between Isaac and Ishmael. Their lack of affection has extended to their descendants, for Isaac was one of the patriarchs of the nation Israel, and Ishmael became the forerunner of the Arabic peoples. Today the middle east is a steaming cauldron of conflict because of the timeless struggle between the Arabs and the Jews. That sibling rivalry of so long ago has certainly had far-reaching consequences.

The Family Album

Let's turn now to Genesis 37, and begin to read of the experiences of another who grew up in an atmosphere of parental favoritism. In this case, our subject, Joseph, was on the receiving end of his father's good pleasure, a bonafide daddy's boy in nearly every sense of the term. Considering his family background, it is no wonder that this was true.

You see, Joseph's father Jacob had not one but four women traipsing about his tent. His marital history is the stuff of which cheap soap operas are made. Jacob's experiences give us the first truly messy picture in scripture of the consequences of polygamy, and make it graphically clear that monogamy is God's ideal.

You recall that after he stole Esau's blessing from their

blind father Isaac, Jacob rightly feared the wrath of his enraged older brother. Esau was prepared to kill him (Genesis 27:41). Rebekah sent her younger and favored son packing, directing Jacob to journey to Paddan-Aram where he could dwell in safety with his uncle Laban (Genesis 27:42-45).

There the fugitive fell head over heels for Laban's younger daughter, Rachel, a luscious beauty who knocked him off his feet at first sight. She must have been something special, because Jacob agreed without reservation to labor seven years for his uncle in order to marry the girl. On the morning after the long-awaited wedding night, Jacob awoke to find that the woman sharing his bed was not his beloved Rachel, but her older sister Leah! No doubt Laban, who had engineered the switch, had guffawed about the deception the entire night. Instead of beautiful Rachel, he had been able to palm off her less attractive, "weak-eyed" sister onto an unsuspecting husband. Not only that but, since Jacob still wanted to wed Rachel, Laban was able to squeeze another seven years' contract labor out of his son-in-law in exchange for her (Genesis 29).

In Jacob's household, four babies came in rapid succession: Reuben, Simeon, Levi, Judah (29:31-35). All were sons of Leah. Rachel was barren. In desperation she opted to follow the custom of the day and use a sort of surrogate mother, sending her handmaid Bilhah in to Jacob. Dan and Naphtali were born (30:3-8). Leah, who had stopped bearing, responded blow for blow by offering her handmaid Zilpah for the same purpose; Gad and Asher were the result (30:9-13). Pause for a moment and think about those statistics: two wives, two concubines, and eight children, all under the same roof. How much peace and harmony do you think existed in Jacob's home?

Then, to make matters worse for poor Rachel, Leah started having babies of her own again (30:17-21). Two sons, Issachar and Zebulun, and daughter, Dinah, were born. Rachel was still childless, although she lived in a home with eleven children.

But finally God answered Rachel's pleas, and a child was born to her: Joseph (30:22-24). Jacob saw the birth as a long-awaited miracle, and so it was. Rachel was his greatest love, and she at last had a son! No wonder Jacob was partial to Joseph. No wonder he was the very special light of his father's life.

Just to complete the story, Rachel prayed for another child, and her prayer was answered a few years later when she became pregnant with Benjamin. She died giving birth to him, and was buried in a remote place in the wilderness of Judea on the road to Bethlehem (Genesis 35:16-20).

Making a Good Impression—Genesis 37:1-2

> Jacob lived in the land where his father had stayed, the land of Canaan. This is the account of Jacob. Joseph, a young man of seventeen, was tending the flocks with his brothers, the sons of Bilhah and the sons of Zilpah, his father's wives, and he brought their father a bad report about them.

With Rachel's death, undoubtedly Joseph became even more precious to his father. Let's pick up the story as we turn to the pages of Genesis 37.

As the chapter opens, Jacob is 108 years old; thirty-nine years are left of his earthly pilgrimage. He has returned to the land of blessing, Canaan, and has settled his family in Hebron, the place—some thirty to forty miles south of Jerusalem—where his own father Isaac had stayed.

Joseph is a boy of seventeen. It is time for his father to give him additional responsibilities, so Jacob sends him out into the fields to tend the flocks with his half-brothers, Dan, Naphtali, Gad, and Asher, the sons of the handmaids, Bilhah and Zilpah. Perhaps Joseph is even placed in charge of his older brothers at the job site, though we are not certain of this. Regardless, he takes his duties very seriously, and he is extremely loyal to his father.

Scripture tells us that Joseph brings Jacob "a bad report" about the behavior of his brothers in the field (37:2). Evidently the conduct of Gad, Asher, Naphtali, and Dan is not a credit to their father, and Joseph feels compelled to inform Isaac about the sordid situation. Some accuse Joseph of being nothing more than a tattletale here, the spoiled son of his father's old age who ensures his position by bad-mouthing the other boys. I disagree.

Rather, I believe that Joseph is a great deal like the kid who has just received his Social Security number, earned his driver's license, and landed his first job. He wants to do well. He is eager to please. In the middle of the first day on the job, he observes that his brothers are not performing their duties properly, so he is faced with a problem. Should he tell his father or not? He chooses to remain loyal to his parent. Naturally, Joseph's decision to inform Jacob of the facts, while morally correct, does nothing to endear him to his siblings.

A Father's Favorite—Genesis 37:3-4

> Now Israel loved Joseph more than any of his other sons, because he had been born to him in his old age; and he made a richly ornamented robe for him. When his brothers saw that their father loved him more than any of them, they hated him and could not speak a kind word to him.

The report given their father by Joseph antagonizes the brothers, and Jacob—referred to here as Israel, the name given him by God in Genesis 32—does little to help the tense situation. Genesis 37:3 tells us that "Israel loved Joseph more than any of his other sons, because he had been born to him in his old age." True, Benjamin had been born during his father's old age as well, yet his birth had also been the occasion of his mother's death.

Joseph was the boy whose childhood Jacob and his beloved Rachel had enjoyed together. It was Joseph who brought his mother great joy while she lived, Joseph whom she cradled in her arms, Joseph who clutched at her skirts as he toddled along, Joseph who fell asleep against her breast, Joseph who undoubtedly gave his aging father poignant memories of the woman he had loved with all his heart.

Because of his great affection, perhaps in gratitude for a job well done in the incident with the disreputable brothers, Jacob makes his favorite boy a special present: a "richly ornamented robe" (37:3). The King James Bible refers to this garment as "a coat of many colours," but it is probably more elaborate than that text suggests. It is a coat fit for a king, a regal robe likely reaching to Joseph's wrists and ankles, signifying achievement and position. Like the high school senior who struts around proudly in his slick, new letter jacket even on a day too warm for such a garment, Joseph wears his fancy new robe wherever he goes.

Clearly Jacob plays favorites in gifting his teenage son with such an obvious mark of status as this ornamented cloak. But Joseph *is* the son of his old age, and most of us tend to spoil our younger children a bit. My wife, Pearl, and I have discussed this often. Of our five children, it has been our youngest, Julea, whom we have unconsciously pampered just a little more than the rest. It's fair to point out that she would probably disagree with this, but the other kids sure wouldn't. "You never let us do that!" they've been heard to exclaim after we've given Julea permission to go somewhere. "She always gets away with murder!" they've cried.

We have tried not to play favorites, but in all honesty, it has been Julea of whom we've been both more protective and indulgent than the others. We don't love her more than the rest, but she *is* the baby of the family. She is the only one of our children, for example, to whom we gave a 'vette when she received her driver's license. She couldn't believe it when I asked her if she'd like one. Of course, she was expecting a new Corvette . . . while I was referring to a used Chevette, which is what she got before heading off for college. Even so, I hope my point is plain: it is easy to be more lenient with the younger ones in the family. If you're still not convinced, just ask any teenager if his or her younger brother or sister is spoiled, and see what response you get.

Besides, as we have discussed, Joseph is a tangible reminder of Jacob's wife Rachel. Yet I believe that there is more to Jacob's attachment to Joseph than these reasons. I think Jacob desperately wants to give his favored son something he never had: a father's full attention and love. Jacob's older brother Esau, the rugged outdoorsman, was their father Isaac's favorite child. Esau always held first claim on Isaac's affection, while Jacob was left to latch onto his mother Rebekah's apron strings. You'd think Jacob, who had grown up experiencing only the crumbs of his own father's good pleasure, would have avoided playing favorites among his own sons at any cost. But—like father, like son— Jacob repeats the mistakes of Isaac.

The reaction of Joseph's brothers to his privileged position is predictable. Genesis 37:4 tells us that when the older boys observe Jacob's preferential treatment of Joseph, they begin to hate him, and cannot bring themselves to utter a civil or charitable word in his presence. The very sight of him repulses them, and they are engulfed with understandable feelings of jealousy and resentment.

Adding to the Hatred Ledger—Genesis 37:5-11

> Joseph had a dream, and when he told it to his brothers, they hated him all the more. He said to them, "Listen to this dream I had: We were binding sheaves of grain out in the field when suddenly my sheaf rose and stood upright, while your sheaves gathered around mine and bowed down to it."

> His brothers said to him, "Do you intend to reign over us? Will you actually rule us? And they hated him all the more because of his dream and what he had said.
>
> Then he had another dream, and he told it to his brothers. "Listen," he said, "I had another dream, and this time the sun and moon and eleven stars were bowing down to me."
>
> When he told his father as well as his brothers, his father rebuked him and said, "What is this dream you had? Will your mother and I and your brothers actually come and bow down to the ground before you?" His brothers were jealous of him, but his father kept the matter in mind.

Do you know what a hatred ledger is? It's that private mental list we keep of everything we hold against another person. Husbands and wives are often guilty of keeping extremely long hatred ledgers on file. Mrs. Smith forgets to wash her husband's softball shirt, and there goes one mark in the hatred ledger. Next she dents the car while backing out of the garage, and there's mark number two. Later she burns the pot roast and mark three finds its place. Finally she neglects to pick up the dry cleaning . . . and look out! The journal entry on Mr. Smith's hatred ledger is filled, and he lashes out at Mrs. Smith. "What's wrong with you? Can't you do anything right? I can't depend on you for anything!" Fireworks exploding in her face would have done less damage to her self-image than her husband's tirade.

Joseph's brothers have been consistently adding to the blacklist of their own hatred ledger concerning him. So far we've seen that they have three reasons to resent their little brother:

1. Joseph has given a bad report about some of the brothers to their father.

2. Joseph is obviously loved more by Jacob than they are.
3. Joseph is clearly treated preferentially by their father when Jacob gives him the robe.

Now the brothers add still another entry into the mental ledger, because Joseph has some dreams that he cannot keep to himself.

Visions of Grandeur

"Listen to this dream I had," Joseph implores his brothers with the innocent enthusiasm that only a seventeen-year-old can muster. With no ulterior motive in mind, Joseph relates the fantastic dream to the siblings who can barely tolerate his presence. It is not the wisest move he will ever make, but it is understandable and forgivable; he is long on enthusiasm and short on experience.

What Joseph says serves to alienate his brothers further; its effect is much like rubbing salt into an open wound. He explains that in his dream he saw his brothers and himself binding sheaves of grain in a field. Suddenly Joseph's sheaf stood upright, while all the other sheaves bowed down before it. The meaning is easy to interpret, and the brothers don't have to be prophets to exclaim, "Do you intend to reign over us? Will you actually rule us?" (37:8). Their feathers are more than a tad ruffled. Doubtless they wonder: Will you listen to our baby brother! Who does this kid think he is? What a pompous fool! How much of this does he think we can stand?

To top things off, Joseph has a second dream. Again, oblivious to the resentment with which his brothers have greeted the first report, he eagerly tells them the details of this second vision. This time Joseph saw the sun, moon, and eleven stars bowing down to him. The brothers catch on quickly, realizing immediately that the eleven stars in the dream plainly represent them. Their envy and antipathy mount. When the fur has been rubbed the wrong way long enough, the cat stiffens, and there is a long, low growl announcing the arrival of claws. Sirens of alarm should be wailing in Joseph's brain, but there is no indication that he even suspects his brothers are angry with him.

The sun and the moon in Joseph's vision symbolize the boy's own parents. When Jacob hears the account of the dream, he recognizes this and exclaims, "What is this dream you had? Will your mother and I and your brothers actually come and bow down to the ground before you?" (37:10). He is incredulous, at least at first. Notice that Jacob mentions Joseph's "mother." To whom is he referring? It cannot be Rachel, for she is long dead and buried. It must be Leah.

The Pieces Falling Together

Sometimes we feel rejected and unloved because of circumstances in our lives. Leah surely did. Life with Jacob and Rachel must have been a lonely experience for her. Certainly her children kept her busy, but she never had sole possession of her husband's heart. Then Rachel died. After that, who changed Benjamin's diapers? Who washed Joseph's face and bandaged his skinned knees? Who became the mother to Rachel's sons? Leah did. She took her sister's place, and it is next to Leah that Jacob would eventually be buried (Genesis 50:12-13). It can be argued that perhaps Leah was the wife God intended for Jacob all along. Indeed, Leah, not Rachel, was the mother of Judah, the one of the twelve from whom Christ is descended. After years of isolation and competition, God allows her to become mistress of her husband's household—the stepmother of even Joseph and Benjamin.

From Rags to Riches

The implications of Joseph's dreams at age seventeen are clear. They depict a rags-to-riches story: pauper becomes prince, laborer becomes premier, mailboy becomes president. Joseph's visions reveal that one day he will be placed in a position of power, prestige, and privilege, and that even his own family members will honor him.

At first it appears that Jacob is at least questioning Joseph's dream, if not downright rejecting it, but he is not. Scripture reveals that while the brothers grow more jealous of Joseph, his father keeps "the matter in mind" (37:11). We remember that the virgin Mary, reflecting upon the visit of the shepherds after Christ's birth, "kept all these things and pondered them in her heart" (Luke 2:19 KJV). Jacob files Joseph's visions safely away in his memory bank. He well understands the importance of dreams, for God has revealed much to him in this manner over the years (Genesis 28:10-17; 31:11-13). By age 108, Jacob is wise enough to recognize when the Lord is speaking.

Going the Extra Mile: To Shechem and Beyond—Genesis 37:12-18

> Now his brothers had gone to graze their father's flocks near Shechem, and Israel said to Joseph, "As you know, your brothers are grazing the flocks near Shechem. Come, I am going to send you to them."
>
> "Very well," he replied.
>
> So he said to him, "Go and see if all is well with your brothers and with the flocks, and bring word back to me." Then he sent him off from the Valley of Hebron.
>
> When Joseph arrived at Shechem, a man found him wandering around in the fields and asked him, "What are you looking for?"
>
> He replied, "I'm looking for my brothers. Can you tell me where they are grazing their flocks?"
>
> "They have moved on from here," the man answered. "I heard them say, 'Let's go to Dothan.' "
>
> So Joseph went after his brothers and found them near Dothan. But they saw him in the distance, and before he reached them, they plotted to kill him.

Tempers flare around Jacob's household after Joseph relates his dreams. Possibly concerned about his older sons' increasing hostility toward their younger brother, Jacob decides to separate the principal players. He sends the older boys away from Hebron to pasture his flocks near Shechem. Maybe some constructive activity—some good old-fashioned hard work—will defuse the boys' anger. Since Shechem is sixty miles north of Hebron, it will be no small task to drive the livestock up there, and will certainly keep the brothers busy.

Shechem is probably also one of the last places in the world that the older boys want to go. Like Dallas after the assassination of President Kennedy or Memphis after the murder of Dr. Martin Luther King, Jr., it is a city with bad memories. Shechem is the place where the brothers' young sister Dinah had been raped five years earlier (Genesis 34). She was assaulted by the prince of the city, who afterward proposed marriage. Simeon and Levi tricked the prince and the men of Shechem into undergoing the Jewish rite of circumcision, before the supposed marriage could take place. Then, while the male population was unable to defend itself adequately, they murdered them all. Jacob's sons, particularly Simeon and Levi, are not welcomed in Shechem. Sending them there is risky, to say the least.

Only a Moment

Some time after the boys depart, Jacob instructs Joseph, "Go and see if all is well with your brothers and with the flocks, and bring word back to me" (37:14). Perhaps Jacob is concerned about his sons' welfare. He ought to be—as I've mentioned, the boys would win no popularity contests in Shechem. Yet the moment Jacob tells Joseph to leave on this mission is one he likely never forgets. Probably he rehashes his words time and time again, agonizing, wondering why, for this is the last occasion he will see his beloved boy for more than twenty years. Indeed, he will believe the young man to be dead. Joseph's journey will irrevocably affect the course of his entire life.

In God's plan for our lives, it sometimes takes only a minute—a split-second decision, a brief reflex action—to change things completely. David's father, Jesse, sent him sixteen miles away to check on the welfare of his brothers who were battling the Philistines . . . and this brief decision put the youngster in the right place at the right time to face off with the giant Goliath (1 Samuel 17). The rest is history.

One of the students in the youth group I led after graduating from seminary a invited friend for a joy ride in his dad's car. That night his car struck another vehicle head-on. The victim driving the other car was a pregnant woman; both she and the unborn baby died upon impact. "A split-second changes lives," said the boy's father, tears filling his eyes, as we cried together at the hospital at 3:00 that morning.

Lest we become complacent, we must not forget that father's advice. Life can change instantly. Years after the traffic incident mentioned above, an orthopedic surgeon who was on the board of directors of our ministry was packing the car for a family ski trip. He pulled at the elastic cord holding the luggage carrier on top of his vehicle, and the supposedly secure cord snapped on the other side. It recoiled in his face, doing such damage to his eye that he was forced to retire from his orthopedic practice. Just like that, all was drastically changed.

Things like these happen so unexpectedly and with such amazing speed. Sometimes it may seem that they happen to everybody else, but not to us. Yet that is not necessarily the case, as Jacob soon discovers. With a few words, father sends son to check on the brothers, and it will be the last time in more than two decades that he will set eyes on the youngster. Truly, as scripture tells us in Proverbs 27:1, "Boast not thyself of tomorrow; for thou knowest not what a day may bring forth" (KJV).

Giving 110 Percent

In obedience to his dad, Joseph sets off on the sixty-mile trip to Shechem. He is surely aware of the dangers of such a long journey, but his compliance to Jacob's wishes is immediate, his submission to his father's authority, absolute. God always blesses the obedient heart and the submissive spirit.

Once in the area of Shechem, Joseph begins to wander about the fields searching for his brothers. He can find no sign of them, but before he has time to start worrying about their welfare, a man walks up to him with the question, "What are you looking for?" (37:15). Isn't it terrific how the Lord brings people into our lives at exactly the right time?

"I'm looking for my brothers," replies Joseph. "Can you tell me where they are grazing their flocks?" (37:16).

"They have moved on from here," answers the man in the field. "I heard them say, 'Let's go to Dothan' " (37:17).

Things may have become pretty hot pretty soon for the brothers in Shechem. Memories of massacres die hard. It's no wonder that they leave the city quickly. Joseph, after receiving the man's report, immediately sets out for Dothan in search of the boys.

When you think about it, Joseph's unhesitating departure for Dothan is remarkable. He has already done what his father asked in traveling to Shechem. And anyway, there is no proof that the boys have actually gone to Dothan. The stranger who spoke to him had merely overheard a chance remark to that effect. The brothers could easily have changed their minds enroute. How easy it would be for Joseph to turn around from Shechem and return to Hebron. Once there, he could explain to Jacob that he tried to locate the boys but failed. The mission was accomplished to the best of his ability.

But Joseph doesn't see things that way. He is no half-hearted employee, so he lugs his pack and provisions an extra twelve miles of dust, sweat, dirt, and danger to Dothan. His example suggests a good principle for Christians to follow in their lives: the principle of going the extra mile, of giving 110 percent. I wonder how many of us function as employees with the conscientiousness of Joseph. Do we go beyond what is simply expected? Do we do more than our duty? And what about in our Christian service? If we allow God to use us in going the extra mile, then we bring glory to him. Sadly, some of us will never hear, "Well done, thou good and faithful servant," because we'll never be more than halfway finished with what God has for us to do (Matthew 5:40-41).

In Dothan, Joseph does find his siblings. As he approaches from a distance, the brothers spy him. Probably they recognize the rich robe he wears, sparkling and shimmering in the bright sunlight. The sight of him immediately stirs up their anger and resentment. They see red! We even read in verse 18 that "they plotted to kill him." Not exactly your idea of a warm welcome, is it? Let's read on.

The Dreamer in the Pit—Genesis 37:19-24

> "Here comes that dreamer!" they said to each other. "Come now, let's kill him and throw him into one of these cisterns and say that a ferocious animal devoured him. Then we'll see what comes of his dreams."
>
> When Reuben heard this, he tried to rescue him from their hands. "Let's not take his life," he said. "Don't shed any blood. Throw him into this cistern here in the desert, but don't lay a hand on him." Reuben said this to rescue him from them and take him back to his father.
>
> So when Joseph came to his brothers, they stripped him of his robe—the richly ornamented robe he was wearing—and they took him and threw him into the cistern. Now the cistern was empty; there was no water in it.

John 1:11 says of Jesus Christ, "He came unto his own, and his own received him not" (KJV). Being God, Christ anticipated his own hostile reception in the world. It is doubtful that Joseph, with the naivete of a seventeen-year-old, imagines in his wildest dreams the greeting that awaits him as he approaches his brothers at Dothan. He has gone to so much trouble to find them. He has made so many sacrifices. Surely they will welcome him with open arms. How excited they will be to see the food and provisions he has brought from home! Unfortunately, Joseph has another sort of greeting awaiting him.

As the boy draws nearer he must notice that his brothers are grouped together. What he doesn't realize is that they have formed an unholy huddle and are plotting his death. "Here comes that dreamer!" they exclaim when they first spot him. "Come now, let's kill him. . . . Then we'll see what comes of his dreams" (37:19).

Reuben, aware of his responsibilities as firstborn, talks his brothers out of this drastic step. Scripture indicates that he intends to rescue Joseph later—if he has the chance.

Finally Joseph arrives in the camp. What is the first thing his brothers do? They strip off his ornamented cloak. They hate the dreams; they despise the robe and the love of Jacob for Joseph which it represents. The brothers can do nothing about their father's affection for Joseph; neither can they touch their brother's dreams. But they can do something about the dreamer himself, and they do. They seize Joseph and violently throw him into a nearby empty well (37:23-24).

God's Will Will Be Done

The brothers are of a mind to thwart the purpose of God in destroying the life of their younger brother. Their conduct is in direct defiance to the will of God as revealed through Joseph's visions. Reuben's interference stays the execution, but his is more than a human act of covering his flank. It is an example of divine providence.

After all, who moves Reuben's heart to this sudden show of responsibility and compassion? None but the Lord, whose purpose will always be worked out. The brothers, while consciously seeking to subvert God's purpose, actually work to fulfill it. But then, isn't that often the case?

Satan probably figured that Christ's death upon the cross meant an end to the Lord's plan for the salvation of mankind. The tables were turned on Lucifer, however, when that death was followed by a resurrection and the offering of redemption to all who believe (John 3:16; 1 Thessalonians 5:9-10). When it comes to fulfilling his will, God is always the winner.

Recognizing the immensity of the power of God is a lesson every Christian should learn—and learn well. As professional golfer Lee Trevino reflected, following a brush with death in which he was struck by lightning on the golf course, "When God wants to play through, you let him!" Our Lord is capable of anything and everything. Even if the brothers had slain Joseph and tossed his lifeless body into the pit, God's purpose would not have been thwarted. But the brothers spare the boy, though their hatred seethes.

In the Nick of Time—Genesis 37:25-28

> As they sat down to eat their meal, they looked up and saw a caravan of Ishmaelites coming from Gilead. Their camels were loaded with spices, balm and myrrh, and they were on their way to take them down to Egypt.
>
> Judah said to his brothers, "What will we gain if we kill our brother and cover up his blood? Come, let's sell him to the Ishmaelites and not lay our hands on him; after all, he is our brother, our own flesh and blood." His brothers agreed.
>
> So when the Midianite merchants came by, his brothers pulled Joseph up out of the cistern and sold him for twenty shekels of silver to the Ishmaelites, who took him to Egypt.

Stripped of his precious cloak, the exhausted Joseph languishes in the dry, dusty cistern where his brothers have thrown him. Think about how he must feel—a mere teenager, away from home for perhaps the first time. The Lord has given him wondrous dreams of grandeur; he is trusting in God and is excited about his future. Suddenly he finds himself half-naked and at the bottom of a dark hole. How unfair it must seem! Why, he is only doing what his father asked him to do! Worse, the brothers he has gone to so much trouble to track down have been the ones to put him where he is. It is probably more than Joseph is able to stand.

Tears well up in his eyes and spill over. We know from the account in Genesis 42 that he cries out for mercy to the brothers who have treated him so cruelly. Years later memories of these tears of anguish will rise up from the recesses of their guilty consciences to plague the brothers (Genesis 42:21), but for the moment they appear to be not at all affected by Joseph's sobs. His wails of misery fall upon insensitive ears, but twenty-two years of smoldering regret will eventually burn the memory of these moments into their very souls.

Scripture records in Genesis 37 that the brothers sit down to eat their meal (37:25). The unbelievable coldheartedness of this action waxes all the more callous when we realize that the food they consumed had likely been brought to them by Joseph. Then, in the distance, the brothers spy a caravan of "Ishmaelites coming from Gilead," a city some twenty-five miles northeast of Dothan (37:25). Their camels are loaded with spices, balm, and myrrh to be traded in Egypt (37:25). Who but God himself could have worked out such minute details? Feeling pangs of hunger, the boys settle down to a tasty meal after tossing their baby brother into a pit. At that exact moment a caravan of traders approaches . . . and we can be certain that their arrival on the scene is no chance happening. The caravan does not make its appearance as a result of coincidence. Unbeknown to any of the players in this drama, the brothers, Joseph, and the traders are keeping an appointment set by God.

When he spots the caravan, immediately a brilliant idea pops into Judah's head. "What will we gain if we kill our brother and cover up his blood? Come, let's sell him to the Ishmaelites and not lay our hands on him; after all, he is our brother, our own flesh and blood" (37:26-27). Genesis 37:28 tells us that when "the Midianite merchants came by, his brothers pulled Joseph up out of the cistern and sold him for twenty shekels of silver to the Ishmaelites, who took him to Egypt." In later times, twenty shekels was the value set by Jewish law for a male of Joseph's age who had been dedicated to the Lord (Leviticus 27:5). And Judas Iscariot centuries later betrays Christ for thirty shekels (Matthew 26:14-15).

The fact that the traders are described as both Ishmaelites and Midianites may seem confusing. These men are probably Ishmaelites who live in Midian, and who are heading toward Egyptian markets. On to Egypt, some 250 miles away, the caravan continues, with its newly acquired property. And Egypt is precisely where God wants Joseph to be.

DECEPTIONS—GENESIS 37:29-36

> When Reuben returned to the cistern and saw that Joseph was not there, he tore his clothes. He went back to his brothers and said, "The boy isn't there! Where can I turn now?"
>
> Then they got Joseph's robe, slaughtered a goat and dipped the robe in the blood. They took the ornamented robe back to their father and said, "We found this. Examine it to see whether it is your son's robe."
>
> He recognized it and said, "It is my son's robe! Some ferocious animal has devoured him. Joseph has surely been torn to pieces."
>
> Then Jacob tore his clothes, put on sackcloth and mourned for his son many days. All his sons and

> daughters came to comfort him, but he refused to be comforted. "No," he said, "in mourning will I go down to the grave to my son." So his father wept for him.
>
> Meanwhile, the Midianites sold Joseph in Egypt to Potiphar, one of Pharaoh's officials, the captain of the guard.

While the transaction for Joseph's freedom is being made, Reuben is evidently not present. Maybe he has wandered off to care for the stock or to figure out how he will handle his brothers. He misses out on the dickering and, upon his return to camp, stops by the cistern to check on baby brother. Joseph is not there!

"Where can I turn now?" a panic-stricken Reuben exclaims to his other brothers (37:30). Jacob will want an explanation of Joseph's whereabouts. He'll never believe that the boy simply wandered off. Joseph would never leave home like that. Deception breeds deception, so, to protect themselves, the brothers take Joseph's richly ornamented cloak and dip it in the blood of a goat they've just slaughtered. They carry the bespattered evidence back to their father and ask him to identify the garment. Of course it can be none other than the beautiful robe he had made for his much-loved boy.

"It is my son's robe!" Jacob wails. "Some ferocious animal has devoured him. Joseph has surely been torn to pieces," he cries, immediately thinking the worst (37:33). The man who deceived his father and brother years before is himself deceived by his sons. Jacob falls victim to a false assumption.

False assumptions lead to unnecessary anxiety. In Jacob's case, a convincing piece of circumstantial evidence prompts him to forget Joseph's dreams. He is guilty of looking only at the immediate circumstances and not at the broader picture. Doing that frequently causes us to jump to the wrong conclusions. And wrong conclusions can cause much harm. They are what prompt Shakespeare's Ophelia to drown herself, Romeo to lap up poison, Othello to murder his wife.

It is ironic, but not surprising, that Jacob succumbs to his sons' scheme. Galatians 6:7 states, "Be not deceived; God is not mocked: for whatsoever a man soweth, that shall he also reap" (KJV). Years earlier Jacob had tricked Isaac and Esau in the matters of the birthright and the blessing. Now he approaches the final decades of his own life, and will have to live over half of that time under the deception of his boys. Our sins always find us out, of that we can be certain. The mills may grind slowly, but they grind exceedingly sure, and God eventually, inevitably, accomplishes his purpose. Jacob learns some lessons from these years, awash in tears for his lost son, that he could learn no other way.

And bathed in his own tears is how we leave Jacob in Genesis 37. He shreds his clothes in grief and refuses to be comforted by his other children. With characteristic dramatics, he swears that his sorrow for Joseph will accompany him to the grave. Meanwhile, Joseph, the object of this intense mourning, finds himself taken to Egypt and there sold to Potiphar, the captain of pharaoh's guard.

The Cellar of Affliction

Someone once said that when we are in the cellar of affliction, we should start looking for the wine of God's purpose. That's excellent advice. Precisely in the cellar of affliction is where we leave Joseph at the end of this chapter. Over the next several years, God permits the hole to be dug deeper and deeper as Joseph undergoes test after test. He is in the process of *becoming*, as are we all. The question is, will he become the type of man God wants him to be? That we shall see.

The cassette tape series of this group of studies on the life of Joseph has found its way into a state prison in Texas. It's a true story that one inmate, a new Christian about to be released on parole, actually asked the warden if he could hang around a couple more days so that he could find out what happened to Joseph! It's not that my lectures are so fascinating, but that God's word is that dramatic, hard-hitting, and relevant to our lives. Joseph has a lot to teach us, and I hope that you'll "hang around" for the duration, too.

LESSONS

As we reach the close of Genesis 37, let's review some of the major lessons of the chapter.

Lesson one: *God the father's purpose, power, and promise are all at work in the life of Joseph and his family.* The chapter illustrates the overruling power of a sovereign God, a power that is wonderful in its counsel and mighty in its operation. It will accomplish his purposes and fulfill his promises.

Lesson two: *while the Lord may give a promise, he may also do a work in our lives to prepare us to receive that promise.* Right now, Joseph is being prepared to receive that which has been promised him in his dreams.

Lesson three: *Joseph's dreams are given partly to sustain him in the time of trial.* When things seem impossible, he'll have the graphic memories of the visions God has given to help pull him through.

Lesson four: *all things do work together for good to those who love the Lord and are called according to his purpose.* If we think we've reached the end of the rope, the best alternative is to tie a knot and hang on a while longer.

Lesson five: *one sin begets another.* The brothers' envy turns into hatred which then becomes a murderous anger. This hardheartedness spurs them to rid themselves of their brother, and that dastardly deed compels them then to lie to Jacob.

Lesson six: *our sins will find us out.* Years after it took place, Jacob bears the foul fruit of his own deceitfulness as he falls prey to the deception of his children.

Lesson seven: *Joseph is an example of submission to his father's authority and obedience to his command.* While it may look like he comes up with the short end of the stick because of his obedience, in the long run he will be rewarded by God for his right attitudes. Submission and obedience to the father—that's what God wants from each of us, too. Think about it.

Food for Thought

As we prepare to continue the adventures of Joseph, let me leave you with two thoughts.

First, Acts 7:9 tells us that "the patriarchs became jealous of Joseph and sold him into Egypt. *And yet God was with him*" (NASB, italics mine). The constant presence of the Lord accompanies Joseph from cistern to caravan to strange country, and beyond. The young man is never alone. Neither are we, if we know Christ as savior and lord, and are submissive to God's purpose.

And second, let us remember the words of the apostle Paul, who exclaims in Romans 8:31, "If God is for us, who can be against us?" How true! God is in Joseph's corner, and if we know him through Jesus Christ, he is in ours, too.

Questions for Study

1. In what way does Jacob treat Joseph preferentially? Look at your own family. Are there unnecessary jealousies among your own children because of something *you* have done—maybe favoritism you have shown?

2. Like Joseph's brothers, are you keeping a "hatred ledger" on file? Is there another person against whom you have a grudge, and the bitterness keeps mounting? If so, confess your attitude to the Lord, and ask him to change it. If necessary, discuss the matter with the one you've resented, and apologize. The time to act is now.

3. What visions does God allow Joseph to dream? How do the brothers react as Joseph relates what he has seen? Could Joseph have handled the situation more tactfully? If so, how?

4. God's plans unfold with minute detail. Split-second decisions change lives. In your own words, outline the incredible series of events that bring Joseph from the safety of his father's home to the clutches of the caravan bound for Egypt.

5. When Jacob sees Joseph's blood-spattered coat, he jumps to the wrong conclusion. Are

you guilty of looking only at the circumstances in some area of your life and possibly doing the same thing? Share your response if you wish.

2

Just Say No

Genesis 39

A humorist once said that the average number of times a man says no to temptation is once, *weakly.* Some say it's easier to run than to say no—but the problem with running from temptation is that we're always leaving a forwarding address!

Those statements have more than a ring of truth to them. How difficult it is for us to police ourselves in the matter of temptation. Even Christians have a tough time saying no. Witness the scandals in 1987 television-land religion, if you don't believe me. If a prominent TV minister can succumb to sexual promiscuity, who's to say any of us is immune to moral failure? We're not. Neither were many of the men in the Bible. At times, David, Solomon, Abraham, Jacob, Samson, Abner, Amnon, Lot, and others gave in when they should have resisted. Since shortly after the creation, Satan has been slithering like a snake in and out of the lives of men and women. He incessantly tries to catch us off guard and do his dirty work of devastation and destruction.

It's not as if society today isn't trying to get us to clean up our acts. In the "enlightened eighties" we are urged by a variety of extraneous influences to shout no from the rooftops. Media ad campaigns featuring newly cleaned-out sports stars urge us to "just say no" to drugs. Experts estimate that by the end of 1988, at least fifty percent of all major companies will require applicants to undergo drug testing before they can sign on as employees. The armed services already conduct random tests of this type in an all-out attempt to curb drug abuse. Members of the organization, Mothers Against Drunk Driving, caution us against taking the wheel while under the influence, and, nationwide, anyone wishing to imbibe legally must now wait till he or she is twenty-one. Sexual monogamy, if not morality, is urged upon us by such notables as the Surgeon General of the United States. While promiscuity historically often resulted in such irritating inconveniences as venereal disease, now being heterosexually or homosexually promiscuous can mean death from Acquired Immune Deficiency Syndrome.

Human Nature Being What It Is

I am not bemoaning the loss of freedom as others might. On the other hand, I am grateful to see the attempt made to sway the country back into the practice of old-fashioned morality. Yet I am also enough of a student of human nature to realize that no public health campaign, no dried-out basketball star, not even the ominous threat of fatal disease, will permanently change people's behavior patterns. Once we allow ourselves to become used to giving in to temptation, it is hard to stop.

I saw that truth vividly illustrated while watching a TV special on AIDS. One of the panelists interviewed was a doctor from the Kinsey Institute, the well-known center for research on human sexuality. When questioned as to whether or not she felt that the threat of AIDS has changed the sexual behavior of Americans, she replied that according to Kinsey research, it has not. Yes, people are talking about changing their lifestyles, but the actual statistics show that very little behavior modification has taken place. People are still sleeping with a variety of sexual partners, and the use of contraceptive safeguards has not increased significantly. It is a sad but true testimony to human nature. Bad habits are easy to acquire and tough to break.

To Everything There Is a Season

Now don't get me wrong—God intends us to enjoy the pleasures of life, as long as these pleasures are kept within the boundaries he establishes. "To every thing there is a season," writes Solomon in Ecclesiastes (3:1a KJV). That is certainly true of what are euphemistically called the "good things" of life. For example, the money we earn may buy us enjoyable things, but we must never forget our responsibility to use part of our financial resources for the Lord's service—not because God needs our money, but because we need to give it to him. Sex is another incredible gift of God, meant for the enjoyment of his children, but it is only pleasing to him—and ultimately satisfying to us—if it is kept within the context of marriage.

God is the author of pleasure, but like any good father, he knows our natures well and gives us guidelines in his word for maximum happiness and fulfillment. The old adage, "You can't get too much of a good thing," doesn't hold water in the seamy reality of life. Just ask the child bent over double with a stomachache after stuffing himself with too much Halloween candy! Or ask the man whose extramarital flings have infected him with a disease for which there is no cure and no hope.

Temptation is unavoidable. Each of us eventually faces the desire to exceed the speed limits in the Lord's overall plan for Christian living. Scripture actually promises us that we will be enticed by the allure of that nasty, three-letter word, sin, during our days upon the earth. In 1 Corinthians 10:13, we read the comments of the apostle Paul to this effect:

> No temptation has overtaken you but such as is common to man; and God is faithful, who will not

> allow you to be tempted beyond what you are able, but with the temptation will provide the way of escape also, that you may be able to endure it (NASB).

Yes, temptations are "common to man." We'll all be tempted, but then we have a choice to make. Do we flee the temptation, or do we leap from the fry pan into the fire? Jesus was able to resist the temptations of the devil in the wilderness because he is God and because he was empowered by the Holy Spirit before he was led out to be tested (Luke 4:1-13). As Christians, we have the same resources as Christ (Hebrews 4:14-16). We, too, possess the power of God's spirit to enable us to resist Satan and run from temptation (James 4:7; 1 John 4:4; Ephesians 6:10-18).

There is always a God-given escape hatch where sin is involved. Even so, it can be difficult to follow through on what we know we ought to do. If the bait dangled is enticing enough, we find it very easy to step into the jaws of the trap. We are all susceptible to the lure of the world, the flesh, and the devil. Unreasoning desire all too easily masters us, causing us to forget the creator in our lust for the creature. Victories are won when we but keep our eyes, hearts, and minds focused on the savior instead of upon the seducer. God, through our relationship with his son and our reliance on his spirit, must of necessity remain real to us if we are to overcome temptation's threat.

What is particularly beautiful about Joseph is that God never ceases to be real to him. As we continue to look at the account of this remarkable young man, we'll see that it is possible to *just say no,* provided that God is on our side because we have been submissive and obedient to him. Submission and obedience to the father characterize Joseph's entire life, and we can learn much from his response when tempted to the absolute limit. Let's turn to the pages of Genesis 39.

Sold into Slavery—Genesis 39:1

> Now Joseph had been taken down to Egypt. Potiphar, an Egyptian who was one of Pharaoh's officials, the captain of the guard, bought him from the Ishmaelites who had taken him there.

Their hatred ledger against baby brother filled to overflowing, Joseph's brothers neatly dispose of their younger sibling by selling him to a caravan of Ishmaelite traders passing through Dothan. The merchants, with their newly acquired cargo, continue the dusty, dirty, dangerous 250-mile trek to the land of Egypt, where the markets are rich and the gold is plentiful. No doubt their handsome Hebrew slave will fetch an equally handsome price there (Genesis 37:26ff).

Picture yourself in Joseph's position at this point. Having been gifted with visions of grandeur and promise from God, he leaves on a mission of mercy for his father. Far from bowing before him, the brothers that he has expended incredible energy to locate cruelly betray him. Now he is no more than a piece of property destined to be sold into slavery in a strange land. Perhaps he will never see his family again. For all practical purposes, his fate rests in the hands of the one who is to purchase him. How he must pray that his master will be a kind and just man. Everything seems so uncertain.

Trudging alongside the slave caravan, what must Joseph think of the dreams he had earlier been given? Does he actually still believe in them? Is he assuring himself that every step he takes, every injustice he suffers, every humiliation he endures, are part of God's plan? Is he reminding himself to be patient and expectant that the Lord will use these present, dismal, discouraging circumstances to produce his desired results?

And what of God? Does he send any messages of comfort and hope to the lonely teenaged boy in this darkest hour? Scripture records no such heavenly reassurance, but I cannot help wondering if Joseph receives some anyway. When his father Jacob fled the anger of Esau, God certainly sent ample doses of comfort his way. As the sun set on his first night out, Jacob stopped in a desolate place. Exhausted, he found stones upon which to rest his head and fell fast asleep. A marvelous vision then materialized in his dreams. The sleeping Jacob saw a ladder or stairway, upon which angels ascended and descended, stretching from heaven to earth. The voice of God reverberated from the topmost rung, proclaiming, "And, behold, I am with thee, and will keep thee in all places whither thou goest, and will bring thee again into this land; for I will not leave thee, until I have done that which I have spoken to thee of" (Genesis 28:15 KJV). Perhaps as the dark of night falls, Joseph, too, far away from family and friends, lying wrapped in whatever thin blankets his captors have thrown to him, experiences the presence of God in an equally comforting and vivid way.

Certainly one of his prayers is answered, for we read in Genesis 39:1 that the Egyptian Potiphar—a VIP, the captain of pharaoh's guard—buys the young Hebrew in the slave markets of Egypt (see also Genesis 37:36). In his capacity as an important official of the king of the land, Potiphar evidently resides in the capital city of Memphis (Unger 290), and serves pharaoh however the ruler desires. Among his duties, he is responsible for carrying out all public executions, and he is in charge of the ancient Egyptian equivalents of the secret service and the FBI. The only problem with working for a man like this is that one mistake could well mean Joseph's handsome neck will meet the executioner's axe. Yet things could be much worse for Joseph, and he is certainly equal to the challenge, because God is with him even in the house of Potiphar.

Still, he is a slave. In a matter of days, his status in life has degenerated from that of preferred son to unprivileged servant. Once heir apparent, he now has no rights, no prerogatives, nothing he can call his own except a

God who loves him. His humble circumstances remind us of those experienced centuries later by Jesus Christ, who, as Scripture reveals:

> . . . although He existed in the form of God, did not regard equality with God a thing to be grasped, but emptied Himself, taking the form of a bond-servant . . . being made in the likeness of men (Philippians 2:6-7 NASB).

Christ voluntarily surrendered his position at the right hand of the father to come to earth as God in flesh. Joseph doesn't volunteer for service in the slave ranks, but rather finds himself forced into servitude. Yet he is willing and able to handle the challenge.

In the House of Potiphar—Genesis 39:2-5

> The Lord was with Joseph and he prospered, and he lived in the house of his Egyptian master. When his master saw that the Lord was with him and that the Lord gave him success in everything he did, Joseph found favor in his eyes and became his attendant. Potiphar put him in charge of his household, and he entrusted to his care everything he owned. From the time he put him in charge of his household and of all that he owned, the Lord blessed the household of the Egyptian because of Joseph. The blessing of the Lord was on everything Potiphar had, both in the house and in the field.

Perhaps the whole of Joseph's life is summed up in the first words of Genesis 39:2: "The Lord was with Joseph." It doesn't matter that Joseph has been torn from Canaan to serve another man in Egypt. God is still with him. Why?

The Obedient Heart and the Submissive Spirit

There are two reasons why Joseph experiences God's presence in his time of trial: the obedient heart and the submissive spirit. As we've mentioned before, Joseph possesses both. Of his great-grandfather Abraham, it is written in Genesis 15:6 that he "believed the Lord, and he credited it to him as righteousness." Likewise, Joseph believes his God, and this is the key ingredient in having an obedient heart and a submissive spirit. It involves following the advice of the writer of the book of Hebrews:

> Keep your lives free from the love of money and be content with what you have, because God has said,
> "Never will I leave you;
> never will I forsake you."
> So we say with confidence,
> "The Lord is my helper; I will not be afraid.
> What can man do to me?" (Hebrews 13:5-6).

Joseph is not bound by his circumstances. He is wrapped up in his God. He is content, submissive, and obedient to the father's wishes, completely convinced that the Lord has ordered his situation.

Sometimes it is hard for us to accept that the Lord ordains even the difficult times. He permits the highs and the lows. When the going gets tough, we start figuring that God isn't taking care of us too well. Maybe he has forgotten about us, we think. Let me tell you, that is never true. God never forgets, and he never neglects.

Today many of us are suffering financial, physical, and emotional woes. How can we be submissive and obedient like Joseph in the face of adversity? We can start by asking ourselves some questions. Have we invited the Lord along? Do we want his will? Do we crave his company to the point where we will allow our lives to become open books before him? Are we where he wants us to be at this moment? Are we willing to go and to do and to be the kind of people he wants us to be? Joseph was.

If there are even well-intentioned disobediences in our

lives, then it's entirely possible that we've never wholeheartedly asked God to come along for the ride. We may have accepted Christ as savior, but we've never made the decision to give him top priority in our lives, so we don't feel fulfilled, we don't feel satisfied, we don't feel prosperous.

I think it is important to note that scripture tells us that Joseph actually "prospered" in the house of Potiphar (39:2). He does well; he accomplishes much; his projects meet with success. Why? It's because he is obedient and submissive, satisfied to serve another because that is the lot the Lord has given him for the moment.

Just because Scripture tells us that Joseph prospers does not mean that he becomes a rich man. He is, after all, a slave. Besides, the Bible doesn't teach that by spreading a little spiritual seed, the sower automatically becomes wealthy. God never intended his church to be completely composed of millionaires. What we can expect, as Joseph, is that if we put the Lord first in our lives, if we are obedient to his word, then we shall receive his blessings because he will lead us directly into the center of his will. Essentially, that is the promise of Joshua 1:8, where General Joshua, about to lead the children of Israel into the promised land at last, is instructed by the Lord:

> Do not let this Book of the Law depart from your mouth; meditate on it day and night, so that you may be careful to do everything written in it. Then you will be prosperous and successful.

Men after His Own Heart

To tell the truth, I actually think that crises, even such as Joseph faced, are good for Christians. It's a beautiful thing to witness Christians becoming more open, more cohesive, more loving, as they are driven to be dependent upon one another in times of trial. Hard times make us recognize that many of the things we are living for aren't first place with God. It's knowing his word, obeying his voice, yielding to his authority, that count. This describes Joseph.

Years after Joseph's experience with slavery, he is present at the farewell address of his aged father. Upon his deathbed, old Jacob calls for his sons to gather around him. He blesses Joseph, calling him "a fruitful bough" (Genesis 49:22 KJV). What an apt description that is! Joseph is the type of individual described in Psalm 1:3: "A tree planted by the rivers of water, that bringeth forth his fruit in his season; his leaf also shall not wither, and whatsoever he doeth shall prosper" (KJV). 2 Chronicles 16:9 says, "For the eyes of the Lord range throughout the earth to strengthen those whose hearts are fully committed to him." God actively searches for people like Joseph, men and women who long to follow him, who are willing to completely trust him. These he will bless. These he will prosper.

As far as God is concerned, there are three factors that are crucial if we are to experience the prosperous life of blessing. These enable us to be men and women after his own heart.

The first is fellowship with him. That means spending time with him in prayer and in the study of his word. We have to get to know him before we can fully experience and appreciate his blessing.

The second is depending upon his faithfulness. It's believing that God's mercies are new every morning. It's hanging in there when everything seems to grow cold. It's trusting in his power and love even when the fog rolls in and the lights flicker.

The third involves bringing forth fruit. It's a byproduct of the first two. "By this is My Father glorified," states Jesus in John 15:8, "that you bear much fruit, and so prove to be My disciples" (NASB). Joseph does this in his life because he remains in fellowship with God, and because he continually trusts in the faithfulness of his heavenly father. The result? His life gives evidence that someone, greater than he, is in control.

The Place of Preparation

Where is Joseph when the Lord prospers him so in Genesis 39? He is living "in the house of his Egyptian master," according to verse 2. And God keeps him there for a purpose. Joseph is in a place of preparation. The time spent in the house of Potiphar will ready him for events that will happen two or three episodes down the pike, when he ascends to the palace.

God allows us to be put in places of preparation, too. Sometimes it can be tough. Maybe you're facing some trials and tests. But regardless of whether things are easy or difficult at the moment, the fact is that the Lord is preparing you for the palace, too. If not on this earth, he is surely readying you to occupy the mansion that he has gone ahead to prepare for you if you are his child (John 14:2).

All of earthly life is temporary, the adversities merely part of a pruning process. God is at work in the life of each individual, clipping and snipping at the dead branches, the diseased wills, the distorted affections. His motive? He desires to bring each of us into a saving relationship with Jesus Christ, and to nurture that relationship so that it bears fruit.

It has been said that adversity is often the father of great things, and that throughout history some of the greatest visions were born of trial. Giving birth can be an intensely painful process. Yet the agony of labor is worth it all in the end, as a precious baby emerges from the contracting womb. Who is to say that the tough times in life don't produce similar results? They can be the birth pangs of something special, because they are all part of the Lord's process of preparing us for what he has in store. The pain, the hurt, the misunderstanding, the suffering, all fit together in the end. As Paul puts it in Romans 8:18, "For I consider that the sufferings of this present time are not worthy to be compared with the glory that is to be revealed to us" (NASB).

The Watching World

Something we need to remember during the weeks, months, and even years of black or gray circumstances is that others will be watching. Joseph isn't the only one to observe that God is blessing him in the midst of slavery. Potiphar also takes note, according to Genesis 39:3.

Isn't that terrific? What a tremendous testimony to the Lord's power that a pagan onlooker notices the success of a slave. What a joy it is to have someone outside (or inside) the body of Christ say, "Hey, you've got it all together. You're happy. You're satisfied." When it's obvious that the Lord is blessing us, believe me, it will be noticed by the watching world.

No Working Man Blues

Just how does Potiphar manage to see the Lord's hand in the life of his slave? I'd venture to say that it's because of Joseph's terrific attitude in a terrible situation. In Colossians 3:23 the apostle Paul instructs us, "Whatever you do, do your work heartily, as for the Lord rather than for men" (NASB). That sums up Joseph's philosophy, as he rolls up his sleeves and dives eagerly into whatever task Potiphar gives him. All the master probably has to do is hand him a job description, and Joseph gets to it without grumbling or disputing, wailing or whining. As in his younger days, herding sheep for his father, he deeply desires to be a reliable employee and a good servant. He does the best he can, and because the Lord is with him, he is extremely successful.

How much Joseph's attitude toward work differs from the typical outlook in our modern society. Today we live in an age where the clamor for individual rights far exceeds the call of duty. This is perhaps most glaringly obvious in the world of big-time athletics. We can't attend a ball game any more without being reminded that some third baseman, running back, or power forward reported late to training camp because his agent was busy right up to the eleventh hour negotiating his multimillion-dollar contract. Money—not competition, contribution, or commitment—is the name of the game.

Far from the pizazz of pro sports, we hear a great deal about strikes and employee demands and very little about employee responsibility in the workaday world. By and large, we aren't a nation of servants in the marketplace. Instead, the idea is to "get all we can, *can* all we get, and forget the rest!" Chrysler president Lee Iacocca exposes the myth of the modern American work ethic in his autobiography, as he describes the average Japanese employee. Writes Iacocca:

> The Japanese worker is highly disciplined. If something's crooked, he'll straighten it. If there's a problem on the assembly line, he'll stop the line until it's fixed.
>
> These guys have a lot of pride. They see their work as a mission. You don't hear stories in Japan about workers showing up with a hangover. There's no industrial sabotage and no visible worker alienation.
>
> In fact, I once read that some Japanese companies had to fine their supervisors because so many of them insisted on working on holidays as well as on their days off. Could you imagine that happening in Michigan or Ohio? (Iacocca 322).

I'm not suggesting that we turn into a nation of workaholics. Far from it. As we'll see from Potiphar's example, one over-zealous workaholic can spoil an entire home. Yet Joseph's positive work habits should convince us that it is essential for Christian employees to put forth maximum effort in their jobs. What a tremendous witness it is for us, like Joseph, to roll up our sleeves and plunge into even distasteful tasks without complaint. It becomes easier if we remember that, while the name of our earthly firm may be printed on our paychecks, it is our heavenly father for whom we are truly working. Joseph certainly knows that God, not his human master, is the ultimate boss.

Life over Lip

Even as a young man, Joseph recognizes that through acts of unselfish service, he brings honor and glory to God. That's an idea we've taken to heart at Don Anderson Ministries. Before we dive headlong into a week's worth of family or youth camp activities, we remind ourselves as a staff that the teaching sessions are only a small part of the overall picture. What really counts is not what happens when one of us is sitting on a stool expositing scripture. The things that are most important about the week occur outside the meeting room. What especially reflects Christ are the loving acts of service performed behind the scenes for the glory of God. This is how we touch people's lives. This is how we show them the savior who cares so much.

When it comes to telling others about Jesus Christ, many of us feel that our tongues are tied in granny knots. I've known men and women guiltridden over their inability to verbalize their Christian faith. We do need to be ready to give an account of our beliefs, but the concentration in the meantime should be on what we are, not on what we are able to say. I repeat, top priority is what we *are*. It's life over lip.

Think of the instructions given by Peter to women married to unbelievers. Writes the apostle: "In the same way, you wives, be submissive to your own husbands so that even if any of them are disobedient to the word, they may be won without a word by the behavior of their wives" (1 Peter 3:1 NASB). Does Peter admonish the wives of non-Christians to display tracts at breakfast time and tape Bible verses to the bathroom mirror in order to win their men to the Lord? Does he coach them to recite the plan of salvation over the supper table? No.

Instead, he exhorts them to win their husbands to Christ through their own pure, gentle, submissive, loving behavior. Actions speak louder than words.

In the Sermon on the Mount, Jesus tells his followers that they are the "salt of the earth" and "the light of the world" (Matthew 5:13-14). Joseph is, too. His light is not snuffed out simply because he finds himself captive in a foreign land serving a foreign official. Rather, Joseph's light radiates with such brightness that Potiphar cannot help but notice his unbreakable yet thoroughly unselfish spirit.

Moving On to the Bigger and the Better

Because the hand of God is so obviously evident in the life of Joseph, he finds favor in the sight of his master. Genesis 39:4 tells us that Joseph becomes Potiphar's "attendant," and that he is placed "in charge of his household." So great is his confidence in the young Hebrew that Potiphar actually entrusts Joseph with everything he owns.

We've seen that Joseph is a loyal employee. Remember, he didn't shy away from informing his father about the misdeeds of his half-brothers, which occurred while they all tended Jacob's flocks together (Genesis 37:2). And recall that he willingly traveled the extra miles to Dothan from Shechem to search out his siblings (37:17). Joseph isn't afraid to do the dirty work. And he can be trusted.

It's certain that he has the gift of administration as well. He works for a relatively short amount of time in Potiphar's house, and soon his talent and ability become so evident that he's running the whole show. God doesn't waste experiences in our lives. The little opportunities of leadership lead to bigger and better things. The management training Joseph acquired in the fields with his brothers enables him to tackle the vastly more difficult chore of running Potiphar's affairs. His promotion is earned and well deserved.

We, too, need to see the opportunities God drops in our

laps as chances to exercise the gifts and abilities he has given us. This is the way we make our greatest contributions in our families, our jobs, and in the Christian community. We fit the mold he's made for us. We find fulfillment instead of frustration.

Potiphar's decision to give Joseph additional responsibility turns out to be a good one. We read in Genesis 39:5, "From the time he put him in charge of his household and of all that he owned, the Lord blessed the household of the Egyptian because of Joseph. The blessing of the Lord was on everything Potiphar had, both in the house and in the field." Things go well for Potiphar because he is cooperating with an unseen hand—the hand of God. But events are soon to become very, very interesting, indeed.

JUST SAYING NO—GENESIS 39:6-10

> So he left in Joseph's care everything he had; with Joseph in charge, he did not concern himself with anything except the food he ate.
>
> Now Joseph was well-built and handsome, and after a while his master's wife took notice of Joseph and said, "Come to bed with me!"
>
> But he refused. "With me in charge," he told her, "my master does not concern himself with anything in the house; everything he owns he has entrusted to my care. No one is greater in this house than I am. My master has withheld nothing from me except you, because you are his wife. How then could I do such a wicked thing and sin against God?" And though she spoke to Joseph day after day, he refused to go to bed with her or even be with her.

With Joseph in charge, Potiphar is relieved of many of his responsibilities at home. As verse 6 reveals, so explicitly does the master trust his slave that he concerns himself with nothing except the food he eats. Evidently

Potiphar still desires to have some say in the menu planning. But choosing lamb chops or sirloin for supper is hardly the only domestic decision a man should make. There are some things that you just cannot turn over to others. One of these is your wife.

Too Busy to Notice, Too Tired to Care

I'd venture to say that before Joseph arrives on the scene, Potiphar probably spends a little too much time at the office. He is a politician on the rise, and that demands long hours, but there is still much to be handled in the house. When Joseph proves to be so capable and dependable, Potiphar sees his chance. Leave this Hebrew in charge, he thinks, and I can devote more time to the job. I won't have to be bothered with the budget, the yard work, the chariot repair, the myriad details of maintaining a home. And if he wasn't before, it's probable that Potiphar becomes a full-blown workaholic, freed from his worries at home, wrapped up in his administrative duties as captain of pharaoh's guard. He certainly seems to have traveled a lot, because we rarely read of his being around the house. Meanwhile, he leaves behind him an unfulfilled woman.

We also read in Genesis 39:6 that Joseph is "well-built and handsome." Joseph is no slouch in the looks department. His face is handsome, and his body taut and firm from the job. He exudes sex appeal without trying. Today ad agencies would line him up for toothpaste or after-shave commercials. He is what my daughters would refer to as a "hunk." If we estimate that Joseph's total time of service in Potiphar's house is some ten years, then he is around twenty-six or twenty-seven years of age when Mrs. Potiphar sits up and takes notice of him. And when she notices, she doesn't waste any time. "Come to bed with me!" she exclaims to him (39:7).

Potiphar's wife may come on fast and furious with Joseph, but it's only because she has a serious problem. Rather than being some sort of nymphomaniac, she is, I believe, simply neglected. Potiphar is rarely at home; he has delegated these responsibilities. He is so caught up in his work that he has no time for her. The only time he pays attention to her is when he desires her sexually, or when he escorts her to a social function so he can show her off. She is probably quite pretty. She is certainly very lonely.

How can Potiphar's wife fill the empty hours of her day? Lonely women today can schedule dates with their golf and bridge buddies. They go to Jazzercise classes, Junior League meetings, garden club events. I imagine Mrs. Potiphar does whatever the ancient Egyptian versions of these things were, yet she finds herself spinning her wheels in a vain effort to erase the boredom. No wonder she begins to look for attention elsewhere. No wonder Joseph, the kid who in the last ten years or so has become a very good-looking man, starts to seem terribly appealing.

The Danger of High Places

There is another woman in scripture very much like the wife of Potiphar, and that is Bathsheba. Bathsheba was literally a military widow. Her husband Uriah, a Hittite, lived, breathed, and ate warfare. He probably slept in his combat boots, his shield by his side. What Bathsheba most desired in the whole world was a child, and this Uriah had not given her. Once more her monthly cycle ran its course with dreary regularity. Her husband was off fighting for his adopted country when she ascended to the roof of their home to bathe and ceremonially cleanse herself of the impurity of her menstrual cycle. And it just so happened that the king of the land was next door, watching.

It was a high point in David's life and career when he spotted Bathsheba bathing atop her roof. At fifty years of age, he stayed behind in the capital while others fought his country's conflicts. He was too valuable to his people to risk his life on the battlefield any more. He had already won the greatest of the victories and extended the boundaries of his land substantially. He had whipped the Philistines, conquered Jerusalem, and made it his capital instead of Hebron. He had built a magnificent palace and had returned the ark of the covenant to its proper resting place in Jerusalem. David had but to rest upon his laurels for the remainder of his days. Then he spied the beautiful young woman next door, and he was overcome by temptation (2 Samuel 11).

That tells me something. Temptation is less of a problem when we're suffering than when we're successful. It's at times of blessing, not adversity, that we face the severest urges to sin. You don't catch a person in moral trouble when his hands are shaky and his cup is empty, because then he is concentrating on the things he ought to be concentrating on. He is climbing the mountain. Get him on top, and watch out! He is wide open for an attack by the evil one. As Chuck Swindoll writes in *Three Steps Forward, Two Steps Back*, "It is tougher to *remain* victorious than it is to *become* victorious" (Swindoll 176).

How the Snare Works

Just how are we tempted? James 1:14-15 puts it well: "But each one is tempted when he is carried away and enticed by his own lust. Then when lust has conceived, it gives birth to sin; and when sin is accomplished, it brings forth death" (NASB). Something appeals to our senses. Usually it is the eyegate that opens wide to let in a flood of desire. That's what happened to Achan following the battle of Jericho. "I saw . . . I coveted . . . I took," he confessed concerning the forbidden gold, silver, and clothing that he plundered from the burning city (Joshua 7:21). Years later, had David kept his eyes from straying, he might never have committed adultery with Bathsheba.

We don't expect temptation; it strikes us unawares. We may be minding our own business, then it hits us. The key is to determine not to succumb *before* the temptation ever hits, then pray like crazy and hit the ground running when the bait of the snare dangles in front of us!

Purposing in His Heart

Like Daniel centuries later, Joseph "purposed in his heart that he would not defile himself" (Daniel 1:8 KJV). When Potiphar's wife comes on to him with her tawdry invitation, Joseph simply refuses. He utters what is at times the most difficult word in the English language to say: "No" (39:8). That two-letter word is the secret to overcoming temptation. Speaking it requires predetermination. We have to decide—before temptation rears its seductively pretty head—what our answer will be. And it is much harder to say no after we've said yes once before. Joseph doesn't allow himself to make that mistake.

Don't make the error of assuming that Joseph is not tempted by Mrs. Potiphar's advances, either. He is under stress, and he is no unemotional mummy. He possesses all the natural desires of the flesh of any twenty-seven-year-old, red-blooded male. Seducing the wife of his master could only minister to his pride. Such a conquest could feed his ego for months. It may be that he pauses for a moment and thinks, why not? Who'll ever know? No one will get hurt. Besides, everybody else is doing it. I'm not living in Canaan any more, with all those restrictions. I'm in a different culture and, when in Egypt, do as the Egyptians do! It may even help my career. Besides, if anyone finds out, she'll certainly shield me. She really thinks I'm something. Letting her have her way would be the easiest way out of this predicament. Why disappoint her? I might as well get a little sexual satisfaction in return for all this service.

But Joseph doesn't equivocate. He refuses to rationalize. Instead he answers emphatically. "My master has withheld nothing from me except you, because you are his wife," he tells her. "How then could I do such a wicked thing and sin against God?" (39:9).

Principles to Ponder

In his response to the woman, Joseph acknowledges that he would be violating two principles if he were to give in. First, each husband and each wife has the right to expect the other to remain faithful. Second, God has the right to expect us to walk openly and purely before him.

Joseph recognizes that yielding to temptation (not simply being tempted) is sin against God. He may be flattered by the lady's attention, but he realizes that giving in to temptation will damage his horizontal relationships with Potiphar and others in the house, and, more importantly, will mar his vertical relationship with the Lord.

"How could I do such a wicked thing and sin against God?" What a refreshing statement Joseph makes as his innocence is transformed into virtue by means of temptation. How much his attitude contrasts with that of the society in which we live. In the United States this year alone twenty million pornographic magazines will be sold. Over two million Americans will contract gonorrhea. Thousands will die of AIDS. Hundreds of thousands will experiment with mind-altering substances. Thousands will be diagnosed as alcoholics. Homosexuals will continue en masse to campaign for gay rights. As a matter of convenience, countless children will be killed before they are born. What the world calls the new morality—but what God calls immorality—will run rampant.

Consequences to Consider

It's a dangerous world we live in. It's especially deadly if we do not decide *before* the bait is dangled that we'll not give in to temptation. Great is the devastation when we allow ourselves to be susceptible.

I think of the trips that Pearl and I so love to make to the northwest. We look forward to driving along the highways and seeing the lush, green forests. Yet one of the things we dread is to come upon a charred mountainside whose towering trees have been reduced to blackened, splintered toothpicks, vestiges of their former beauty. The grandeur is gone, vanished in the raging forest fire that, sparked by a burst of lightning or the fallen match of a careless camper, devastated the area.

Forest fires are a horrendous problem in Oregon and Washington. Once they ravage a region, all that is left are ugly evidences of what was once beautiful. Sin does that to a life, too. If allowed to run amok, its searing flames scar the landscape of a person's life. To love this destructive force, sin, is to love what literally drove Jesus Christ to the cross.

It is Satan's pleasure to minimize sin. He calls it by other names. In his jargon, homosexuality becomes "an alternate lifestyle"; promiscuity, "sexual liberty"; drunkenness, "a social disease"; murder through abortion, "freedom of choice." Satan points us to the pleasure and never to the pain of disobedience. Joseph is a model for us as he says, "I'm not going to do it. Others may sow their wild oats, but not me. I'll not sin against God."

How to Keep On Keeping On

And he has to keep on saying it. Verse 10 reveals that Potiphar's wife will not take no for an answer. She persists. Day after day she attempts to seduce Joseph, and day after day he refuses her. He even begins avoiding her, and who can blame him? She persists; he resists. Finally, he wisely retreats.

That tells us a great deal about Joseph's character. Often we can be victorious on the first shot, but come the second or the third or the fourteenth, and we give in. Sometimes the evil one just lets the temptation barrage continue until we can take no more. Eve resisted eating the forbidden fruit the first time the serpent tempted her, but she caved in on round two (Genesis 3:1-6). Samson did well in resisting Delilah the first three times, but he succumbed to the fourth volley of her charms, and revealed the secret of his strength (Judges 16:4ff).

When it comes to moral temptation, there is also often a weakening of the will that comes with emotional involvement. If we don't run from a touchy situation, we may well become emotionally involved. We're lost. The best recourse is to flee. Joseph does that. If he were to allow himself to feel sorry for Mrs. Potiphar, if he were to hold long, tender talks with her trying to defuse her desire, he might well wind up in bed with her. Comforting counsel and concern can too easily carry one into intimacy. The answer takes firm resolution. It takes just saying no, and then getting out of the way—fast.

BEATING A WELL-TIMED RETREAT—GENESIS 39:11-18

> One day he went into the house to attend to his duties, and none of the household servants was inside. She caught him by his cloak and said, "Come to bed with me!" But he left his cloak in her hand and ran out of the house.
>
> When she saw that he had left his cloak in her hand and had run out of the house, she called her household servants. "Look," she said to them, "this Hebrew has been brought to us to make sport of us! He came in here to sleep with me, but I screamed. When he heard me scream for help, he left his cloak beside me and ran out of the house."
>
> She kept his cloak beside her until his master came home. Then she told him this story: "That Hebrew slave you brought us came to me to make sport of me. But as soon as I screamed for help, he left his cloak beside me and ran out of the house."

It has to happen sometime. Try as he might to avoid her, Joseph inevitably walks into the woman's clutches. On this particular day, Genesis 39:11 tells us, "none of the household servants" is inside as Joseph, oblivious to the danger, walks within the mansion to attend to some of his duties. Mrs. Potiphar and he are alone in the house. Seizing this opportunity born of isolation, Potiphar's wife zeroes in on the handsome Hebrew like a heat-seeking missile. Her sensors are ready, and he is caught totally unawares.

And he is caught literally. Mrs. Potiphar grabs Joseph by his cloak. "Come to bed with me!" she begs with not much subtlety.

What does Joseph do? He runs. He takes off like a bolt of greased lightning. He doesn't even bother to retrieve his cloak. She can have it! He's getting out of there! This is the second coat Joseph has lost since his biography began. The first, you remember, was torn from him by his brothers before they threw him in the pit. This one remains in the grip of his would-be seductress, as he flees from her presence. He may be losing his coats, but at least Joseph is keeping his character!

Resisting the Devil and Running from Temptation

Is Joseph right in his response to the advances of his master's wife? Does he handle the situation as he should? In a word, yes.

I believe that one of the biggest problems we Christians have with temptation is that we handle it all wrong. As we've discussed earlier, we can count on being enticed by the world, the flesh, and the devil.

The world constantly tries to lure us to conform to its priorities and its patterns. What are we supposed to do? Romans 12:2 puts it well: "And be not conformed to this world, but be ye transformed by the renewing of your mind, that ye may prove what is that good, and acceptable, and perfect, will of God" (KJV). In certain situations, we'll have to say, "No, I'm a Christian and that's not my lifestyle." We have to determine, for example, that we will not spend seven hours a day in front of the television. Neither will we pour ourselves into materialistically keeping up with the Joneses. There are better things to do and better places to go than what the world would have us believe, and we can find fulfillment in not conforming to many of its standards.

Then there's the devil. What do we do when the evil one hits us with his darts and arrows? He always aims at the spiritual tender spots, you know. If we haven't taken time yet today to pray for our families and to meditate on God's word, Satan has already won. He has struck us right where we live. He's centered us in his sights and, finding us with neither shield nor sword, he's nailed us. We've been slow-moving, easy-to-hit, virtually defenseless targets. All he wants is to keep us out of the word, away from the Lord, and empty of gratitude.

What do we do with the devil? We resist him. We stand up to him and say, "You are a defeated foe! I am going to get into the word and, in the power of Jesus Christ, I have victory over you!" As James 4:7 puts it, "Submit therefore to God. Resist the devil, and he will flee from you" (NASB). If we've accepted Christ as savior, he has already won the war for us. In the heat of the battle, the devil has no choice but to turn tail and run when we resist.

What about moral temptation? What do we do when we're faced with the flesh? That's easy. Like Joseph, we run. 1 Timothy 6:11 says of moral temptations, "But flee from these things, you man of God; and pursue righteousness, godliness, faith, love, perseverance and gentleness" (NASB). Often we get it all backwards. We flee from Satan and try to resist temptation. Let me tell you, the devil likes that, too, because when we try it, we lose on both counts. The devil chases after us, and we succumb to the seductress if we stick around long enough in the same room with her.

Joseph wins the battle. He loses his coat but keeps his character. Fortified by the grace of God, he doesn't fail and he doesn't fall. The way to get rid of temptation is never to yield to it, always to gallop away from it. Yes, yielding may be more popular, acceptable, exhilarating, but the person who is the happiest, least guilty, most fulfilled in the long run is the one who has said no.

After the Lusting?

Perhaps startled by Joseph's rapid retreat, Mrs. Potiphar, left holding the cloak, calls for her household servants.

"Look," she exclaims, "this Hebrew has been brought to us to make sport of us! He came in here to sleep with me, but I screamed. When he heard me scream for help, he left his cloak beside me and ran out of the house" (39:14-15).

What Mrs. Potiphar's reaction to Joseph's running tells us is a principle worth noting. Intense hatred always follows either a satisfaction of lustful passion, or the inability to gratify such. The issue at stake is not love, but pride. Amnon and Tamar, half-brother and sister, children of David, are an example of how lust becomes disgust when indulged (2 Samuel 13).

Feigning illness, Amnon lured his sister to his quarters, where he implored her to make love to him. When Tamar refused and attempted to dissuade him, Amnon violently raped her. After the act, according to 2 Samuel 13:15, "Then Amnon hated her with intense hatred. In fact, he hated her more than he had loved her. Amnon said to her, 'Get up and get out!' " His lust turned to loathing as quickly as his appetite was appeased.

For Mrs. Potiphar, there is no satisfaction. She is left holding the coat. The sting of such obvious rejection gets to her, and hell truly hath no fury like a woman scorned. Frustrated, embarrassed, angry, her passion is transformed to hostility. With rancor, she thirsts not for romance, but revenge. She screams for her servants and lies about what has happened, accusing Joseph of attempting to force himself upon her (39:14-15). When Potiphar gets home that evening, she brandishes Joseph's cloak as evidence, and repeats the lie (39:16-18). Finally, she has her husband's full attention, but at what a tremendous cost.

Falsely Accused . . . Found Guilty as Charged—Genesis 39:19-23

> When his master heard the story his wife told him, saying, "This is how your slave treated me," he burned with anger. Joseph's master took him and

> put him in prison, the place where the king's prisoners were confined.
>
> But while Joseph was there in the prison, the Lord was with him; he showed him kindness and granted him favor in the eyes of the warden. So the warden put Joseph in charge of all those held in the prison, and he was made responsible for all that was done there. The warden paid no attention to anything under Joseph's care, because the Lord was with Joseph and gave him success in whatever he did.

Potiphar listens to his wife's false but plausible account. He glares at the coat Joseph left behind. He begins to burn with anger (39:19). Enraged, he seizes Joseph and throws him in jail, into "prison . . . where the king's prisoners were confined" (39:20).

What do you suppose Joseph is thinking at this point? Well, Lord, here we go again. You sure have a funny way of fulfilling dreams, God. Maybe those are his thoughts. But we don't read of Joseph's grumbling and protesting the situation. True, he is in prison, but that in itself is a fairly mild penalty, considering Potiphar could well have ordered Joseph's execution for attempting to rape his beautiful wife. And it is not such a bad jail, as prisons go. It is the place where political prisoners are kept, not a human cesspool where hardened criminals are caged. Don't misunderstand—the prison experience will not be a picnic for Joseph. Jail beats the pit into which his brothers had tossed him, but it is also a far cry from Potiphar's comfortable abode.

What is marvelous is that Joseph is not *under* his circumstances, he is *on top* of them. He is facing the situation in confidence and trust, and great is his victory. The Lord is still with Joseph, and grants him "favor in the eyes of the prison warden" (39:21). Just like Potiphar, the official recognizes talent, trustworthiness, and the touch of God, and places Joseph in charge of the entire prison. We read that the warden doesn't even bother to watch over Joseph's shoulder, so confident is he in the young man's character and ability. Chapter 39 concludes with these encouraging words: "The Lord was with Joseph and gave him success in whatever he did" (39:23).

What Is Your Captivity?

As she traveled around the world, the late Corrie ten Boom often carried with her a small piece of tapestry. One time I was privileged to hear her speak and I watched as she displayed the piece of cloth to the audience. At first glance, it was an ugly item, its threads tangled, ragged, and snagged. But when Corrie turned it over, the onlooker knew that he had merely been viewing the back of the piece. Beautifully embroidered on the reverse side of the tapestry were the words, "God Is Love." Anyone looking at Joseph's situation right now might see only a tangled mass of loose ends, a snarled, ugly snafu. He's been misjudged and mistreated in an enormous miscarriage of justice. Yet from God's perspective above, the prison experience is simply a thread woven into the tapestry of a beautiful life.

What is your captivity? Perhaps you are bound by the four walls of an accident, anxiety, disappointment, loneliness, depression, illness, financial reversal, misunderstanding, tragedy, or sorrow. How are you handling it? Or, to revise the question: *Are you letting God handle it?*

William Tyndale, a contemporary of Martin Luther, is revered as one of the leaders of the Protestant Reformation. Deeply convicted that the people needed scripture in their own language, he was the first to translate and publish the New Testament in English, despite tremendous ridicule and intense adversity. He also translated the books of Jonah and the Pentateuch. Excommunicated, hunted, shipwrecked, betrayed, jailed, tortured, sentenced, like Joseph he too awaited his fate in prison. How did he handle the situation? Lying in his dank cell, Tyndale mentioned to friends that the date of his execution had not been set and that winter was coming on. "Bring me a warmer cap, something to patch my leggings, a woolen shirt, and above all, my Hebrew Bible!" he implored (Gunther 23). William Tyndale managed the adversity by placing his confidence in the creator, by laying his fears at the feet of the master, by serving the savior until the hour he was strangled and burned at the stake. Even then, the final words he loudly proclaimed at the time of his execution were, "Lord, open the king of England's eyes!" (Gunther 17).

Joseph and William Tyndale were kindred spirits. Both knew that God never promises us rose gardens, but that he will enable us to navigate through the thorns. He will always be with us. H.G. Wells once said that "God is an ever absent help in the time of adversity." Far from it, my friends, far from it indeed. We may think he isn't there, but he is waiting to minister. Our hardship can become a cocoon from which something lovely will emerge.

We grow in life by losing, leaving, letting go. Joseph of necessity does that. He leaves his homeland. He loses his position in Potiphar's house. He is forced to let go of the past. And in the midst of the training ground of affliction, God is with him, and he is victorious.

LESSONS

This episode of Joseph's life suggests many powerful lessons. Let's consider these briefly.

Lesson one: *the Lord is with Joseph, and he becomes a successful man.* We can experience this God-given success, too, if we possess obedient hearts and submissive spirits.

Lesson two: *the blessing on Potiphar's house occurs because Joseph is working there, and because God upholds Joseph.* And what a terrific attitude he has!

Lesson three: *in succumbing to temptation, the sin is*

really against God. It is never wrong to be tempted; it is always wrong to give in and sin.

Lesson four: *let's remember the Lord's guidelines for godly living: be not conformed to this world, resist the devil, flee temptation.*

Lesson five: when we are facing unexplainable circumstances, we must realize that *God is going through the affliction with us, and he has permitted the situation for our growth and his glory.* He is in control.

Lesson six: *it is better to lose one's coat than one's character.*

Lesson seven: *we can only give away our virginity once.*

Lesson eight: *Satan will point to the pleasure and not to the pain of sin.*

Lesson nine: *Satan also will minimize sin in our eyes.* He'll call it by other names. He'll disguise its danger and misrepresent its consequences.

Lesson ten: *properly handling temptation comes easier when we're in the pit than atop the pinnacle.* Success brings with it its own snares.

Counting the Cost

Lest we forget, there are consequences to sin. Joseph avoids them because he runs away from an immoral situation as fast as his legs will carry him. His is the intelligent response. We must never forget that we are all liable to give in when we should say no.

I am reminded of one of our sailing excursions in the northwest. My love of salmon fishing is not the least of the reasons our ministry has sponsored these trips from time to time! On one particular evening, we glided the boat into a small cove that promised to be flush with salmon, and spent the night there. The next morning, as the grey mist rolled away to reveal a brilliant blue sky, I hooked a live one! What a fish! How it fought! Finally I managed to reel it in and net it, and we gathered to admire my trophy. The salmon was a magnificent creature, one of the prettiest I had ever caught. Its silvery scales shimmered in the sunlight. Its beauty seemed absolutely flawless, until I flipped it over. On the other side of the fish there was a long black mark down near the tail, which marred its appearance.

"What is that?" I asked a fellow from the area.

"That's nothing," he replied. "At one time your fish almost became a meal for a seal, and the mark is what is left of the experience."

I thought to myself, isn't that tragic? The salmon escaped being the main course of a seal's banquet, only to be fooled into snatching a fisherman's bait.

That happens in life, too. Just about the time we're pounding ourselves on our chests and whooping a Tarzan yell of victory, we are hit from behind by the darts of Satan, and our hides are nailed to the wall. That's why the Bible exhorts us, "Therefore let him who thinks he stands take heed lest he fall" (1 Corinthians 10:12 NASB; see also Galatians 6:1). We cannot be too careful when it comes to dealing with temptation.

And What If?

And what if we've failed in the past? What if we've said yes when we should have said no? The answer is easy. It is never too late for us to come before the Lord in honest repentance. If we have not accepted him as savior, the opportunity is there for us to ask him into our lives (John 3:16). If we are Christians already, then the attitude of David in Psalm 51 is one we should adopt as we seek forgiveness and the restoration of our fellowship with the father. There the psalmist writes, following his sin with Bathsheba:

> Be gracious to me, O God, according to Thy lovingkindness;
> According to the greatness of Thy compassion blot out my transgressions.
> Wash me thoroughly from my iniquity,

And cleanse me from my sin.
For I know my transgressions,
And my sin is ever before me.
Against Thee, Thee only, have I sinned,
And done what is evil in Thy sight,
So that Thou art justified when Thou dost speak,
And blameless when Thou dost judge
(Psalm 51:1-4 NASB).

Questions for Study

1. Can we avoid temptation (1 Corinthians 10:13)?

2. How does Joseph respond when tempted by Potiphar's wife?

3. How should we respond to temptation? To the devil? Think of an experience from your own life when you have either rightly or wrongly reacted to temptation or the devil. Share the incident, if you wish.

4. What spiritual resources do we have to turn to when we are tempted (Hebrews 4:14-16; James 4:7; 1 John 4:4; Ephesians 6:10-18)?

5. Describe Joseph's attitude as he works in Potiphar's house and later in prison. How does he approach the duties that are assigned him? From his example, what principles might we apply to our own work?

3

On Hold

Genesis 40

Good things come to those who wait—so goes the old adage. Yet isn't this the typical American perspective: good things come a lot faster to those who won't wait? I'm afraid so.

Although our lives many times are slowed because of crawling traffic jams, crowded store lines, and creeping banking lanes, we never get used to waiting. It is excruciating for us. We detest delays of almost any kind. So we pop frozen waffles into the toaster rather than whipping up the real thing. We stir spoonfuls of instant coffee into mugs of microwaved boiling water instead of waiting for the percolator to do its stuff. We fume at ticket agents when flights are behind schedule. We run our credit cards to the limit rather than saving for major purchases. Simply put, we hate to wait.

I'm worse than most when it comes to putting up with delays. To my way of thinking, every minute should fit into a schedule, and itineraries are made to be followed. God is working on me to make me more flexible, however. I recall one recent Monday morning when I was driving to Dallas in order to catch a flight to Austin for my study series there. I'd left home in plenty of time to make it to DFW International before takeoff. Then on the radio, the all-news network informed me that an overturned vehicle was blocking the freeway I was on, and that traffic was backed up for miles. No problem, I thought, exiting I-20 and heading onto the loop. But the loop was jammed, too, thanks to a couple of accidents. I limped along, getting dangerously close to flight time. Turning south onto the tollway in a last-ditch effort to make my plane, I ran smack dab into a third backup. There was nothing I could do but creep along with the others. I arrived late at the airport, no longer steaming but resigned. There, God allowed me to discover a truth that before had eluded me: all delays aren't bad. It turns out my plane was late, too, and I made it to Austin in time for class anyway.

As I am more often than I'd like, most Americans are obsessed with the tyranny of the urgent. We're infected by the gotta haves: We want what we want and we want it now! But the truth of the matter is that good things often really do come to those who wait.

Waiting: Required Curriculum in the Divine School

Attendance in the school of patient expectation has been mandatory for many a man and woman of God. The plain truth is that the Lord often wants us to wait. He uses the delays in our lives to construct character, to train us to trust, to develop dependence on him.

If you feel your life is stuck in a holding pattern just now, you are not alone. Biblical examples abound of people forced to deal with required waiting. Abraham and Sarah were put on hold twenty-five years from the moment God promised them a son to the day of Isaac's birth. Moses spent forty years doing postgraduate work herding sheep on the backside of the desert, and learning the lesson that any old bush will do as long as God is in it. The prophet Samuel anointed David king when the future monarch was but a boy, yet David found himself spending the years of his young adulthood holed up in caves or hiding out in foreign lands, fleeing from the vengeful Saul. The apostle Paul desperately yearned to journey to Rome, but in the meantime ended up spending two long years in prison in Cesarea, waiting.

Church history literally teems with accounts of men and women who experienced definite direction from the Lord, yet then had a time of waiting upon him thrust into the curriculum of life. Before Scotland adopted the Protestant faith as its national religion, John Knox was forced to spend some twelve years in exile, nineteen months of these as a slave chained to a French galley. John Bunyan became a Christian shortly after his marriage. Joining the Bedford Baptist Church, he felt the call of the Lord to exposit scripture, but in 1660 was thrown in jail for preaching without permission from the established church. There he would remain for over twelve years. Of the fourteen years Adoniram Judson, nineteenth-century missionary to Burma, spent among his pagan flock, two were passed in the confines of a dank, foul, prison cell.

To give a more recent example, a lovely Christian lady I know has gradually lost her ability to communicate. Once a vibrant speaker and writer, active in a prison ministry, involved in leading Bible studies and teaching, this woman now cannot sign her name to a check or even clearly verbalize her frustration. She knows what she wants to say and do, but the words and actions will not come. Doctors are certain that her problem is organic, not psychological, but the affliction is a rare one. They have not isolated a cause, and they are experimenting with treatments and medications. For five years she has waited on modern medicine, waited on sundry physicians, and, most of all, waited on her Lord. How often she has longed to touch the hem of his garment and be made well! As she will haltingly tell you, waiting can be tough.

While We Wait

What do we do while waiting for open doors from God? When we experience delays in our lives, let's remember that the Lord is looking on. He wants to see how we handle things. He desires that we bear fruit in circumstances that would confound others. He longs for us to stay under the stress, persevering with patience, progressing in our Christian lives, all the while leaning totally upon him. He wants to see us pore over his word for indications of his will. He hopes that we'll be driven to our knees in earnest prayer. He desires that we come to the end of ourselves, for that is the beginning of truly trusting him. He wants to make us fruitful, especially in the land of our affliction!

It is possible to bear fruit when the four walls of delay crowd in. While in prison those twelve years, John Bunyan penned two allegories, *Pilgrim's Progress* and *The Holy War*, another work, *Life and Death of Mr. Badman*, and his autobiography, *Grace Abounding*. During his period of exile in Europe, John Knox met and conversed with John Calvin. Martin Luther translated the New Testament into German while imprisoned at Wartburg Castle. German theologian Dietrich Bonhoeffer wrote *The Cost of Discipleship* while jailed by the Nazis. Four of the apostle Paul's letters are called the prison epistles, scripted under lock and key. In exile on the Isle of Patmos, the apostle John produced the book of Revelation. And on a no-less grand scale in the eyes of God, the woman I mentioned previously whose life seems a murky quagmire of illness, spends hours praying for and playing with her much-loved grandchildren. That is bearing fruit in the midst of what most would consider thoroughly stifling circumstances.

While He Waits

Our hero, Joseph, is fruitful in the land of his affliction as well. As a slave in the house of Potiphar, he is successful in all he undertakes. Relatively speaking, the ten years at Potiphar's place are good ones—sunshine compared to the gloomy cloud of prison. But God had given the young Hebrew dreams about being served, not about serving (Genesis 37:5-10). Thus, in the years he runs the home of his Egyptian master, Joseph is forced to learn much about handling delay.

After he runs from sensual temptation virtually into prison, Joseph learns even more about waiting upon God. As the scene in Genesis 40 opens, he is around twenty-eight years old, and has been stuck in jail for about a year. Can you imagine celebrating your twenty-eighth birthday in the cold confines of a prison cell to which you've been unjustly sentenced? As his birthday approaches, with a sinking feeling in the pit of his stomach, Joseph perhaps thinks of his family far away in Canaan. It has been eleven years since he's seen his father, his stepmother Leah, his younger brother Benjamin, or his older siblings. Benjamin is now in his twenties, Jacob confronting old age, his other brothers approaching mid-life. Joseph has spent over a third of his life in captivity. God has not seen fit to deliver him yet.

It was ten years from the time God promised Abraham that his descendants would become "a great nation" until the day when Sarah suggested that her husband go in to her handmaid Hagar (Genesis 12:2; 16:1-4). It took ten years for Sarah and Abraham to decide wrongly to assist God in fulfilling his vow. Joseph has made it eleven years without resorting to machinations of his own to help the Lord get him out of this mess. He hasn't plotted or schemed, hasn't attempted to escape, hasn't slept with Mrs. Potiphar so that she would influence her husband in his favor, hasn't done anything but wait upon God to change his circumstances. After eleven years, he must be wondering if it is time now to assume that "God helps those who help themselves," and get busy manipulating himself out of prison. We shall see.

Deliverance?—Genesis 40:1-5

> Some time later, the cupbearer and the baker of the king of Egypt offended their master, the king of Egypt. Pharaoh was angry with his two officials, the chief cupbearer and the chief baker, and put

them in custody in the house of the captain of the guard, in the same prison where Joseph was confined. The captain of the guard assigned them to Joseph, and he attended them.

After they had been in custody for some time, each of the two men—the cupbearer and the baker of the king of Egypt, who were being held in prison—had a dream the same night, and each dream had a meaning of its own.

Although stuck in prison, Joseph, remember, has been given the run of the place. The warden puts the young man in charge of "all those held in the prison," and Joseph is answerable "for all that was done there" (39:22). He possesses extraordinary responsibility, more than any modern trustee in a minimum security lock-up would even dream of. And two more prisoners are admitted to the same prison as he (40:2).

These jailbirds aren't typical men either, but rather individuals of prominence in pharaoh's administration, bonafide Egyptian VIPS. The cupbearer to the king—a sort of butler—is the man responsible for tasting pharaoh's wine to assure that it is not poisoned before it touches the king's lips. His frequent access to the throne and the confidential nature of his duties give him great influence at court. The same may be said of the chief baker, the man responsible for overseeing the baking of the many varieties of cakes and breads consumed at the palace. He is in charge of the whole dining room operation at court.

Why does pharaoh become angry with these two powerful servants? We are not certain. Some speculate that one, the other, or both, of the officials had entered into a plot to assassinate the Egyptian ruler. Perhaps some poison was to be inserted into a loaf of the monarch's bread or used to spike the royal wine. Possibly the baker and the cupbearer simply hadn't been performing their duties up to snuff. Tough, chewy meat, stale bread, and flies in the grape juice would irritate any diner, especially the king of the land.

Seeing God's Hand

Genesis 40:3 tells us that pharaoh orders the two men into the "custody . . . of the captain of the guard, in the same prison where Joseph was confined." The words, "in the same prison where Joseph was confined," are words of providence, of purpose, indications that God is at work. As Joseph is probably thinking, things like this just don't happen without a reason, do they?

However, as we shall observe shortly, the Lord is not at work in this situation as Joseph expects him to be. The roles the cupbearer and baker play in his eventual release are not exactly the parts Joseph envisions for them. God often approaches us in different ways than we anticipate. That much we can count on! He came to Moses in a burning bush, Jacob on a lonely night at Bethel, Saul while the future king was fetching his father's lost donkeys, Gideon when he was threshing enough grain to keep his family alive, David while he was feeding sheep, the apostle Paul when he walked along the Damascus road. Now God unexpectedly allows two Egyptian officials to be placed in the same jail as Joseph, and thereby gives evidence once again of his sovereign ability to intervene in the affairs of man.

We, too, can see God's hand in directing certain individuals into our lives. There are no chance encounters for a Christian. Wherever we are, also are men, women, and children whom the Lord has providentially placed there. Maybe they are where they are to give us a blessing, a bit of encouragement, a special insight into what it means to serve God. Perhaps we are there to do the same for them. It is a beautiful thing to be sensitive to the places, positions, and people the Lord permits us to run across. He never makes a mistake, but we do if we become selfish and withdrawn and fail to reach out. A number of times people have shown up at our classes and have offered a smile or word of encouragement. They've just happened by, but they've also happened to meet a real need because they've been sensitive to the Lord's leading.

The Benefits of Keeping On . . . and Looking Up

Of the chief baker and cupbearer, we read that the "captain of the guard assigned them to Joseph, and he attended them" (40:4). Joseph cannot avoid meeting up with these two. They become his direct responsibility.

Who assigns these officials to Joseph's care? The "captain of the guard" takes care of this detail. And who is he? None other than Potiphar himself! Obviously Potiphar's anger has cooled. Apparently he isn't totally convinced of the accuracy of his wife's accusations, but he has to save face, so Joseph must remain in jail. Be that as it may, Potiphar still gives Joseph the same types of duties the young man had assumed in his house.

As Proverbs 16:7 says, "When a man's ways are pleasing to the Lord, He makes even his enemies to be at peace with him" (NASB). When we give the Lord time and we trust him to work out the details, he can do that for us, too. Joseph's consistent, faithful, positive attitude, his willingness to persevere and serve when everything seems to be crumbling, eventually results in a restored relationship with Potiphar. Joseph's warden and fellow prisoners aren't going to remember him as a whining complainer, but as a man triumphant in the face of adversity.

Church history is filled with accounts of men and women like Joseph, people who kept on keeping on even when the going became incredibly rough. When we get to heaven, we'll find ourselves among tall timber, company of character. We've already talked about a few of the giants of the faith: John Calvin, John Bunyan, Martin Luther. Thousands of early Christians died in the jaws of wild beasts, in flames at the stake, in dungeons of horrible torture. I know times are tough for many of us, yet, in the wake of such suffering saints, who then are we to bemoan the hand we've been dealt? In the words of the hymnwriter, "Must we be carried to the skies on flowery beds of ease while others fought to win the prize and sailed through bloody seas?"

I hope this doesn't sound harsh or callous, but who are we to cry constantly about our jobs, our illnesses, our heartaches? When we die, our friends won't long regret our passing if all we've done is indulge in self-pity about our difficult lives. They'll be relieved that death has freed us from our misery! "Poor John, how he suffered," they'll sigh. What people recall with warmth and tenderness and longing are the blessings of our lives. The incredible ability to conquer that God gave us, the amazing victories we experienced over impossible situations—these are what friends reflect upon with joy and gladness long after we're gone.

This is what people are going to remember about Joseph, too. They'll recall that he stays on top of his circumstances in prison. They'll reflect on his winning the hearts of his jailers, his fellow inmates, and even Potiphar, the one who threw him in there in the first place.

It's a principle that the secret to winning the victory in traumatic circumstances is to see, with the eye of man, the hand of God. Joseph does that in jail. Circumstances are difficult, but he has learned to be quick to hear, slow to speak, and slow to anger. He is a silent servant, a man who hangs in there and keeps ministering to others, even when his own life seems virtually shipwrecked (for a similar example from the life of Paul, see 2 Corinthians 4:5).

Dreams, Dreams, Dreams, Dreams

Time passes. Then one amazing evening, both the chief cupbearer and baker have unusual dreams. Genesis 40:5 tells us that "each of the two men . . . had a dream the same night, and each dream had a meaning of its own." Thus we witness more of God's sovereign influence over the lives of men. While under Joseph's care, these fellows each have strange visions. As Joseph will realize, these dreams are no chance occurrences, no products of random coincidence. They are videos projected into the subconscious from the same source, God himself.

Being a Sensitive Servant—Genesis 40:6-8

> When Joseph came to them the next morning, he saw that they were dejected. So he asked Pharaoh's officials who were in custody with him in his master's house, "Why are your faces so sad today?"
>
> "We both had dreams," they answered, "but there is no one to interpret them."
>
> Then Joseph said to them, "Do not interpretations belong to God? Tell me your dreams."

The next morning, like every morning, Joseph approaches the chambers of the cupbearer and baker. Since he is there to serve them, he likely brings a razor, shaving cream, and a bowl of hot water, and sets it all down with a big smile. "Good morning, gentlemen," he perhaps brightly greets them. Probably they just stare at him in return.

We know why the baker and cupbearer are downcast, but Joseph does not. He asks them, "Why are your faces so sad today?" (40:7). How sensitive and compassionate it is of him even to notice their depression! Surely Joseph has enough trials of his own without borrowing trouble. Prison has not made him self-absorbed; he is able to immerse himself in the difficulties of the other inmates. He has taken the time to establish relationships with those also confined. Like Jesus, who washed the feet and patiently answered the questions of his men in the upper room just hours before his arrest, Joseph knows that the best tonic for sorrow is ministry to others. What a marvelous attitude!

"We both had dreams," reply the baker and cupbearer to Joseph's inquiry, "but there is no one to interpret them" (40:8).

"Do not interpretations belong to God?" responds Joseph. "Tell me your dreams" (40:8). His answer reminds me of the story of two little boys who were overheard talking one time. "My dad and I know everything!" proudly exclaimed one of the lads.

"Okay," said the second boy, "try this one on for size. Tell me, how big is God?"

"Uh, that's one for my father," stammered the wide-eyed youngster who had been bragging! Likewise, Joseph immediately recognizes his limitations, and that his heavenly father is the one who will reveal the meaning of the dreams.

I like to think that I would have responded to those two fellows as Joseph does. I like to imagine that I'd have been sensitive, caring, concerned, and convinced of God's purpose and goodness. I'm afraid, though, that after more than a decade as a slave and a jailbird, I wouldn't have been very enthusiastic about the subject of dreams. "Look, guys," I might have said to the two, "don't tell me about dreams. I had some dreams eleven years ago; delusions of grandeur, that's all they were. Look where they got me. My advice to you is to forget them."

But Joseph, the sensitive servant, doesn't respond that way. Rather, he acknowledges God as the giver and interpreter of dreams, and he requests that the baker and cupbearer relate their experiences. What amazing confidence Joseph places in his God, even after eleven years spent sidelined in slavery and prison. He fully realizes that man's disappointments are God's appointments, that delays are not denials, that nothing can separate him from the love of the father (Romans 8:38-39). And he asks his friends to reveal the visions they have seen.

The Cupbearer's Delight—Genesis 40:9-15

> So the chief cupbearer told Joseph his dream. He said to him, "In my dream I saw a vine in front of me, and on the vine were three branches. As soon as it budded, it blossomed, and its clusters ripened

into grapes. Pharaoh's cup was in my hand, and I took the grapes, squeezed them into Pharaoh's cup and put the cup in his hand."

"This is what it means," Joseph said to him. "The three branches are three days. Within three days Pharaoh will lift up your head and restore you to your position, and you will put Pharaoh's cup in his hand, just as you used to do when you were his cupbearer. But when all goes well with you, remember me and show me kindness; mention me to Pharaoh and get me out of this prison. For I was forcibly carried off from the land of the Hebrews, and even here I have done nothing to deserve being put in a dungeon."

The cupbearer is the first to speak up and describe the vision of the night before. He tells Joseph that in his dream he saw a vine with three branches, which budded, then blossomed. The clusters ripened into grapes, and these grapes the cupbearer squeezed into pharaoh's cup, and then placed the wine into the ruler's hand (40:9-11).

"This is what it means," says Joseph. "The three branches are three days. Within three days Pharaoh will lift up your head and restore you to your position, and you will put Pharaoh's cup in his hand, just as you used to do when you were his cupbearer" (40:12-13).

Talk about good news! Can't you see the cupbearer dancing around the cell when he receives God's message through Joseph? Only three days left in this hole, then it's back to work as usual! Obviously they have found he is not guilty. All is forgiven! Probably he begins numbering the hours, and even minutes, till his release.

Remember Me . . . Won't You Please Remember Me?

So wrapped up in his own good fortune is the cupbearer that he must not pay close attention to what Joseph says next. It is a simple request, a completely natural, understandable desire that Joseph voices in a moment of weakness.

"But when all goes well with you, remember me and show me kindness; mention me to Pharaoh and get me out of this prison," asks Joseph (40:14). Then he goes on to explain to the Egyptian that he had not only been kidnapped from his homeland, but also jailed unjustly (40:15). It is remarkable that Joseph says nothing unkind about his brothers, or about Potiphar and his wife. He refuses to accuse, to smear the reputation of others, even when such may be well deserved. He is not bitter toward those who have mistreated him; his response is one of loyalty, silence, and service, even to Potiphar. He only requests that the cupbearer mention him to pharaoh and recommend his release. Yet there are two problems with the young man's methods.

First, God has another idea. Joseph is jumping to the conclusion that the cupbearer will provide a means of immediate escape for him. He is presuming upon God, anticipating his will before that will is made clear. He is resorting to his own efforts in an attempt to help out the Lord, and God doesn't need or want that sort of assistance. Assumption, anticipation, and assistance will usually get us into trouble as far as God's program is concerned.

Second, Joseph is vastly overestimating human nature. The old saying really ought to be, "To *forget* is human, to *remember*, divine," because we often have very short memories when it comes to fulfilling our obligations or showing our gratitude. How quickly we forget!

Oh, we harp at our kids when they forget to clean their rooms, wash the cars, dry the dishes, mow the grass, but are our memories really any more dependable? Do we ever go back and say heartfelt thank you's to the special people who have inspired us? Do we show our appreciation to the pastors and Sunday school teachers who so diligently ministered to us as they served the

Lord in pulpit or classroom? Do we ever, after resigning a position in a company, volunteer to return and assist in the training of our replacements? In a word, no. Usually, in the hustle of moving on to the next school, the next job, the next area of ministry, we forget our indebtedness to the ones remaining behind.

God knows our natures well! Did not Jesus himself, on the night in which he was betrayed, take bread, give thanks, and distribute it among his disciples, saying, "This is My body which is given for you; do this in remembrance of Me" (Luke 22:19 NASB)? The Lord knows how prone we are to forget . . . and to neglect! He is, after all, the one who healed ten lepers, instructed them to show themselves to the priests, and then waited as only one returned with words of praise and thanksgiving (Luke 17:12ff). "Were there not ten cleansed?" asked Jesus of the single leper who remembered to show his gratitude, "But the nine—where are they?" (Luke 17:17 NASB).

Joseph is probably deeply hurt by the ingratitude of the cupbearer who, according to Genesis 40:23, promptly forgets him as soon as he is freed from prison. It is better to acknowledge reality and accept the fact that people are essentially selfish. While it may seem pessimistic to say so, the truth is that the closer our expectations are to reality, the happier we will be. Godly acts of service should spring from hearts that expect nothing in return. Joseph figures that the timely dream of the cupbearer is part of God's providential plan to get him out of prison. And actually, he is right, but the deliverance will not be when he expects. Release won't come till God is ready to open the door. It never does.

THE BAKER'S DISMAY—GENESIS 40:16-19

> When the chief baker saw that Joseph had given a favorable interpretation, he said to Joseph, "I too had a dream: On my head were three baskets of bread. In the top basket were all kinds of baked

> goods for Pharaoh, but the birds were eating them out of the basket on my head."
>
> "This is what it means," Joseph said. "The three baskets are three days. Within three days Pharaoh will lift off your head and hang you on a tree. And the birds will eat away your flesh."

So excited is the baker at the good news given the cupbearer that he blurts out the details of his own, very similar, dream. Without waiting for an invitation from Joseph to speak, he tells the young man that, in his vision, three baskets of bread rested atop his head. The uppermost basket was filled with assorted breads and pastries, and these were plucked and eaten by birds (40:16-17). Without hesitation, Joseph reveals the interpretation of this dream.

"This is what it means," he candidly informs the baker. "Within three days Pharaoh will lift off your head and hang you on a tree. And the birds will eat away your flesh" (40:18-19).

Not exactly cheery news, is it? We can almost sense the excitement, the anticipation, of the baker as he awaits the interpretation. Then Joseph hits him with a bombshell and the baker's countenance collapses in dismay, disappointment, disbelief. Surely he sinks to his knees in despair—his heart pounding against his chest, his hands shaking, his brow dripping sweat.

Some have criticized Joseph here as showing a lack of compassion, a genuine coldheartedness. I think not. The text does not convey how tenderly and gently he delivers the bad news to the baker. We do not know what tone of voice he uses, or if tears fill his eyes. We do know that he answers directly, candidly, truthfully. God has revealed the meaning of the dream, and he can do nothing but impart his God-given knowledge.

It wouldn't be surprising if Joseph were tempted, just a bit, to tamper with the report, to give the baker a more favorable response. But he handles the Lord's word with the same care and accuracy that we are instructed to use when dealing with Scripture. Paul exhorts his younger disciple in 2 Timothy 2:15, "Be diligent to present yourself approved to God as a workman who does not need to be ashamed, handling accurately the word of truth" (NASB). The apostle also writes the church at Corinth, "We do not use deception, nor do we distort the word of God. On the contrary, by setting forth the truth plainly we commend ourselves to every man's conscience in the sight of God" (2 Corinthians 4:2). Joseph is not afraid to handle a message from God with that kind of boldness and care. He isn't worried about receiving the approval of men, but is concerned with satisfying God, before whom he will ultimately stand.

The Camps of Death or Deliverance

In prison, Joseph is wedged between two men. One is destined to live, the other to die. How much his situation reminds us of that experienced by the Lord Jesus Christ at Calvary centuries later. As Jesus dangled from the cross, two thieves flanked him on either side. One called him Lord; the other spit out a tirade of verbal abuse at him. One passed from death into eternal life; the other crossed over to meet judgment (Luke 23:39-43).

As Christians, we too stand between individuals who have the choice of death or life. It is our responsibility as believers to convey the message of the cross, to communicate that Christ died for our sins, and that only through faith in him can we achieve an eternal relationship with God the father. As Paul puts it in 2 Corinthians 2:15, "We are a fragrance of Christ to God among those who are being saved and among those who are perishing" (NASB).

As the baker momentarily dwelt under the false supposition that he would be delivered from death, so too do scores of men and women who assume that their good works, their churchgoing, their contributions to charity, will earn them a chunk of heaven. The Bible says otherwise. In the words of Jesus Christ, "I am the way, and the truth, and the life; no one comes to the Father, but through Me" (John 14:6 NASB). And as the apostle Paul writes in Ephesians 2:8-9, "For by grace you have been saved through faith; and that not of yourselves, it is the gift of God; not as a result of works, that no one should boast" (NASB).

We may be good at fooling ourselves, yet it is an agonizing truth that many people are living spiritually dead, diseased, and deceived lives. They figure they've got it all together, but the reality is that if they've never accepted Christ as savior, they're going to end up in hell. In his book, *Facing Death and the Life After*, Billy Graham puts it this way:

> A lot of people talk about hell, use it to tell others where to go, but do not want to be confronted with the thought that it might be their destination. Hell, for them, is only where the Hitlers and Stalins should end up, along with murderers, rapists, or child pornographers. But most think that "Good People" who mind their own business, pay their taxes, and put a few dollars in the collection plate will have some "eternal rewards" (Graham 37).

Unfortunately for the "good people" of whom Graham speaks, they'll never be good enough. We can never—apart from a relationship with Christ—be considered good enough to be called children of God, even if we aren't mass murderers or pedophiles. What counts is not what we are, but whom we know. Says Jesus himself of the destiny of those who try to go it alone, "Many will say to Me on that day, 'Lord, Lord, did we not prophesy in Your name, and in Your name cast out demons, and in Your name perform many miracles?' And then I will declare to them, 'I never knew you; depart from Me, you who practice lawlessness' " (Matthew 7:22-23 NASB).

We really have no reasonable alternative except to take the Lord's statements at face value. We might say "faith value," because only through faith in the finished work of Christ can we receive salvation. In the end it will not matter how many eastern religions we've embraced, how many Protestant churches we've graced, or how many self-help books we've read, if we do not know the son as savior. All the positive things in the world cannot change the negative reality of sin. We are sinners by birth and we will die that way unless we experience a new birth in Christ.

Does that mean God is unfair? Certainly not. But we must remember that God is God and he has the right to do as he will. In the early days of man, he accepted the sacrificial lamb presented by Abel because that was part of his predesigned program. He rejected the fruit of the ground brought by Cain (Genesis 4:1-7). He gives us clear-cut instructions in his word concerning our salvation. We are to be modernday Abels, placing our trust in the ultimate sacrificial lamb of them all, the lamb of God, Jesus Christ (John 1:29). We are to place no faith in work done under our own efforts, for it will never earn us a place of favor with God, even as it failed to do for Cain so many thousands of years ago. God offers only one way for us to arrive on earth physically, and that is through birth. Likewise, he offers only one way for us to come into heaven eventually, and that is through rebirth—belief in Jesus Christ (John 3:3). The options are clear: life or death. The choice is ours.

EVENTS COME TO PASS—GENESIS 40:20-23

> Now the third day was Pharaoh's birthday, and he gave a feast for all his officials. He lifted up the heads of the chief cupbearer and the chief baker in the presence of his officials: He restored the chief cupbearer to his position, so that he once again put the cup into Pharaoh's hand, but he hanged the chief baker, just as Joseph had said to them in his interpretation.
>
> The chief cupbearer, however, did not remember Joseph; he forgot him.

Three days pass, and pharaoh decides to celebrate his birthday with a bang. He orders the imprisoned baker and cupbearer brought into his presence and, in front of all his officials, decrees that the cupbearer will resume his former position. The baker does not fare as well. Just as Joseph has predicted, he is hanged upon a tree (40:20-22). Perhaps Potiphar had tracked down enough leads to ascertain the baker's guilt in a plot against pharaoh; maybe the king had just grown sick of the man's cooking. At any rate, the baker is executed while the cupbearer is restored.

And then we read a sad verse: "The chief cupbearer, however, did not remember Joseph; he forgot him" (40:23). Overjoyed with his return to power, he doesn't look back. He completely forgets the young Hebrew who had said it would be so, who had served him so sacrificially in prison, who had comforted him so effectively with wisdom sent from the Lord.

Jacob had served Laban for fourteen years when he decided it was time to pack up and return to Canaan (Genesis 30:25ff). God said no to that desire. Jacob would have to serve his father-in-law for six more years before the Lord would again open the door to the promised land. There were still years left in God's program for the patriarch.

Jacob's boy Joseph is at the eleven-year mark in his own period of service. Probably he expects deliverance any day . . . and then the weeks stretch into months because the cupbearer has forgotten him, and because God has said, "No, it's not time yet. Wait on me." And, as we shall see in the next chapter, the time of waiting upon him will stretch to two more years.

Some Things Left to Learn

Why is Joseph forced to spend two additional years in prison? It's because he still has some things to learn. God desires him to learn that deliverance will not come through the memory of a mere cupbearer. It will occur in God's own time and in his own way.

In *When the Hurt Won't Go Away*, Paul Powell includes the reflections of Andrew Murray on suffering. Paraphrased below are the valuable principles suggested by Murray to help us cope with trial, trouble, and delay as we wait upon the Lord.

> First, we should realize that God is the one who has brought us to this place of trial. It is his will for us at this time. In that knowledge we must rest.
>
> Second, we must recognize that the Lord will sustain us with his love, and will give us grace in this trial to behave as his children.
>
> Third, we can trust that God will turn the trial into a blessing, teaching us the lessons he intends us to learn, working in us the grace he means to bestow.
>
> Finally, we must rest assured that in God's good time, he can bring us out of the trial. Only he knows how and when (Powell 48).

Thirteen humiliating years after leaving his home, Joseph will finally taste freedom once again. It will be in God's time and in God's way and, in the meantime, his grace will prove to be totally sufficient for the young man. So it can be for us, no matter what our own "prison" experiences involve.

LESSONS

There is a great deal we can learn from Joseph's time of delay, and much that can be applied to our own lives. Let's look at a few of the lessons straight from prison.

Lesson one: as we go through times of difficulty, we must remember three principles: *God's way is the best way; God's time for deliverance is the best time; God's grace is always sufficient for us.*

Lesson two: *we are to put no confidence in man.* As Psalm 118:8 states, "It is better to take refuge in the Lord

/ Than to trust in man" (NASB). Man at his best will only fail us—witness the cupbearer and Potiphar. God will always come through.

Lesson three: *we need to learn to wait upon the Lord.* As David so comfortingly puts it in Psalm 27:14, "Wait for the Lord; Be strong, and let your heart take courage; Yes, wait for the Lord" (NASB).

Lesson four: *it is necessary to be faithful in the presentation of God's message.* It was hard for Joseph to confront the baker with the news of his coming demise. We, too, cannot mince words when telling others about God's love and about God's judgment. We are obligated to explain the Lord's word with accuracy and care.

Lesson five: *the cure for bitterness in our relationships with one another is to recognize God's providential use of human vehicles.* Joseph could easily have resented the cupbearer for his ingratitude, but nothing is recorded in scripture of such resentment. Instead, it's safe to assume that Joseph realized God's sovereign hand was somehow at work in the circumstances.

Lesson six: *the closer our expectations are to reality, the happier we'll be.* People forget. "There is no remembrance of men of old," writes Solomon in Ecclesiastes 1:11, "and even those who are yet to come will not be remembered by those who follow." Should we quit serving and sacrificing when people disappoint? No! Let's just remember that we're really serving the Lord, and that his memory never fails.

Lesson seven: *we must never let circumstances adversely affect our relationships with God.* We mustn't lose confidence in the Lord when the tough times hit. Joseph doesn't. We cannot afford to, either.

Lesson eight: *a question that must not be overlooked is this: Are you in the camp of deliverance or in the camp of death?* You are in the camp of deliverance if you have come to Calvary to receive Christ as savior. You have stepped from death into life. It is a challenge you should consider today.

TAKING THE STEP

Perhaps you are wondering exactly how to take that step of faith which will transport you from the camp of death into that of deliverance. Would you right now be willing to bow your head and do the following?

1. Acknowledge your sin and need of a savior (Romans 3:23; 6:23).
2. Believe that Jesus Christ died for your sins and is waiting to come into your life (Romans 5:8; Revelation 3:20).
3. Invite him into your life by faith. Talk to him. Tell him that you believe his death paid the penalty of your sin and that you want him as your savior (John 1:12; 3:16).
4. Thank him for responding to your prayer.

The moment you invite Christ into your life by faith, you are born again into God's family. The date this happens is your spiritual birthday. Record it in a permanent place as a defense against future doubt. On the authority of scripture (1 John 5:11-12), you are now God's child and will spend eternity with your heavenly father. Welcome to the family!

Questions for Study

1. Jumping ahead of God can be both disappointing and dangerous. What does Joseph do to try to "assist" God in getting himself out of prison? What is the tragic result?

2. How do Joseph's experiences in Genesis 40 teach us that the less we expect from men, the happier we'll be? In whom should we place our confidence? (See Psalm 118:8.)

3. Describe how accurately Joseph relays God's message to the baker. Does Joseph tamper with the facts? What does his example teach us about our own use of scripture?

4. Are you experiencing any delays in your own life right now? Are you frustrated by them, or are you acting in faith by trusting the Lord to deal with them?

5. What are the camps of death and deliverance? Where do you stand?

4

In His Time

Genesis 41

You may have noticed that I've dedicated this book to our daughter Becky. There is a reason for this. Through Becky, as with Joseph, we have witnessed both the agony of sustained delay and the unspeakable joy of deliverance.

Shortly after her eleventh birthday, Pearl and I noticed that Becky was becoming increasingly listless. Her skin seemed more pale each day, her body more frail. She complained of a persistent sore throat. We grew concerned, and made arrangements to consult a doctor, but never had the chance to keep the appointment. One afternoon Becky rolled off her bed, falling onto the floor with a tremendous thud. We rushed into her room and found we could not rouse her. With our daughter in my arms, we raced to the car and sped to the hospital, with Pearl feverishly laboring to keep Becky semiconscious while I covered the miles.

An intern in the emergency room saved Becky's life. She had lapsed into a nearly comatose state by the time we made the twenty-minute trip to the medical center. With the fruity smell on Becky's breath serving as a tip-off, the young doctor rapidly diagnosed the problem as diabetes. Within seconds insulin was administered, and she soon began resting comfortably.

Diabetes was not an entirely new thing to us. My dear grandmother, the lady who first told me about Jesus Christ, had also suffered from the disease. We dimly understood the severity of the illness, but were soon to witness its devastating effect on our little girl. From that awful night onward, Becky's life became one long holding pattern of illness—punctuated by glimmers of hope, pinnacles of anticipation, pits of despair . . . and finally, deliverance.

Almost immediately after her release from the hospital, Becky began giving herself insulin injections three, sometimes four, times per day. While her teenaged friends, sisters, and brothers gorged on shakes, fries, burgers, pizza, and ice cream, she tried to stick faithfully to the restricted diet prescribed by her doctors. Yet, as the time approached for her to enter college, it all became too much to handle.

After seven years of battling the disease, Becky lapsed into a well of depression that appeared bottomless. The reality that she'd never be normal and the ominous, ever-present possibility that she would eventually die from the disease or from related complications, dragged her spirits into the dust and quenched her will to live. She became lax in maintaining her diet and grew sick of sticking herself with the dreaded needle. Physically, her problems worsened. Her eyesight began to fail; her feet became swollen because of poor circulation. She began to think of suicide as a pleasant alternative to making it through yet another day as a diabetic. She truly wanted to die. It seemed Pearl and I could do nothing to chisel even a small chink in the wall that separated us from our girl. She was irrational and untouchable during her time at college, and these were literally the worst years of our lives.

Finally, a pinpoint beam of hope pierced the wall of despair when Becky reached her early twenties. A doctor at Parkland General Hospital in Dallas asked her to participate in a pilot program involving a computerized insulin pump, and Becky became a test case. The portable machine was hooked onto her body and it administered insulin as needed. No more needles! No more guesswork! The several months that Becky spent at Parkland were among the happiest of the ten years since her disease had been diagnosed. We began to think, as Joseph must have after the cupbearer's release, that deliverance was at hand. But—as with Joseph in prison—it was not to be so at that time.

Although the insulin pump worked well, it was bulky and uncomfortable. Besides, we were not in a financial position to afford to purchase one for Becky's personal use. She grew weary of staying at Parkland and tired of being a test case. Eventually she came home to face the needle once more.

It was then that God began to work unexpected miracles in the life of our daughter. The Lord had sustained Becky through the years of the disease—more often than not it was only by his strength that she had survived at all. At what might have been her lowest moment, by God's grace a genuine ray of sunshine came into Becky's life. I'm talking about the young man who is now our son-in-law, Ray Devine (see the letter Becky wrote which is included in the dedication of this book).

This fellow has been a gift of God—of that Pearl and I have no doubt. For Becky and Ray, it was love at first sight. And though the song goes, "Love and marriage . . . go together like a horse and carriage," I made sure that Ray understood the full implications of the decision he made when he asked Becky to become his wife. In a heart-to-heart talk, we discussed the heavy responsibilities he'd be assuming once they said, "I do." Becky was going to face continual medical problems. Her eyesight had not improved and now a new complication had developed which made insulin injections pale by comparison: her kidneys had begun to fail. Rounds of dialysis were inevitable. All this Ray understood . . . and not once did he waver in his intention to become Becky's husband.

As we'll see in this episode of the biography of Joseph, when God starts to do a work in the life of one of his children, he is capable of moving with incredible speed. Within a few short years after her marriage, Becky found herself hooked up to a dialysis machine several times a week. The inconvenience of giving herself insulin injections was nothing compared to the discomfort of the kidney machine. But, to chalk one up for the miraculous sovereignty of God, Becky also found herself accepted as a patient in Parkland Hospital's transplant program. For most practical purposes, the years of hopeless waiting were over.

Of course there were setbacks. In early June of 1985 a suitable donor was found. The staff at the hospital made arrangements to transport the donor kidney to Parkland. They notified the doctors and nurses, and scheduled the operating room. They informed everyone involved about the timetable for the transplant—everyone, that is, except Becky. No one phoned her until it was time to wheel her into surgery. At that moment she was one hundred miles away at her home in Tyler. There was no way we could rush her to Dallas in time.

The disappointment, the dashed hopes, the shattered dreams, gave way to elation within a couple of weeks. In late June another kidney was found, and this time everything went relatively smoothly. Oh, surgery was tough and recovery difficult as Becky battled infections and the threat of rejection. But within two months she felt well; her color was good, her energy level higher than it had been in years. Besides, she had Ray.

Following her marriage and transplant, Becky became a far different young woman from the one we had despaired of in college. Medically she still has a tough row to hoe. Since receiving her kidney, she has, for example, suffered a blackout and near-accident while driving. But she is happy and high-spirited. Although physically she will never run in the Olympics, she is wholeheartedly engaged in a marathon of her own as she strives to live her life with as much normalcy as possible. She loves to cook and now is often able to assist Pearl with entertaining. Ray and Becky also teach Sunday school and help with numerous youth activities at our churches. The years of desperate suffering—nearly eighteen of them—are behind her. Like Joseph in the chapter we're about to study, Becky has been delivered—not freed from the past but reconciled to it and finally able to handle new challenges. She still must inject herself with medication, but there is no more dialysis and there is the hope of a satisfying life with a man she loves deeply. I'd call that deliverance on a grand scale!

When Two Full Years Had Passed

At the end of Genesis 40, Joseph is waiting to be delivered as well. He still languishes in prison—biding his time, trusting, hanging on to his hopes. The men whose dreams he has interpreted have met their fates: the baker executed at the gallows, the cupbearer restored to his former position of prominence in the court of pharaoh. We remember that before the cupbearer escapes the confines of his cell, Joseph, in a moment of sheer human vulnerability, implores the man to remember him and to make mention of him to the king. It is a completely natural request, but one that falls on deaf ears, for Genesis 40 closes with these woeful words: "The chief cupbearer, however, did not remember Joseph; he forgot him" (40:23). And, like Becky after removing herself from the hospital test program, Joseph remains on hold.

In some places scripture is divided illogically—some might say even tragically. The text of the Bible itself is wholly inspired by God; the verse and chapter divisions are strictly manmade. At times some of the intense drama which marks the word of God is lost in the shuffle. This is starkly evident in the separation of the final verse of Genesis 40 from the first verse of Genesis 41, where we read that it is "two full years" after the cupbearer's release from prison before events again evolve that concern Joseph.

Two entire years go by after the cupbearer forgets Joseph, and our hero spends the entire twenty-four months in jail. Think of what he goes through. Seventy-two hours after his interpretation of the cupbearer's dream, the man is set free. Joseph eagerly waits, fully expecting release. Hour seventy-three comes, and stretches into hour seventy-four, then seventy-five. The hours become days, which become weeks, which lengthen into months, and finally, years. More specifically, it's 17,520 hours, or 730 days, or 104 weeks, or twenty-four months that we're talking about here! Anyway you figure it, the numbers add up to a vast period of enforced—and certainly excruciating—waiting.

The impressive thing about Joseph's time of trial is that never do we read of him slumping into depression or angrily bouncing accusations against God off the walls of his cell. Not once do we hear him place blame for his troubles on the Lord, or on those who have treated him abominably. Instead, his attitude is one of worship. In speaking of the Lord, he can say along with David, "You have made known to me the path of life; you will fill me with joy in your presence, with eternal pleasures at your right hand" (Psalm 16:11).

Joseph is thirty years old as Genesis 41 opens. Nearly half of his life—thirteen years—has been spent in slavery or confinement, and yet he has achieved incredible emotional and spiritual maturity. Such a man is Joseph that portions of Rudyard Kipling's immortal poem "If" might well have been written about him. Just read over Kipling's words and see if you don't agree.

> If you can keep your head when all about you
> Are losing theirs and blaming it on you;
> If you can trust yourself when all men doubt you,

But make allowance for their doubting too;
If you can wait and not be tired by waiting,
Or, being lied about, don't deal in lies,
Or, being hated, don't give way to hating,
And yet don't look too good, nor talk too wise;

If you can dream—and not make dreams your master;
If you can think—and not make thoughts your aim;
If you can meet with triumph and disaster
And treat those two impostors just the same;
If you can bear to hear the truth you've spoken
Twisted by knaves to make a trap for fools,
Or watch the things you gave your life to broken,
And stoop and build 'em up with wornout tools;

If you can make one heap of all your winnings
And risk it on one turn of pitch-and-toss,
And lose, and start again at your beginnings
And never breathe a word about your loss;
If you can force your heart and nerve and sinew
To serve your turn long after they are gone,
And so hold on when there is nothing in you
Except the Will which says to them: "Hold on";

If you can talk with crowds and keep your virtue,
Or walk with kings—nor lose the common touch;
If neither foes nor loving friends can hurt you;
If all men count with you, but none too much;
If you can fill the unforgiving minute
With sixty seconds' worth of distance run—
Yours is the Earth and everything that's in it,
and—which is more—you'll be a Man, my son!

As Genesis 41 opens, Joseph, like the subject of Kipling's poem, has waited and not grown tired of waiting. He's been lied about, but has not dealt in lies. He has been hated, but has not given way to hating. In all and through all, he has kept steady perspective. His life has been God-centered rather than man-centered, and he himself has become more than a man. He has become a man of God.

How has this happened? As the words of the prophet Isaiah both promise and exhort us, "The steadfast of mind Thou wilt keep in perfect peace, Because he trusts in Thee. Trust in the Lord forever, For in God the Lord, we have an everlasting Rock" (26:3-4 NASB). And that is what Joseph does.

God never intends to dwell along the perimeter of our lives; he desires to be at the center. He made that clear when he determined the arrangement of the camp of the nation Israel in the days of Moses (see Exodus 25-28; Numbers 2:1,17). In the midst of the camp, the tabernacle of the Lord was to be located. In the center of that tabernacle was a section known as the holy of holies; in the center of the holy of holies rested the ark of the covenant; in the center of the ark dwelt the spirit of God himself. God was not on the periphery, the outskirts of town. He was the vital central heartbeat about which the camp pulsed and throbbed. Like that Israelite camp, neither should God be delegated a peripheral spot in our lives. We get into trouble if he is not center, as he was with Joseph.

God Speaks to Pharaoh—Genesis 41:1-7

> When two full years had passed, Pharaoh had a dream: He was standing by the Nile, when out of the river there came up seven cows, sleek and fat, and they grazed among the reeds. After them, seven other cows, ugly and gaunt, came up out of the Nile and stood beside those on the riverbank. And the cows that were ugly and gaunt ate up the seven sleek, fat cows. Then Pharaoh woke up.
>
> He fell asleep again and had a second dream: Seven heads of grain, healthy and good, were growing on a single stalk. After them, seven other heads

> of grain sprouted—thin and scorched by the east wind. The thin heads of grain swallowed up the seven healthy, full heads. Then Pharaoh woke up; it had been a dream.

We read in Genesis 41:1 that "when two full years had passed" following Joseph's episode with the baker and cupbearer, "Pharaoh had a dream." What is God teaching Joseph, and us, through this? In sending pharaoh special delivery visions, it is as if the Lord is instructing Joseph, "Son, I realize that two years ago you thought the dreams of the cupbearer and the baker would be the keys to your freedom, but I've got a surprise for you. The time is now. It's going to be done my way and at my appointed hour. It'll be accomplished through dreams, but not those of a butler and a baker, because I've got a better idea."

Is God's timing flawless? You'd better believe it is—always! He consistently awaits the perfect moment; then and only then does he act. We read in Galatians 4:4-5 that it was not until "the fulness of time was come" that the Lord "sent forth his Son" (KJV). After thirty-three years upon the earth in human flesh, the time was ripe for that son to die as a sacrifice for the sin of man. John 13:1-4 states, "Jesus knowing that His hour had come that He should depart out of this world to the Father . . . rose from supper, and laid aside His garments, and taking a towel, girded Himself about" (NASB). And the savior of the universe then gave his disciples a final object lesson in service by humbly washing their dirty feet (John 13:5ff). The point is that Jesus knew; he knew the hour of his trial was at hand. He knew this because he is God the son.

The Lord alone knows the moment he will take action; we usually do not. Joseph doesn't. He sits in prison two years longer than he anticipates; then God keeps his appointment. As a result, pharaoh has a dream.

What a dream it is, too! Genesis 41:2-4 tells us that the

Egyptian ruler envisions himself standing beside the great Nile. Seven sleek, fat cows come up from the river to graze alongside the shore. Then seven ugly, gaunt cows approach the healthy beasts. First, the newcomers stand alongside the other cows; then, the seven scrawny animals devour the seven plump ones.

Pharaoh abruptly wakes up. I imagine sweat pours in bucketfuls off his brow. Maybe he pinches himself to make sure he's not asleep. Soon he falls fitfully asleep again, dreaming of wheatfields—and another weird occurrence.

In pharaoh's second dream, seven full, healthy, plump heads of grain grow upon a single stalk. Then seven thin, shriveled heads, scorched by the east wind, sprout upon the same stalk. These wretched, withered heads proceed to swallow the healthy ones! At this, pharaoh wakes up (41:5-7). What a night! Scripture doesn't tell us, but I imagine he stays awake well into the early hours of the morning, pacing, pondering what the strange visions mean that have invaded to interrupt his slumber.

Delay Is Not Denial—Genesis 41:8-14

> In the morning his mind was troubled, so he sent for all the magicians and wise men of Egypt. Pharaoh told them his dreams, but no one could interpret them for him.
>
> Then the chief cupbearer said to Pharaoh, "Today I am reminded of my shortcomings. Pharaoh was once angry with his servants, and he imprisoned me and the chief baker in the house of the captain of the guard. Each of us had a dream the same night, and each dream had a meaning of its own. Now a young Hebrew was there with us, a servant of the captain of the guard. We told him our dreams, and he interpreted them for us, giving each man the interpretation of his dream. And things turned out exactly as he interpreted them to us: I was restored to my position, and the other man was hanged."

> So Pharaoh sent for Joseph, and he was quickly brought from the dungeon. When he had shaved and changed his clothes, he came before Pharaoh.

We know that the nightmares bother pharaoh, because Genesis 41:8 tells us, "In the morning, his mind was troubled, so he sent for all the magicians and wise men of Egypt." Pharaoh relates his dreams to these fellows, but none can help him. There is no relief, no understanding. Then an unexpected event occurs. After two long years of forgetfulness, the cupbearer suddenly remembers Joseph!

"Today I am reminded of my shortcomings," exclaims the cupbearer to his master (41:9). The servant goes on to remind pharaoh of the time the baker and he were imprisoned, and to explain about their fellow inmate Joseph's uncanny ability to decipher dreams (41:10-13). One can only wonder why the man hadn't remembered the young Hebrew earlier.

The Natural and the Supernatural

Yet upon reflection, the cupbearer's forgetfulness is not surprising. First of all, two years earlier he was probably so relieved to be alive and again in the service of pharaoh that he could think of little else. Besides, it might have been awkward to mention a foreign prisoner. Pharaoh had just recently pardoned the cupbearer, and who was he to make waves? It just wasn't the time to be asking for favors. Doing so would have amounted to asking the boss for time off just after taking a vacation. It's likely the cupbearer wanted to remain in the background, working hard and with humility to regain pharaoh's full favor. Naturally, thoughts of Joseph slipped from his mind altogether.

Naturally, the cupbearer forgets Joseph. Supernaturally, he remembers him. The chief reason why the servant suddenly recalls Joseph has nothing to do with humanity and everything to do with divinity. Simply put, the man remembers because God is ready for him to do so!

For twenty-four months the Lord blots out the memory of Joseph from the cupbearer's mind because it is not yet in his time schedule for the man to remember. Then the day finally arrives, and behold, the fellow shamefacedly recalls his shortcomings.

What are these shortcomings? They are three in number, and they are ugly when found in a group of Christians. The cupbearer possessed an ungrateful spirit, a selfish attitude, and was forgetful of a favor. God did not make him this way, but God used these unattractive qualities to cause the cupbearer to become consumed with the present and remiss in recalling the obligations of the past.

Our Delay—God's Prerogative

The Lord allowed the cupbearer's memory lapse. That is the way he operates. Think about that the next time the contract doesn't come through, the check isn't in the mail, the project isn't pulled off. God is at work in the delay. He has his own purposes and plans, and it is his prerogative to do things in his way and in his time. If we'll trust him to take charge of a situation, eventually things will all come together in an exciting, cohesive whole. God will be glorified; we will be edified. All it takes is time and trust—and occasionally heavier doses of both than we'd honestly like.

God loves to have us on hold. When we're waiting for results and it seems there is no provision coming forth and no answer to our prayers, these are the occasions when we truly learn what it is to trust. We depend upon him. We search his word, making ourselves sensitive to his leading, forcing ourselves to seek his will. Finally things gel, sometimes with more speed and intensity than we imagined possible. It all comes together for Joseph as God nudges the memory of the cupbearer. Thus starts a chain reaction of events that can only be described as amazing.

Pharaoh, frustrated by the inability of his own advisers to decode his dreams, listens intently to the cupbearer's description of Joseph. The ruler wants this young man! Quickly the king fires off a message to Potiphar (41:14) which probably reads something like this: "Do you have a Hebrew slave in the dungeon? Get him up here—now!"

Quickly, Joseph shaves and slips on fresh clothes, then makes his way into pharaoh's presence . . . from the pit to the Pentagon, just like that (41:14)! How beautiful it is when the Lord permits this type of rapid-fire rescue from the realm of apparent hopelessness. Yes, God moves in mysterious ways, his wonders to perform.

To God Be the Glory—Genesis 41:15-32

> Pharaoh said to Joseph, "I had a dream, and no one can interpret it. But I have heard it said of you that when you hear a dream you can interpret it."
>
> "I cannot do it," Joseph replied to Pharaoh, "but God will give Pharaoh the answer he desires."
>
> Then Pharaoh said to Joseph, "In my dream I was standing on the bank of the Nile, when out of the river there came up seven cows, fat and sleek, and they grazed among the reeds. After them, seven other cows came up—scrawny and very ugly and lean. I had never seen such ugly cows in all the land of Egypt. The lean, ugly cows ate up the seven fat cows that came up first. But even after they ate them, no one could tell that they had done so; they looked just as ugly as before. Then I woke up.
>
> "In my dreams I also saw seven heads of grain, full and good, growing on a single stalk. After them, seven other heads sprouted—withered and thin and scorched by the east wind. The thin heads of grain swallowed up the seven good heads. I told this to the magicians, but none could explain it to me."
>
> Then Joseph said to Pharaoh, "The dreams of Pharaoh are one and the same. God has revealed to

> Pharaoh what he is about to do. The seven good cows are seven years, and the seven good heads of grain are seven years; it is one and the same dream. The seven lean, ugly cows that came up after they did are seven years, and so are the seven worthless heads of grain scorched by the east wind: They are seven years of famine.
>
> "It is just as I said to Pharaoh: God has shown Pharaoh what he is about to do. Seven years of great abundance are coming throughout the land of Egypt, but seven years of famine will follow them. Then all the abundance in Egypt will be forgotten, and the famine will ravage the land. The abundance in the land will not be remembered, because the famine that follows it will be so severe. The reason the dream was given to Pharaoh in two forms is that the matter has been firmly decided by God, and God will do it soon."

Joseph, cleanshaven like an Egyptian rather than a bearded Hebrew, soon stands before pharaoh. The young man has barely had time to blink before he is whisked from prison to palace. No doubt pharaoh eyes him appraisingly. The ruler then begins to speak.

"I had a dream," explains the king when addressing Joseph, "and no one can interpret it. But I have heard it said of you that when you hear a dream you can interpret it" (41:15).

But Joseph responds to pharaoh's request with neither anger nor sarcasm, as well he might have. He doesn't complain about the cupbearer's ingratitude, Potiphar's injustice, Mrs. Potiphar's indiscretion, or any of the sundry people who have mistreated him. Instead, he answers the king in honest humility, "I cannot do it, but God will give Pharaoh the answer he desires" (41:16).

What about that? God will give pharaoh the answer. God—not Joseph—will interpret the dreams. How cocky and self-righteous Joseph could have been! But he isn't.

Rather, Joseph recognizes his own inadequacy and acknowledges the Lord's all-sufficiency. When we, too, do that—when we realize our limitations and admit that our only hope lies in someone stronger than ourselves—we demonstrate our confidence in God.

Surrender to the Savior

The first step of confidence vital to anyone wishing to become a Christian involves giving up on human performance as a means of salvation. As we've discussed, salvation comes through faith in the savior—nothing else. In a moment of determined abandonment, we must surrender to God through Jesus Christ. We can't go it alone. Apart from Christ, we are lost.

Once we surrender to the savior, we have the option of yielding ourselves further. We have the potential to become instruments, tools in God's hands, if only we allow him to wield us. Joseph has reached this point. He knows without doubt that the Lord will use him to decipher pharaoh's dreams, and that any knowledge he imparts will come from outside of himself, specifically, from God almighty.

What is particularly touching about Joseph's ready reply to pharaoh's request is that it is obvious that the young Hebrew has never lost confidence in God. He's been waiting, but he has kept the faith. Not only has he retained confidence in the Lord, but Joseph is willing for God to do whatever he wants with his life. He knows that God's plan is being worked out—be it in three days, three years, thirteen years. God is always faithful to keep his promises, and we'd better not try to time him with a stopwatch. We reach the height of frustration if we demand immediate answers to prayer. This Joseph avoids, and he is the better for it. Submissive trust leads him (and us) into rest (Isaiah 32:17).

Evidently pharaoh recognizes that Joseph functions as an instrument of the Lord, for without hesitation he relates the details of the dreams, closing with the statement, "I told this to the magicians, but none could explain it to me" (41:24; see 17-24). Each of pharaoh's advisers has failed. Is Joseph the least bit intimidated by the fact that so many others have not been able to figure out the meaning of the dreams? No! He trusts completely in the ability of the Lord to reveal the message inherent in the visions. We can almost hear the hymn, "To God Be the Glory," reverberating in the background as Joseph proceeds to explain what pharaoh has dreamed.

Boom and Bust

The meaning of the dreams is this. The items appearing in sevens in the visions denote periods of seven years. A time of tremendous prosperity will come to the land of Egypt. Following seven years of this boom economy, the bust will come. The agricultural surplus will soon give way to seven years of famine and intense poverty. So severe will the down period be that the years of abundance will be completely forgotten in a massive period of deprivation, the likes of which even our currently economically depressed state of Texas hasn't seen (41:25-31). And believe me, that's bad. Right now it is said that in the city of Dallas, banks are offering either free toasters or titles to oil wells to their new customers. And most are taking the toasters.

What is more, the Egyptian downslide is coming fast! The events symbolically depicted in pharaoh's dreams are going to start immediately. As Joseph explains, "The reason the dream was given to Pharaoh in two forms is that the matter has been firmly decided by God, and God will do it soon" (41:32). His statement suggests two principles we would do well to acknowledge.

Principle one: God is in control of the economy. He was in control in ancient Egypt, and he is today. My advice to businessmen is to place the Lord first in every area of their lives. Cooperate with him. Follow biblical guidelines in relationships with customers, employees, and employers. Don't think of the world of work as a secular jungle, but as an arena as sacred as any other. Christ literally "is all and in all" (Colossians 3:11). He's with us in the pit and in the palace—in the sanctuary, on the assembly line, in the executive suite. What we do in the business world should be determined by our desire to please God, because we are on display. We are living, walking, breathing examples of Christianity. Our pulpits are the everyday environments we find ourselves in; our congregation is the world.

Principle two: When God says something twice, we'd better sit up and take notice. He sends two visions with the same meaning to pharaoh to show he means business, and that he means it now! Do you know what is repeated three times in the book of Hebrews? "Today if you hear His voice, do not harden your hearts" (3:7,15; 4:7 NASB). The Lord is warning us, "Friends, it is a serious matter when you hear truth and yet fail to respond to it." We are called to be doers, not merely hearers, of the word. That means making a commitment to Christ as savior, not just thinking about it. Once we're Christians, it means going about the affairs of the father, not merely talking about them. When we're convinced by God's word that a step should be taken, we can't afford to ignore the message.

Joseph as Economic Advisor—Genesis 41:33-40

> "And now let Pharaoh look for a discerning and wise man and put him in charge of the land of Egypt. Let Pharaoh appoint commissioners over the land to take a fifth of the harvest of Egypt during the seven years of abundance. They should collect all the food of these good years that are coming and store up the grain under the authority of Pharaoh, to be kept in the cities for food. This food should be held in reserve for the country, to be used during the seven years of famine that will come upon Egypt, so that the country may not be ruined by the famine."

> The plan seemed good to Pharaoh and to all his officials. So Pharaoh asked them, "Can we find anyone like this man, one in whom is the spirit of God?"
>
> Then Pharaoh said to Joseph, "Since God has made all this known to you, there is no one so discerning and wise as you. You shall be in charge of my palace, and all my people are to submit to your orders. Only with respect to the throne will I be greater than you."

Joseph could easily stop once he explains pharaoh's dreams but, as is typical of his character, he goes the extra mile. Inspired by the spirit of God, he launches into outlining a plan of action—all part of God's program. He offers administrative and economic suggestions, and so great is his wisdom that it is obvious it could only have come from God.

Joseph first suggests that pharaoh select a "discerning and wise man and put him in charge of the land of Egypt" (41:33). This head honcho will oversee the work of a vast network of subordinates, "commissioners over the land," who will be entrusted with taking "a fifth of the harvest of Egypt during the seven years of abundance" (41:34).

Joseph recommends that pharaoh set up a food administration in preparation for the coming years. This body will have the authority to tax all agricultural production, legally collecting one-fifth of each harvest. The foodstuffs collected will be stored in grain elevators erected at strategic places in the land, and will be held in reserve for use during the seven years of famine (41:35-36).

Pharaoh is clearly impressed by Joseph's advice, and immediately recognizes its source as the young man's God. The text tells us that Joseph's "plan seemed good to Pharaoh and to all his officials" (41:37). But the king is also impressed by the man who has advised him. "Can we find anyone like this man, one in whom is the spirit of God?" asks the Egyptian ruler of his court officials (41:38).

Isn't that terrific? Joseph sticks to his convictions, bringing God into the picture without hesitation and crediting him with revealing the truth. Immediately pharaoh recognizes what Potiphar had earlier noticed and what the chief jailer had realized: that Joseph is blessed of God. Because of this, pharaoh exclaims that he wants this man in his administration. Amazed, Joseph is evidently speechless, for he says nothing.

"Since God has made all this known to you, there is no one so discerning and wise as you," says the ruler to Joseph. "You shall be in charge of my palace, and all my people are to submit to your orders. Only with respect to the throne will I be greater than you" (41:39-40). From prison to the palace, just like that! Isn't it astounding how fast God can work, how quickly he can get things done, how rapidly the pieces can all fit together in his time? Pharaoh simply sees the possibilities, and invites Joseph to join the party. No more dreams now . . . instead, a most remarkable reality sets in.

Making Things Official—Genesis 41:41-49

> So Pharaoh said to Joseph, "I hereby put you in charge of the whole land of Egypt." Then Pharaoh took his signet ring from his finger and put it on Joseph's finger. He dressed him in robes of fine linen and put a gold chain around his neck. He had him ride in a chariot as his second-in-command, and men shouted before him, "Make way!" Thus he put him in charge of the whole land of Egypt.
>
> Then Pharaoh said to Joseph, "I am Pharaoh, but without your word no one will lift hand or foot in all Egypt." Pharaoh gave Joseph the name Zaphenath-Paneah and gave him Asenath daughter of Potiphera, priest of On, to be his wife. And Joseph went throughout the land of Egypt.

> Joseph was thirty years old when he entered the service of Pharaoh king of Egypt. And Joseph went out from Pharaoh's presence and traveled throughout Egypt. During the seven years of abundance the land produced plentifully. Joseph collected all the food produced in those seven years of abundance in Egypt and stored it in the cities. In each city he put the food grown in the fields surrounding it. Joseph stored up huge quantities of grain, like the sand of the sea; it was so much that he stopped keeping records because it was beyond measure.

When pharaoh makes a decision, he does things in style and wastes little time in the process. "I hereby put you in charge of the whole land of Egypt" (41:41), declares the king, and Joseph is sworn into office on the spot. A nobody becomes a somebody, with no apparent time for job training. We must not forget about the thirteen years Joseph has spent on hold, but current events move with blinding speed.

To make things official, pharaoh places his own signet ring—a mark of royal authority—upon Joseph's finger. He dresses the young man in robes of fine linen and hangs a sparkling chain of gold around his neck. This outfit sure beats prison stripes! How much these actions remind us of the way the prodigal son is treated by his father when the wayward boy returns home (Luke 15). The waiting father places a fresh, clean robe on the boy's back, new sandals on his feet, and a ring on his finger. The fatted calf is killed and there is great rejoicing. In like manner does God wait to greet us when we come to him in faith through Jesus Christ. The past is forgotten, the slate wiped clean. We become honored recipients of God's grace, much as Joseph receives pharaoh's good favor.

The king next perches Joseph atop a royal chariot. His coming is heralded by men who shout, "Make way!" He enjoys each benefit the executive vice-presidency of the land has to offer.

Prior Preparations for the Palace . . .

"I am Pharaoh, but without your word no one will lift his hand or foot in all Egypt," proclaims the king. What authority! Can Joseph handle such responsibility at thirty years of age? The answer is a resounding yes. He's been prepared for the position. Now we know why Jacob assigned him to supervise his brothers. Now we realize that the time spent running the house of Potiphar was not put to waste, but was on-the-job training for the future. Suddenly it is clear why the chief jailer handed over the management of the prison to Joseph. Because of his past experiences, the young man has been tried and proven. He is ready to run the kingdom. And that is not all Joseph is ready for, as we shall see.

Genesis 41:45 tells us that pharaoh next gives Joseph a new Egyptian name by which he shall be known: Zaphenath-Paneah. According to Unger, the meaning of the name is "sustenance of the land is the living one" (Unger 1179). Pharaoh barely knows Joseph, but already speaks of him as the sustainer or savior of the land. Isn't it amazing how things come together in God's time?

. . . And for Everything from A to Z

God further rewards Joseph's faithfulness by prompting pharaoh to give him a wife: Asenath, the daughter of Potiphera, priest of On.

Is Joseph prepared for marriage? Yes he is. By resisting the advances of his former master's wife, he has kept himself pure. Now he will experience the wholesome joy of a guilt-free relationship with a special girl. As daughter of the priest of On, a small community some twenty miles away on the east side of the Nile, Asenath grew up in a religious home. We mustn't assume she is a worshiper of Joseph's God, but it is probable that she is open to spiritual matters. Certainly the names given the children they eventually have indicate that she at least acknowledges the presence of the Lord. It's interesting also that Asenath's father is named Potiphera. The similarity between the name of his father-in-law and the name of his former master, Potiphar, will constantly remind Joseph from whence God has delivered him. And God has literally given Joseph everything from A to Z to ensure his happinesss, as Asenath marries Zaphenath. How graciously he works!

Implementing the Policies

Following his marriage, Joseph gets busy directing the program God has designed to save Egypt in the coming years. We read that he begins to travel throughout the land, implementing the policies he has suggested (41:45-46). Things proceed as Joseph has predicted. The land produces plentifully during the seven years of abundance (41:47). Vast crops are hauled in, and one-fifth of each .harvest is collected in federal tax. We know the ground must have yielded huge amounts of produce, because not once is it mentioned that the people complain about the increased taxation.

Joseph orders the surplus grain from each area to be stored in a nearby city. Each region will one day sustain itself from food actually grown there. So immense is the amount collected and stored that scripture describes it as "like the sand of the sea" (41:49). Even a conscientious administrator like Joseph cannot keep track of the tons of grain garnered over the years. It is simply beyond measure (41:49).

Birthdays and the Boom Sours—Genesis 41:50-57

> Before the years of famine came, two sons were born to Joseph by Asenath daughter of Potiphera, priest of On. Joseph named his firstborn Manasseh and said, "It is because God has made me forget all my trouble and all my father's household." The second son he named Ephraim and said, "It is because God has made me fruitful in the land of my suffering."
>
> The seven years of abundance in Egypt came to

> an end, and the seven years of famine began, just as Joseph had said. There was famine in all the other lands, but in the whole land of Egypt there was food. When all Egypt began to feel the famine, the people cried to Pharaoh for food. Then Pharaoh told all the Egyptians, "Go to Joseph and do what he tells you."
>
> When the famine had spread over the whole country, Joseph opened the storehouses and sold grain to the Egyptians, for the famine was severe throughout Egypt. And all the countries came to Egypt to buy grain from Joseph, because the famine was severe in all the world.

Joseph is busy, tremendously so. But he doesn't make the same mistake Potiphar does; he doesn't become so consumed with his career that he neglects his wife. During the seven years of plenty, two precious sons are born to Joseph and Asenath (41:50). Don't you think Joseph is glad he waited for the physical? Don't you imagine he is thankful that he didn't satisfy his desires in the house of Potiphar? When we give God time and we wait for him to act, he blesses abundantly.

Joseph names his first boy Manasseh, Hebrew for "causing to forget." Exclaims the proud father, "It is because God has made me forget all my trouble and all my father's household" (41:51). Joseph hasn't forsaken his roots, his family, but he has fully rebounded from the heartache and pain of the portion of his life that saw him go from pit to prison. By naming his firstborn son as he does, Joseph tells us that he is big enough to leave behind the things of the past. He is able to overlook the wrongs done him over the span of thirteen years. He isn't bitter. If anything, he is better than before, and happier than he's ever been in his life.

Time passes, and it's a boy again! Son number two is called by the Hebrew name Ephraim, or "fruitful." Joseph explains his choice of names this way, "It is because

God has made me fruitful in the land of my suffering" (41:52). And indeed he has. Joseph's life epitomizes John 15:8, where we read the words of Jesus Christ, "Herein is my Father glorified, that ye bear much fruit; so shall ye be my disciples" (KJV).

Managing the Economic Emergency

Joseph's thirty-seventh birthday coincides with the year in which the boom sours. A turning point in the nation's economy occurs, and we read in verse 53 that the seven years of abundance in Egypt come to an end, just as Joseph had said they would. The years of plenty are replaced by a depression more severe than any seen during the Oklahoma dustbowl days. The famine spreads worldwide and, since no other country has had the benefit of Joseph's advance information, only Egypt is ready for the fiasco. When the Egyptians begin to feel the pinch in their bellies, they cry out to pharaoh for assistance. The ruler's reply? "Go to Joseph and do what he tells you" (41:55).

What does Joseph do when the hungry masses approach him? Verse 56 tells us that he opens the storehouses and sells grain to multitudes. Notice, Joseph sells the grain. There are no food stamp programs or federally-funded giveaways in either Joseph's administration or in scripture itself. Because of the type of man he is, we can assume that Joseph's prices are just, but he does not make the mistake of simply handing over the surplus.

You might argue, "That's not fair! The citizens paid one-fifth of what they produced in taxes! The grain is legitimately theirs. They deserve to get it back for nothing." Yet that is not the way the system works. Taxes collected belong to the government, and giveaways do not honor the dignity of man. One of the problems of our own affluent society is centered on the fact that we give so much and we demand so little in return. When they are not required to work for what they receive, men, women, and children often become selfish. They expect life will be a gravy train to glory, but it isn't so. The Egyptians do not have food, but they still have cash, and it is only just that they pay for what they take. As we'll see later in Genesis 47, they'll continue to pay, too, never expecting something for nothing.

The hunger pangs strike more than the people of Egypt, as the famine affects the entire world. Since only Egypt is prepared for the disaster, it is to Egypt that foreigners begin to flock. Joseph sells grain to these folks also; there are no subsidized relief programs in his international policy manual, either (41:57).

Of course, since all the world is starving, it is only logical to assume that the people in Canaan are tightening their belts as well. Pretty soon Jacob and family will find themselves in need of food. And there is only one place to go and one person to see: Joseph. We see unveiling before our eyes the marvelous plan of God, not only to reunite Joseph and his family, but also to transport the children of Israel into the nation of Egypt in accordance with the abrahamic covenant.

LESSONS

Before we witness God's work in motion, let's review some of the most important lessons of Genesis 41.

Lesson one: *when everything is on hold in our lives, God is working out his ultimate purpose.* He possesses the plan; we must possess the patience.

Lesson two: *the Lord's timing is always perfect.* He awaits exactly the right moment to jog the cupbearer's memory, when circumstances in Egypt are ripe for a hero like Joseph.

Lesson three: *Joseph never loses confidence in God's person, plan, and promises, and neither should we.*

Lesson four: *how quickly God can make things happen when he starts to work!* Within hours Joseph is no longer a prisoner, but a palace official.

Lesson five: *Joseph magnifies and glorifies God in front of pharaoh.* Even before the most influential person in the land, Joseph's priorities are straight.

Lesson six: *the world economy is truly in the Lord's hands.* Recessions, depressions, crashes—all are restrained or permitted according to his will.

Lesson seven: *God blesses Joseph and meets his every need.* We've seen him take care of Joseph throughout, and now Joseph is blessed abundantly.

Lesson eight: as the names of Joseph's sons suggest, *God expects us to forget our troubles and to be fruitful in the land of our afflictions.*

Waiting and Watching

Two thoughts come to mind as this chapter ends. First, it is important to maintain a godly attitude in the face of trial, even in the midst of prolonged adversity. Second, it is good to bear in mind and heart that God is always capable of delivering us from trouble with blinding speed.

Like Joseph, Corrie ten Boom was unjustly imprisoned. For her crime—that of concealing Jews in German-occupied Holland during World War II—she was sentenced to solitary confinement in Scheveningen Prison for three months, then sent to a concentration camp in Holland, and finally shipped in an overcrowded baggage car to a destination deep within the heart of Germany: Ravensbruck concentration camp.

Ravensbruck—the very name struck terror into the hearts of Corrie and her sister Betsie, who had also been arrested. In the summer of 1944, the camp gates clanged shut behind the pair, and Corrie wondered if the doors of hell could sound any different. The sisters joined the 1400 women assigned to a lice- and flea-infested barracks designed to hold only 400. Then the ordeal began in full.

The dawn of each new day at Ravensbruck brought with it the possibility of death. With the passing of every twenty-four hours, scores were summoned to meet their creator. Prisoners gave birth to babies in the camp infirmary, only to have their infants left to die. The occasional hot showers the women were allowed to have were greeted with a combination of gratitude and dread, for from the faucets in the large, dank room might pour either steaming water or lethal gas. Recalls Corrie of the particular ordeal of awaiting each shower:

> At such moments you look death in the eye. You stand, as it were, on the edge of eternity. What a joy it was for me to know that Jesus had brought me the assurance of salvation. If it were gas, then after a short time I would go to the house of the Father, where Jesus is preparing a home for everyone who belongs to Him (Brown 61).

Despite the circumstances, the ten Booms, like Joseph, maintained a godly attitude in the face of adversity. They were servants, leading Bible studies, supplying words of comfort, telling any and all about the love of Jesus Christ. On numerous occasions, Corrie, the healthier and more active of the two, would risk her life to visit prisoners in other locations around the camp, and to offer them the living water of spiritual truth. Whenever she did this, the frail Betsie steadfastly prayed.

Months passed. Betsie's fragile health crumbled and she finally went home to be with the Lord in December of 1944. Before her death, she confided to Corrie that the Lord had given her a vision. After the war, they were to travel the world, bringing the gospel to thousands, relying upon God for strength and endurance. With Betsie's demise, the dream might have died, too. But it did not.

Two weeks after Betsie passed away, Corrie was summoned from the ranks at roll call. The other prisoners trembled, knowing such special attention might signal that she was to be executed. For three hours Corrie stood shivering in the bitter, icy weather with the other prisoners who had been singled out. She used the opportunity to speak to those around her of Jesus Christ and of his undying love. Then a guard came and escorted her into the camp office. There she learned that, far from going to her death, she was to be released. Release! How unexpected! Within eight days Corrie walked outside the gates of Ravensbruck, a free woman (Brown 56-65).

Much later, Corrie learned that her release from the concentration camp had come about as the result of a clerical error. A clerical error? Yes. But it was an error allowed by a sovereign God who is ever capable of delivering his children with blinding speed when he desires. He did that for Joseph. He did that for Corrie ten Boom. He can do that for you, too, no matter what your prison is.

With Corrie's freedom, Betsie's dream lived on. Only one ten Boom sister eventually traveled the world telling others of Jesus, but she did so with the comforting knowledge that Betsie was waiting on the other side, safe in their savior's arms.

QUESTIONS FOR STUDY

1. In what ways may God work in our lives when it seems we're "on hold," as Joseph was for so many years?

2. From Joseph's example, we see that God is able to change rapidly our circumstances when he desires. Has that ever happened to you or to someone you know? Share the incident, if you wish.

3. What do the names of Joseph's two sons mean, and what do these meanings tell us about his attitude toward all that has happened in the past thirteen years? Is there a situation from your own past about which you are bitter? Have you confessed your bitterness to the Lord and asked him to remove it?

4. What do Joseph's actions in distributing the government grain to the hungry Egyptians tell us about the biblical attitude toward work?

5. What do pharaoh's dreams suggest about God's control of world economics? In light of what we read in Genesis 41, what lessons can we apply to our own personal and professional lives concerning economic downswings and upturns?

PART TWO

The Testing

5

The Dreams Unfold

Genesis 42

Each spring our ministry holds couples' conferences in the piney woods of east Texas. We frequently stay at Kaleo Lodge, a retreat center operated by the Christian Concern Foundation, the ministry founded by the late Creath Davis. Kaleo, nestled between a shimmering blue, well-stocked lake and a forest of tall pines whose topmost needles brush the sky, is the perfect setting in which to relax, reflect, and renew relationships.

We've only had trouble at Kaleo once in all the years we've used its lovely facilities. Our couples' conference that particular year was unusually promising. We had a full house—many special friends had signed up for the weekend. The program we'd worked so hard to develop promised great fun, fellowship, and opportunity for growth. For months the staff had prayed earnestly that God might use us to touch the lives of the husbands and wives who would attend. We were eager for the weekend to begin.

Friday night went off without a hitch, as did Saturday morning. Then disaster literally slapped us flush in the face. Saturday afternoon the pump that operates the conference ground's water system broke down. That meant no running water, no flushing toilets—and no way could we stay. The group packed up and we all left early, conference unfinished, program partly unpresented, and, I felt, lives largely untouched.

I am rarely quiet under stress. Driving the thirty-odd miles back to our home in Tyler, I fumed, fussed, and fired off a mostly meaningless monologue of my frustrations. As usual in these occasions when I am letting off steam, Pearl kept quiet. In silence she allowed me to voice my disappointment for forty-five uninterrupted minutes. Then, as we turned into our driveway, she looked over at me and simply said, "Don, I think the God who runs the universe could have kept a little old pump going one more day if he had wanted to."

That knocked the wind out of my sails, as you can imagine! How right she was. There are no accidents in the will of God—only preplanned incidents. The ups, downs, and inbetweens of our lives are programmed in advance by a loving heavenly father who seeks proper responses from us. Everything that happens does so because he permits it—even right down to broken water pumps and prematurely-ended conferences.

Trusting during the Stops and the Starts

As we have witnessed in our study of his experiences so far, God's perfect plan is being worked out in the life of Joseph. The stops and starts in that plan are wonderful for us to behold, and our own hearts ought to be encouraged as we see the Lord faithfully meet Joseph's needs at every twist and turn of the road.

We remember the betrayal of his brothers, the decade of servitude, the years of imprisonment. In God's time, Joseph is given the opportunity to interpret the dreams of pharaoh, and he candidly relays both the good news and the bad to the Egyptian king. The Lord reveals to Joseph that pharaoh's visions indicate seven years of tremendous economic growth are at hand for the land of Egypt. Agriculture will boom; production will skyrocket. But then the crash will come, and seven years of severe hardship will follow. The market will bottom out; ranching operations will fold; inflation will climb to new heights; food will be in short supply; intense famine will completely replace the period of plenty.

Joseph goes on to offer pharaoh advice on how the country can prepare for the lean times ahead, and the ruler listens intently. Once the young Hebrew is finished, the king unexpectedly names him executive vice-president of the land. At the age of thirty, Joseph finds himself not only freed from jail, but appointed to head the nation's newly-instituted federal food administration. He is charged with implementing the economic policies that will one day save the land from ruin (41:41). In the meantime, he also finds time for family, marrying Asenath, the daughter of a priest, and fathering two precious sons, Manasseh and Ephraim (41:50-52).

For seven years the economic boom continues, and Joseph keeps busy overseeing the storage of foodstuffs for the tough times ahead. As our study of Genesis 42 begins, he is close to thirty-nine years of age. The seven years of plenty are over; the tide has turned; the depression is coming on full force, affecting not only Egypt, but the entire world. "Go to Joseph," is pharaoh's answer as the people clamor for food to fill their empty bellies (41:55).

It is a time in Joseph's life when he literally holds the fate of hundreds of thousands of people in his hands. He is the acting authority of the land. Pharaoh has delegated huge responsibilities and awesome power to him—serious stuff for the son of a shepherd from Canaan. And Joseph has had time to learn to enjoy the perks and prerogatives of power: the royal chariot, custom-tailored clothes, servants, carte blanche authority.

It is often easier to worship God when the tires are about to go flat than when the ride is smooth. Crises force us to cry out to the Lord; easy times often make us fat, felicitous, and forgetful. When Joseph was in the pit, the house of Potiphar, and the prison, he had no choice except to depend upon God. He could not control his circumstances, and looking to the Lord in the delay and the distress was the only viable way he could handle his situation.

But now the tables are turned. Joseph is the most influential political figure in the land, second only to pharaoh. Does he continue to lean upon the Lord now that he is a man of prestige and power instead of a prisoner? Can he trust God in personal prosperity as he did in times of turmoil?

The answer we have discovered so far is yes. There is no indication at the close of Genesis 41 that Joseph is corrupted by his new position. In prosperity he resists the temptations of pride and arrogance, even as he had done in adversity. The lessons of the Lord's faithfulness have been hammered home over thirteen difficult years, and Joseph is both ready and able to properly respond to the rights and responsibilities of leadership. Never do we observe him withholding his loyalty or withdrawing his gratitude from God.

As we turn to the pages of Genesis 42, we'll watch Joseph face yet another trial in his life, an emotionally gut-wrenching confrontation with men he has not seen in twenty years, the brothers who turned their backs upon him decades before. In dealing with his long-lost family, the questions are not only will Joseph continue to depend upon God, but also will he be able to leave the past where it belongs—behind him? In his heart will he voice the words of the apostle Paul who, in Philippians 3:13, assures us he is "forgetting what lies behind and reaching forward to what lies ahead" (NASB)? Or will Joseph wallow in the miry muck of resentment, thirsting for revenge rather than reconciliation? Let's read on and find out.

MEANWHILE, BACK IN CANAAN—GENESIS 42:1-5

> When Jacob learned that there was grain in Egypt, he said to his sons, "Why do you just keep looking

at each other?" He continued, "I have heard that there is grain in Egypt. Go down there and buy some for us, so that we may live and not die."

Then ten of Joseph's brothers went down to buy grain from Egypt. But Jacob did not send Benjamin, Joseph's brother, with the others, because he was afraid that harm might come to him. So Israel's sons were among those who went to buy grain, for the famine was in the land of Canaan also.

As the curtain opens on Genesis 42, we find ourselves momentarily transported from Egypt to Hebron, in Canaan, Joseph's old homestead. Here we catch a glimpse once again of Joseph's father, Jacob, and his family. The famine has spread to the promised land, and the going is tough. All totaled, there are sixty-six men, women, and children, plus the in-laws, in Jacob's extended family. Their stomachs are growling and their mouths hungry for the food that is in such scarce supply. Naturally, Jacob is deeply concerned.

He learns that provisions are available in Egypt. Perhaps a messenger or traveling merchant relays the news. Somehow, Jacob hears about Egypt's preparedness for the disaster, and he summons his sons together for an emergency family conference.

"Why do you just keep looking at each other?" he demands of his now middle-aged sons (42:1). Their lives are in jeopardy, and the brothers haven't made any inroads in solving the problem. "I have heard that there is grain in Egypt," continues Jacob. "Go down there and buy some for us so that we may live and not die" (42:2). What great news! Their lives may yet be spared from starvation. But the brothers probably greet the information with something less than ecstasy.

Egypt—the word leaves a sour taste in their mouths and a sinking feeling in the pits of their stomachs worse than any hunger pang. Send us anywhere but Egypt, they undoubtedly think. Egypt is where the Midianite caravan carted our brother twenty-plus years ago. Surely Joseph is long gone or perhaps even dead, but still, we'd rather not risk it.

However, there is no choice. Verse 3 reveals that the ten oldest boys set out on a journey of some 250 miles to a land they'd prefer never to see. What an experience it is for them to travel the route Joseph had taken. Perhaps the brothers nurse secret feelings of dread. Maybe they fear they'll run into someone who knows of Joseph and his story. Possibly they are afraid of entering the country and being accused of the crime of selling their brother. No doubt their hearts are as heavy as their saddlebags, which bulge with silver to purchase grain.

Money Can't Buy Me Love . . . or Fix Me Dinner

Billy Graham once said, "Money can't buy health, happiness, or what it did last year." That's for sure! It is interesting that in the midst of his material wealth, Jacob and his family are starving. Their bank accounts bulge, but their stomachs remain empty. Their money is absolutely useless unless it is taken to Egypt and spent there on the bare essentials of life.

Today we scrape to pay the bills and strive to sock some away in savings accounts. We invest in mutual funds, IRAs, and the stock market. Our goal is financial independence, but in reality there is no such animal. Ironically, there are occasions when our well-padded portfolios and passbooks do us little good. National and world economics are capable of fluctuating beyond belief during times of crisis. During the depression of the 1930s, for example, unemployed Americans went through life savings with horrifying speed and stood in bread lines by the thousands. Following World Wars I and II, Germans encountered much the same thing. In the 1970s, Vietnamese and Cambodian refugees coming to America found themselves surrendering lucrative professional practices in their homelands and forced to find work as custodians and dishwashers in the States, their sprawling homes in southeast Asia a far cry from the tiny apartments into which they had to cram their families in the new land.

In the Bible, Jacob and clan find themselves hungry despite their gold and silver reserves. There is another biblical instance in which money proves totally worthless as well. Larry Norman has composed a stirring ballad about the tribulation, an intense period of suffering which will engulf the world in a future day (Revelation 6-7). Of these seven years of horrendous hardship, writes Norman:

> Children died, the days grew cold,
> a piece of bread would buy a bag of gold.
> I wish we'd all been ready.

As Revelation 6:5-6 reveals, in the coming tribulation days, famine more severe than any experienced in prior human history will blanket the earth. A day's wages will but purchase a quart of wheat. Then, as Norman puts it, "A piece of bread would buy a bag of gold." If we're Christians, we'll miss out on the trauma of the tribulation, because we'll have already been transported into the presence of Christ in an event known as the rapture (1 Thessalonians 4:16-18). Norman's lament, "I wish we'd all been ready," is a refrain written about the unbeliever during the last days.

In the meantime, we would do well to recognize that there is no such thing as financial security apart from God. Our trust must not be placed in the bottom line, but in the priceless savior, Jesus Christ, who has promised to take care of our needs. As he said in the Sermon on the Mount:

> Do not be anxious then, saying, "What shall we eat?" or "What shall we drink?" or "With what shall we clothe ourselves?" For all these things the Gentiles eagerly seek; for your heavenly Father

> knows that you need all these things. But seek first His kingdom and His righteousness; and all these things shall be added to you (Matthew 6:31-33 NASB; see also 1 Timothy 6:6-8).

Big bucks in the bank by themselves never necessarily guarantee that we'll have food on the table, because economic disasters may come to wipe out our savings and render our purchasing power useless. Jacob's ranching operations may be successful, but he is dirt poor when it comes to supporting his family at home during the economic crunch of Genesis 42. But God intervenes to provide the means of salvation in Egypt.

Don't ignore the fact that it is God who rescues Egypt from ruin, either! It is God who preplanned Joseph's entry into Egypt, God who gifted him with the ability to interpret dreams, God who gave him the wisdom to save the nation and the world. Now it is by God's prearrangement that Jacob and the children of Israel become connected with Egypt. The Lord's hand is pushing the buttons and turning the dials. It always does.

A Doting Dad

Ten of Jacob's sons mount their camels and begin their trip west. They will be among the many foreigners streaming into Egypt in hopes of purchasing provisions (42:5). Verse 4 reveals that, at their father's discretion, Benjamin does not accompany his big brothers. Why is Jacob hesitant to let the boy, now a man of around thirty years of age, make the trip into the foreign land? Essentially, the old man is afraid for his youngest son's safety.

It's not that Jacob has any specific reason to suspect his sons' reception in Egypt will be less than warm. It's just that Benjamin is so very special to him. He is the last (as far as Jacob knows) surviving son of dearly departed Rachel. Benjamin is Jacob's one remaining link (or so he thinks) with a very pleasant part of his past. Joseph is gone, dead, evidently ripped to shreds by some foul animal, and, as much as is possible, Jacob has substituted Benjamin for Joseph in his affections. The doting dad isn't about to let the baby of the family out of his sight! Soon, though, Jacob will be forced to face the inevitable.

The Persistence of Divine Purpose—Genesis 42:6-17

> Now Joseph was the governor of the land, the one who sold grain to all its people. So when Joseph's brothers arrived, they bowed down to him with their faces to the ground. As soon as Joseph saw his brothers, he recognized them, but he pretended to be a stranger and spoke harshly to them. "Where do you come from?" he asked.
>
> "From the land of Canaan," they replied, "to buy food."
>
> Although Joseph recognized his brothers, they did not recognize him. Then he remembered his dreams about them and said to them, "You are spies! You have come to see where our land is unprotected."
>
> "No, my lord," they answered. "Your servants have come to buy food. We are all the sons of one man. Your servants are honest men, not spies."
>
> "No!" he said to them. "You have come to see where our land is unprotected."
>
> But they replied, "Your servants were twelve brothers, the sons of one man, who lives in the land of Canaan. The youngest is now with our father, and one is no more."
>
> Joseph said to them, "It is just as I told you: You are spies! And this is how you will be tested: As surely as Pharaoh lives, you will not leave this place unless your youngest brother comes here. Send one of your number to get your brother; the rest of you will be kept in prison, so that your words may be tested to see if you are telling the truth. If you are not, then as surely as Pharaoh lives, you are spies!" And he put them all in custody for three days.

What thoughts must run through Joseph's brothers' minds as they guide their camels along the route to Egypt? Imagine for a moment the quiet conversations they must hold among themselves while gathered around campfires at night.

"I wonder whatever happened to Joseph."

"Oh, he's probably serving in some remote place, if he's still alive. I doubt we'll ever see him again."

"Stop worrying. He's long gone."

Little do they know that as they follow the hordes of hungry pouring into Egypt, they will indeed see their younger brother, and he won't be sweating as a slave under the yoke of a master, either.

When Dreams Really Do Come True

The ten men ride into the Egyptian city where surplus grain is sold to foreigners. A large contingent, they are immediately directed to the chief administrator of the food program—namely Joseph, who is described in Genesis 42:6 as "the governor of the land, the one who sold grain to all its people."

When Joseph's brothers approach him, scripture tells us they fall upon their knees and bow down to him, "their faces to the ground" (42:6). Shades of yesteryear! This is exactly what God had said would happen some twenty-two years before, when Joseph dreamed about his brothers' sheaves of grain bowing before his sheaf (37:7). God sometimes works slowly, but he always gets the job done. The persistence of divine purpose is powerful to behold. Finally, after nearly a quarter century of waiting, Joseph receives a first glimpse of the ultimate fulfillment of the visions he has been given.

Why do the brothers bow? It is not because they recognize Joseph. Instead, they are on a serious mission. They desperately wish to avoid trouble in this strange land. They realize that they are at the mercy of the official before whom they bow, and so they sink to their knees in humble obeisance, showing their respect for this leader who holds the lives of their families in the palm of his hand.

Although the men do not recognize Joseph, he immediately realizes who they are. Genesis 42:7 tells us that rather than reveal his identity, he pretends to be a stranger. Some are surprised that Joseph could conceal himself so effectively, but actually such subterfuge would have been relatively easy for him.

As we discussed before, the last place Joseph's brothers expect to find him is in a position of prominence. They assume he is dead, or at least waiting on tables in the house of his master somewhere. It would be highly unlikely even for him to be near the capital city, much less be the prime minister of Egypt! Besides, it has been twenty-two years since they have seen him. Men change quite a bit physically from their late teens to their late thirties.

And Joseph walks, talks, looks, and breathes like an Egyptian. He is dressed as an Egyptian, robed and sporting golden chains. His grooming no longer reflects Israelite customs: he is not bearded; his hair is styled much as that of any nobleman of his adopted country. Rather than conversing with his brothers in Hebrew, he speaks the local language to them, using an interpreter (42:23). He wants to convey the impression that he is an Egyptian through and through, and the brothers have no reason to doubt that he was born right beside the banks of the Nile.

If they cannot recognize him, why is it so easy for Joseph to identify the ten men kneeling before him as his family members? The fact that there are ten of them traveling together is a dead giveaway. Besides, the brothers are older than Joseph. Most were in their twenties, some perhaps even in their thirties, when they threw him in the pit. Now the majority are in their forties. Barring severe illness, not too much happens to the body between the ages of twenty-five and forty-seven. The manly appearance present in the mid-twenties—much more so than in the mid-teens—remains fairly identifiable. It's not surprising that Joseph is able to spot his ten middle-aged siblings without difficulty.

Dealing with the Discovery

How does Joseph handle the fact that his brothers have finally come back into his life? Scripture reveals that he speaks to them harshly, demanding, "Where do you come from?" (42:7).

Some people may wonder why Joseph speaks sternly to his brothers. He has forgiven them, hasn't he? Not once has he made an angry remark about their behavior toward him. Have the long-locked floodgates of bitterness suddenly opened to permit the flow of resentment? Has Joseph been concealing his hatred for twenty-two years, only to have it burst forth unbridled now that he has the chance for revenge? The answer is no.

Joseph has long before allowed God to cleanse him of any feelings of bitterness toward his brothers. Yet he realizes that they may still have some lessons to learn. He desires to put them to the test to see if they have really changed. If not, he must nudge them to repentance, or they will never be the men God intends them to be.

The test that Joseph plans to give his brothers involves none other than his younger brother, Benjamin. Joseph is prompted by principle, and his goal is basically this: he wishes to discover if his brothers are the same types of men today that they were the afternoon they jealously sold him into slavery. Twenty-two years ago they acted with unimaginable cruelty because they deeply resented his favored position in the eyes and heart of their father. Joseph realizes that much of Jacob's affection for him must naturally have been transferred to his little brother, the remaining child of Rachel. If the older brothers are as envious of Benjamin as they once were of him, then they don't deserve assistance. Joseph must discern the truth about his brothers before he can justifiably make a provision of blessing in their lives.

You'll find that God often does the same thing in our lives. He puts us to the test, dealing with us in ways to make us shape up before he brings the promised blessings into our lives.

One day Christ climbed up on a mountain, and thousands followed to hear him. It was the time of the Passover, and the multitudes had brought no picnic lunches. They were hungry. Jesus turned to his disciple Philip and asked, "Where are we to buy bread, that these may eat?" (John 6:5 NASB). Christ's question was a test, for scripture tells us that "He Himself knew what He was intending to do," and that was to feed miraculously the five thousand with the loaves and fishes of a little boy. Philip's response? "Two hundred denarii worth of bread is not sufficient for them, for every one to receive a little" (John 6:7 NASB). In other words, there's no way that we can feed all these people! And thus Philip, who walked alongside the savior, failed the test of trust.

Of course Philip had no idea he was being tested. The truth is that we seldom do. God's pop quizzes are generally unannounced. It would be nice if he'd give us a schedule, but he doesn't, so we should be ready at all times. As far as Philip was concerned, Jesus was giving him a little object lesson to prepare him for the blessing that followed: a massive banquet for more than five thousand, catered exclusively by God on the slopes of that mountain.

Commencing the Test

Joseph is just, as he administrates each trial the brothers will endure. His motives are not self-seeking or cruel. He simply desires to see if his brothers have morally grown up.

"You are spies!" he responds accusingly to their request to purchase food. "You have come to see where our land is unprotected" (42:9).

"No, my lord. . . . Your servants have come to buy

food. . . . Your servants are honest men, not spies," they sputter in reply, astonished (42:10-11). Such a charge is not to be taken lightly, because the penalty for international intrigue against the country of Egypt could easily be death. Joseph's remarks strike fear into the hearts of his brothers. He tells them that they may never see Canaan again, and that they will be very, very lucky if they escape with their lives, much less get to buy food.

The brothers literally cry to Joseph for deliverance. They plead with him concerning their honesty, their lack of guilt. His answer? "No! You have come to see where our land is unprotected" (42:12). How reminiscent this is of the way he pleaded with them to be merciful years earlier, from the depths of the cistern (42:21). Then they turned deaf ears upon his suffering. Now they will experience the same cold response he did. Joseph isn't trying to exact vengeance. This is no eye for an eye, tooth for a tooth, scheme of retaliation. He is merely trying to refresh graphically their memories about the events of twenty-two years past.

I've often wondered why Joseph chose to accuse his brothers of being spies, and then I realized that one of the chief reasons they had angrily tossed him into the pit was that he had reported to Jacob about the foul behavior of Gad, Asher, Dan, and Naphtali in the fields (37:2). Why, the brothers had probably scorned him with such taunts as, "Here comes Daddy's little spy!" Now they receive a taste of their own medicine.

"Your servants were twelve brothers, the sons of one man, who lives in the land of Canaan. The youngest is now with our father, and one is no more," the brothers insist, quaking in their sandals (42:13). At last Joseph receives the whole history. Benjamin is alive; Jacob is alive. Joseph's whole family is convinced that he himself is dead. They've given him up as gone for good.

With this, Joseph introduces part one of the exam he intends to put his brothers through. "It is just as I told you: You are spies!" he exclaims again (42:14). And then comes the description of the test. "And this is how you will be tested: As surely as Pharaoh lives, you will not leave this place unless your youngest brother comes here. Send one of your number to get your brother; the rest of you will be kept in prison, so that your words may be tested to see if you are telling the truth. If you are not, then as surely as Pharaoh lives, you are spies!" (42:15-16).

Finally Benjamin is brought into the picture. Fetching Benjamin from Canaan to Egypt will ostensibly prove the brothers' honesty and innocence. In reality, it will afford Joseph a bird's-eye view of how they treat their baby brother. Then he will know if they have become less selfish, more sensitive, and truly sorry for the sins of the past.

Genesis 42:17 reveals that Joseph then jails his brothers for three days. He had been imprisoned for three years, thanks to their original deceit. Now they would have time—though only a short time—to reflect and remember. He gives them seventy-two hours to sit. We'll see if their consciences have been softened or hardened as the years have gone by.

The Strength of Human Affection, and the Power of a Guilty Conscience—Genesis 42:18-26

> On the third day, Joseph said to them, "Do this and you will live, for I fear God: If you are honest men, let one of your brothers stay here in prison, while the rest of you go and take grain back for your starving households. But you must bring your youngest brother to me, so that your words may be verified and that you may not die." This they proceeded to do.
>
> They said to one another, "Surely we are being punished because of our brother. We saw how distressed he was when he pleaded with us for his life, but we would not listen; that's why this distress has come upon us."

> Reuben replied, "Didn't I tell you not to sin against the boy? But you wouldn't listen! Now we must give an accounting for his blood." They did not realize that Joseph could understand them, since he was using an interpreter.
>
> He turned away from them and began to weep, but then turned back and spoke to them again. He had Simeon taken from them and bound before their eyes.
>
> Joseph gave orders to fill their bags with grain, to put each man's silver back in his sack, and to give them provisions for their journey. After this was done for them, they loaded their grain on their donkeys and left.

On the third day of their imprisonment, Joseph pays a visit to his brothers, and it appears that he has tempered his plans for them a bit. In Genesis 42:18-20, we see the conditions he lays out. Rather than nine of the brothers remaining in custody, only one will be required to stay behind in the Egyptian jail. The rest may return to their families, taking provisions along to feed their starving households, but the nine must still make a return trip to the land of Egypt, this time bringing their youngest brother with them.

Why does Joseph slightly soften the test? I am not sure, but perhaps he fears the traumatic sight of only one brother returning to Canaan will be too much for his father. Jacob is old, and Joseph surely doesn't want to shock him into having a coronary or a stroke. Besides, Joseph also knows Jacob well enough to realize that it may take the voices of nine sons to persuade him to loosen his grip on Benjamin and allow him to make the journey. Maybe Joseph is considering the dangers of the trip itself. One lone traveler would be easy prey for bandits or highwaymen; nine men riding together would be more likely to make it home safely. Anyway, it would be difficult for only one fellow to carry enough grain to feed the starving clan back in Canaan. Whatever the reason,

Joseph relaxes the rules a little, but it is still a tough test that the brothers will undergo.

The Power of a Guilty Conscience: the Beginnings of Repentance

Once Joseph finishes speaking, the brothers begin to mutter among themselves, and it is obvious that the past has not been forgotten. "Surely we are being punished because of our brother. We saw how distressed he was when he pleaded with us for his life, but we would not listen; that's why this distress has come upon us," they wail from their cell in sheer misery (42:21).

What a man reaps, that also will he sow. God promises us that our sins will eventually, inevitably, find us out (Galatians 6:7; Numbers 32:23). In Genesis 42, the chickens are coming home to roost in the lives of Joseph's brothers. The men are arriving at the conclusion that God is allowing the past to affect the present. Oftentimes in our own lives, realizing that we are reaping what we have sown is the first step toward becoming repentant and broken in spirit. Only when we become tangibly aware of our own sins and shortcomings do we acknowledge our need of a savior.

In Joseph's brothers' case, their consciences cause them to proclaim, "Surely we are being punished because of our brother." Their memories flash technicolor images of the wretched episode into their thoughts: "We saw how distressed he was. . . ." And their reason prompts them to conclude, "That's why this distress has come upon us" (42:21). In their anguished comments we witness the fullthrottled power of consciences burdened by decades of guilt. They've lived a lie for twenty-two years, sweeping their crime under the rug and concealing it with a blood-drenched robe and a host of falsehoods. They've even come to believe it themselves but, when stress hits, the shameful events of the past are mentally replayed with the graphic reality of a television documentary.

"Didn't I tell you not to sin against the boy? But you

wouldn't listen!" exclaims the oldest, Reuben. "Now we must give an accounting for his blood" (42:22). Isn't that just like an older brother? "I told you so! I warned you this would happen! But you wouldn't listen to me." Looking again at the events of Genesis 37, we recall that it was Reuben who persuaded his brothers not to murder Joseph. It was Reuben who intended to rescue his younger brother when the others had cooled off (37:21-22). Still, he has been as guilty as any in deceiving Jacob and concealing the crime.

The Strength of Human Affection

While all the verbal banter is taking place among the unfortunate men, Joseph listens closely. They do not realize that he understands their words for, as verse 23 reveals, he has been using an interpreter during his interaction with them. He is unable to ignore the emotion of the moment; their regret pierces him, their sorrow stabs him to the core. He turns from them and weeps hot, bitter tears (42:24).

You see, Joseph isn't enjoying this test. He doesn't really want to prolong his brothers' misery. He loves them. His tears are no sign of weakness, but the mark of a man who has not seen his family in two decades and who desperately wishes to be reunited with his father and brothers. He'd probably like to end the charade at this moment, sending them home to fetch Jacob, Benjamin, and the rest of the Israelites, bringing all to the safety of Egypt. But it is not yet time for that.

The fact that his family reunion will be agonizingly delayed overwhelms Joseph, and prompts his weeping. His are tears of compassion for his brothers—tears of joy because God's promises to him are beginning to unfold and tears of sorrow because he must yet wait.

His tears are not the only ones to have been shed in the face of enforced waiting. John 11 gives the account of Mary and Martha's agonized waiting and weeping as their brother lay dying. If only Jesus would come! For days, their eyes strained to catch a glimpse of a traveler on the horizon. When Christ arrived, it was apparently too late. Lazarus was dead, his body resting in the family tomb. However, the waiting and weeping were worth it all for, with the forceful command, "Lazarus, come forth," Jesus freed him from the grave (11:43 NASB). God is ever and always at work in the delays of our lives.

Continuing the Test

Joseph turns again to face his brothers. He orders that Simeon be seized and bound before their eyes (42:24). It is Simeon who will remain behind as a hostage. What makes Joseph choose him for this dubious distinction?

Simeon is the second oldest of Jacob's sons. Reuben, the eldest offspring of Jacob and Leah, had proved himself to be at least moderately sympathetic toward Joseph in the past. Although he was unable to accomplish it, Reuben had planned to release Joseph from the pit unharmed and return him to their father. Simeon is another story. Nothing in scripture suggests that he is anything other than a lowlife.

You remember that Simeon was one of the brothers who engineered the massacre at Shechem (Genesis 34), and there are no indications that his character improved much with the passage of time. A man capable of mass murder would have had no qualms about killing a younger brother. On that fateful day of twenty-two years ago, I imagine that he was the one who most wanted to slay Joseph, only to have his plan overruled when Judah and the others spotted the caravan of Midianites on the horizon (37:25-26). Surely kindness and mercy were not among his strong suits.

Whatever the reason, Joseph chooses Simeon as the one to be ransomed, and instructs the guards to tie him up. For the entire trek home, the brothers will have before them the eyewitness image of Simeon bound, sweltering in prison, awaiting their return with Benjamin in tow.

Joseph next orders his servants to fill his brothers' bags with grain, and to return secretly to each man the silver he had brought to purchase food (42:25). Joseph's reasoning is simple. He does not intend to become obligated to his family in any way. He freely gives them the food that will save their lives; they owe him nothing in return. How much this action reminds us of Jesus Christ, who offers salvation as a gift, not as an item to be earned. And, with this, the brothers load their grain onto the backs of their donkeys and depart for home (42:26).

The Shortsightedness of Human Reason—Genesis 42:27-38

> At the place where they stopped for the night one of them opened his sack to get feed for his donkey, and he saw his silver in the mouth of his sack. "My silver has been returned," he said to his brothers. "Here it is in my sack."
>
> Their hearts sank and they turned to each other trembling and said, "What is this that God has done to us?"
>
> When they came to their father Jacob in the land of Canaan, they told him all that had happened to them. They said, "The man who is lord over the land spoke harshly to us and treated us as though we were spying on the land. But we said to him, 'We are honest men; we are not spies. We were twelve brothers, sons of one father. One is no more, and the youngest is now with our father in Canaan.'
>
> "Then the man who is lord over the land said to us, 'This is how I will know whether you are honest men: Leave one of your brothers here with me, and take food for your starving households and go. But bring your youngest brother to me so I will know that you are not spies but honest men. Then I will give your brother back to you, and you can trade in the land.' "
>
> As they were emptying their sacks, there in each

> man's sack was his pouch of silver! When they and their father saw the money pouches, they were frightened. Their father Jacob said to them, "You have deprived me of my children. Joseph is no more and Simeon is no more, and now you want to take Benjamin. Everything is against me!"
>
> Then Reuben said to his father, "You may put both of my sons to death if I do not bring him back to you. Entrust him to my care, and I will bring him back."
>
> But Jacob said, "My son will not go down there with you; his brother is dead and he is the only one left. If harm comes to him on the journey you are taking, you will bring my gray head down to the grave in sorrow."

Along the first leg of their journey back to Canaan, I imagine the brothers talk freely among themselves about the unusual experiences they have had. Perhaps they speculate about the identity of the ruler who has dealt with them so severely. Maybe they plan the way in which they will break the news to Jacob, rehearsing their roles, considering the easiest way to convince their father to let Benjamin out of his sight.

Their voices grow quiet as soon as they stop to set up camp for the night. One of them unsuspectingly reaches into his saddlebag to grab fodder for his animal, and discovers the silver. Genesis 42:28 tells us that the hearts of the brothers sink in despair at this discovery. "What is this that God has done to us?" they frantically inquire (42:28).

Imagine what else they must have said. "It's bad enough that the second-in-command in Egypt thinks we're spies. Now he can accuse us of grand larceny, too! How can we go back? We'll be accused of being thieves. But how can we not go back? We've got to think of Simeon—and eventually we'll need more food."

The brothers' question, "What is this that God has

done to us?", reflects their growing awareness of the Lord's sovereign hand in their lives. Indeed, sometimes God must permit our businesses to wither, our fortunes to evaporate, our bodies to be riddled with disease, our hope in ourselves to be crushed, in order to get our attention. His discipline in our lives is designed for our ultimate benefit as his children. As the writer of the book of Hebrews puts it:

> Furthermore, we had earthly fathers to discipline us, and we respected them; shall we not much rather be subject to the Father of spirits and live? For they disciplined us for a short time as seemed best to them, but He disciplines us for our good, that we may share His holiness. All discipline for the moment seems not to be joyful, but sorrowful; yet to those who have been trained by it, afterwards it yields the peaceful fruit of righteousness (Hebrews 12:9-11 NASB).

It can be argued that God uses discipline in the lives of nonbelievers to bring them to a saving knowledge of Jesus Christ. Once an individual is a Christian, then godly discipline functions to conform him or her to the image of the savior. Surely the Lord is at work in the hearts of Joseph's brothers—poking, prodding, pruning away the dead branches to expose the vital roots of faith and trust. No doubt the rest of their trip is spent in silent contemplation. It is perhaps their longest journey ever.

Back Home Again

When they arrive again in Hebron, any rehearsed speeches are quickly forgotten as the brothers spill the news to Jacob of all that has happened (42:29-34). Their account is brief but factual—and honest, unlike the last time they came running home en masse with the bad news of Joseph's apparent demise.

Their story told, the brothers turn to the task at hand:

unpacking. Their families are hungering for a bellyful of the provisions they've brought. While emptying their sacks, however, the brothers receive more than they've bargained for. Inside each bag is a pouch of silver; the money the brothers took into Egypt has been mysteriously returned to each of them (42:35). Verse 35 states that this discovery greatly frightens both father and sons. It's as if one more nail is hammered in their coffins.

Jumping to Conclusions

"You have deprived me of my children. Joseph is no more and Simeon is no more, and now you want to take Benjamin. Everything is against me!" wails Jacob bitterly (42:36). He focuses only on the immediate circumstances and he reaches the wrong verdict, jumping to the conclusion that the entire situation is hopeless.

This is not the first time that Jacob has shut his eyes to the possibilities and leaped to the wrong conclusion. When his brother Esau came to greet him with an entourage of his men, Jacob immediately assumed that his goose was as good as cooked. It wasn't so, for Esau's intentions proved to be friendly (Genesis 32-33). Years later, when his own sons came crying with Joseph's blood-soaked cloak, Jacob promptly figured the worst had happened. Never mind the promises, never mind the dreams—Joseph was gone! As we know, this turned out to be a false assumption. Now Jacob decides that the wheels have fallen off his life for good. Everything is against him! No more Joseph, no more Simeon . . . and they want to take Benjamin away, too!

How many times in our own lives do we hit storms and, like Jacob, assume it's time to pack it in? A few tough trials come our way, and we moan and groan, "Everything is against me." Then months, sometimes years, go by and we are privileged to see the pieces fitting together. God's purpose in our suffering becomes clear. "Thank you, Lord, for what you did because it has put me where I am!" we are able to exclaim.

I'm not saying that we always get to see how the pieces fit together. Many times we don't—and we won't in this lifetime. Not till eternity breaks will we truly know all the whys underlying the Lord's script for our lives. But whether or not we uncover all the answers on earth, we can trust that God is working in each and every event in our daily existences.

In Genesis 42, the plan of the Lord is to get the children of Israel out of Canaan and into Egypt temporarily. This is his purpose, but Jacob cannot see beyond the immediate. All he can think of is Benjamin. And it is clear that he has no intention of letting his youngest son go.

Jacob's reluctance puts the older brothers in a difficult position. More than Benjamin's life is at stake. The grain they've carted home won't last forever, and there are over sixty-six mouths to feed. In desperation, Reuben, with typical recklessness, cries, "You may put both of my sons to death if I do not bring him [Benjamin] back to you. Entrust him to my care, and I will bring him back" (42:37).

But Jacob's answer still is no. "My son will not go down there with you; his brother is dead and he is the only one left. If harm comes to him on the journey you are taking, you will bring my gray head down to the grave in sorrow," he adamantly replies to his eldest son.

The Verdict before the Fact

Someone has said that if we do not have all the facts, we have no right to an opinion. In refusing to permit Benjamin to accompany his brothers to Egypt, Jacob plainly acts without the facts. His resistance to God's purpose is mirrored in the words, "Everything is against me." And, in the meantime, the fates of a clanful of wives, children, and grandchildren hang in the balance.

Jacob's discouragement and failure to try to see beyond the present are attitudes common to many Christians. But the truth is that as believers we've got to expect tests. There will be rough roads to travel as we run the race God expects of us. Making a commitment to Christ never means we'll find ourselves free from trouble. Instead, we'll sometimes find ourselves wallowing in the middle of it all! And yet, there are rewards ultimately. As the apostle Paul writes in 2 Corinthians 4:17, "For our light affliction, which is but for a moment, worketh for us a far more exceeding and eternal weight of glory" (KJV).

As we grow in our faith in Christ, our lives do not become easier, but they do become better! We can expect the crucible of trial. We can even look forward to it, because through it the sovereign is shaping us up so we'll be able to contribute meaningfully to those around us.

So many times we forget that pruned branches are those that bear fruit. So often we prematurely pronounce judgment on the uncompleted process of God's work in our lives. We rely on appearance, not outcome. Like Jacob, we resist our heavenly father's dealings with us because we plant our eyes on the here and now, not the hereafter.

This is precisely where we leave Jacob as Genesis 42 closes—engaged in a wholehearted rebellion against the purpose of God. But the Lord has ways of dealing with his stubborn children, as we shall see by reading more of the continuing saga of Joseph and his brothers.

LESSONS

Let's take a few minutes to review some of the major lessons of Genesis 42, and of the story of Joseph to date.

Lesson one: *God is persistent in working out his purpose.* He doesn't give up.

Lesson two: *as human affection is strong, so also is the power of a guilty conscience.* We see that in Joseph and his brothers.

Lesson three: *true repentance involves acknowledging our failures and admitting our need of a savior.*

Lesson four: *human reason has its limitations.* We are shortsighted if we only focus on what we see, and do not consider God's perspective in what happens in our lives.

Lesson five: as is obvious with Joseph, *God has a purpose for every life.*

Lesson six: *the Lord's purpose calls for discipline.*

Lesson seven: *God proves himself to those who trust him.* His wisdom is verified in the outcome of events.

Final Thoughts

On June 28, 1987, a six-seat, twin-engine Cessna plane en route from White Sulphur Springs, Montana, to a Dallas suburb crashed into the side of Dead Indian Peak in the Absaroka Mountains of Wyoming. The pilot, Hugo Schoellkopf III, and his three passengers, Dr. Trevor Mabery, George Clark, and the Reverend Creath Davis, all of Dallas, perished instantly in the crash. They were heading home from a week-long retreat sponsored by Dr. James Dobson's Focus on the Family organization. Within the twinkling of an eye, these four Christians abruptly found themselves walking across the threshold of their heavenly home.

Two were friends of mine. Trevor Mabery once sat on the board of a Christian conference center I directed. One of my first Bible studies for youths was held in his home. Creath Davis and I rejoiced together some twenty-odd years ago as that conference center and his ministry's Kaleo Lodge were being built simultaneously. As I mentioned at the beginning of this chapter, our own ministry has made extensive use of the facilities at Kaleo over the years.

Why did the Lord see fit to call them home at a time that to us seems premature? We do not know. Probably all the reasons won't be clear till we join them in heaven. But this I do know: the four men now gone to glory have only enriched my anticipation of heaven. What a joyful expectation it is to think of spending eternity with them, and with a host of other brothers and sisters in Christ who also have finished their work down here.

Trevor Mabery, Creath Davis, Hugo Schoellkopf, and George Clark had no inkling that the take-off from White Sulphur Springs would be their last. But they are rejoicing in eternity with the savior who called them there and, to them, his purpose is now clear. God's plan and purpose for Jacob involve some fantastic things, too . . . if only he is willing to trust!

Questions for Study

1. Does Joseph's attitude toward God remain the same in prosperity as it was in adversity? Looking at your own life and your relationship with the Lord, can you say the same?

2. It is ironic that Jacob and his family are nearly starving, despite their material wealth. What does God have to say to us about money worries (Matthew 6:20-24)?

3. Why does Joseph conceal his identity and speak harshly to his brothers? Has God ever put you to the test before bestowing a special blessing?

4. What signs of remorse about their earlier treatment of Joseph do the brothers display in this chapter?

5. "Everything is against me," wails Jacob when only eight of his sons return from Egypt with news he'd rather not hear. What does his response reveal about his trust in God at that moment?

6

Sovereign Stress

Genesis 43

My two grandsons, Ian and Andrew, are real fighters when it comes to bedtime. They are so afraid of missing something that they think up every excuse in the book to delay going to sleep. When 8:00 PM rolls around, the boys acquire sudden desires for stories, drinks of water, lost blankets, and misplaced teddy bears. They do everything they can to resist or bypass their parents' authority in the matter of going to bed. That's the way kids are—whether we're talking about going to sleep, eating vegetables, picking up toys, cleaning rooms, doing homework, or washing the dishes. And, in the end, resistance is futile. Mom and Dad eventually win out. But the rebellion is there anyway, a natural part of growing up.

Unfortunately, rebelliousness doesn't end with childhood. In the Bible, the book of Isaiah contains a scathing condemnation of the rebellion of an entire nation against God. Writes Isaiah of the vision God has given him concerning the sinfulness of the kingdom of Judah and its capital, Jerusalem:

> Hear, O heavens! Listen, O earth!
>   For the Lord has spoken:
> "I reared children and brought them up,

> but they have rebelled against me.
> The ox knows his master,
> the donkey his owner's manger,
> but Israel does not know,
> my people do not understand"
> (Isaiah 1:2-3).

God's chosen people turned from him, forgot him, rejected him. In Isaiah 1 we find the Lord announcing to the inanimate creation the condition of his children. They have rebelled against him. Even the animal creation—the ox, the donkey—does better at understanding his plan, purpose, and provision than his people do.

In *When the Ceiling Is Zero,* Robert Foster tells of Louis Blanc, an arrogant scoffer who epitomized the sort of adult rebelliousness we see characterizing the nation of Israel in Isaiah 1. Claimed Blanc:

> When I was a baby I rebelled against my mother; when I was a young boy I rebelled against my teachers; when I was a teenager I rebelled against my father; when I reached mature years I rebelled against the government; when I die, if there is a heaven and a God, I will rebel against Him! (Foster 31).

What a pathetic picture of a man controlled by selfish anger. With each breath, Blanc defied authority—and with such vehemence that one wishes it were possible to take him aside and explain, "Look, it is easier to cooperate. Besides, it's a lot more fun!" As we turn to Genesis 43, Jacob is about to find that out for himself.

Battling God's Purpose

When we last leave Jacob at the end of Genesis 42, he is fighting God's eternal purpose, which is to reunite Joseph with his family and to get the children of Israel into the land of Egypt. His heels dug in, his jaw set, Jacob refuses to budge in his decision that Benjamin must not leave Canaan. What blessings the patriarch is in danger of missing because of his stubbornness! He has no idea that it is his beloved son Joseph who is governor of Egypt, and who has instructed the other brothers to return there with their younger sibling. Do you think Jacob would have hesitated had he known the true identity of the apparently hard-hearted official who held his son Simeon hostage? Why, he'd hop on the donkey himself and ride day and night just to catch a glimpse of Joseph!

God has a way of dealing with us when we are stubborn and resistant to his plans. He is capable of increasing the volume of stress in our lives until we are brought to the point of turning to him. I think again of the parable Jesus told of the prodigal son. That young man forsook his roots, said goodbye to dear old dad, gathered up his inheritance, had it converted to cash, and left home. Off he went to live the high life in foreign lands, but there was a day of reckoning. There came a time when God turned up the stress level in his life to cause him to reconsider his decisions, repent, and return home to find reconciliation. Luke 15 tells us that once the prodigal spent all his money on wine, women, and song, a severe famine ravaged the area. Penniless, the young man hired himself out to a local citizen who sent him to the country to feed swine. So hungry was he that the garbage he shoveled at the pigs began to look appetizing to him. On a scale of one to ten, I'd call that stress factor eleven! Then the prodigal came to his senses, quit rolling in the filth and husks of the pigpen, and came home to his father (Luke 15:14ff).

As Genesis 43 opens, Jacob, like the prodigal, finds himself underneath his circumstances, fighting a losing battle against God's design. The grain the brothers have brought from Egypt is running out. The Lord is amplifying the stress in Jacob's life to get him to respond . . . and the response he desires is for the old man to let go of his youngest son.

SOVEREIGN STRESS SEEKING SUBMISSION—GENESIS 43:1-10

> Now the famine was still severe in the land. So when they had eaten all the grain they had brought from Egypt, their father said to them, "Go back and buy us a little more food."
>
> But Judah said to him, "The man warned us solemnly, 'You will not see my face again unless your brother is with you.' If you will send our brother along with us, we will go down and buy food for you. But if you will not send him, we will not go down, because the man said to us, 'You will not see my face again unless your brother is with you.' "
>
> Israel asked, "Why did you bring this trouble on me by telling the man you had another brother?"
>
> They replied, "The man questioned us closely about ourselves and our family. 'Is your father still living?' he asked us. 'Do you have another brother?' We simply answered his questions. How were we to know he would say, 'Bring your brother down here'?"
>
> Then Judah said to Israel his father, "Send the boy along with me and we will go at once, so that we and you and our children may live and not die. I myself will guarantee his safety; you can hold me personally responsible for him. If I do not bring him back to you and set him here before you, I will bear the blame before you all my life. As it is, if we had not delayed, we could have gone and returned twice."

Jacob and family have consumed most of their grain reserves when Genesis 43 opens, and we read that the famine remains severe in the land (43:1). Once more there is nearly nothing to eat and no hope of a reprieve on the horizon. The children of Israel are scraping the bottom of the barrel. In reality, God is merely shifting the stress level into high gear. Sovereign stress such as this strikes when God seeks our submission to his authority and his will. This is what he wants from Jacob. He desires that Jacob trust and obey by releasing Benjamin and allowing him to accompany the brothers to Egypt. Still, Jacob isn't willing to move, despite the increasing pressure to do so.

The Lord often uses such factors as economic trends, national policies, and natural forces to prod his children into line. The prodigal son and Jacob are simply two examples of men who face imminent starvation until they submit to what God would have them to do.

Many people think that in chapter 3 of Ecclesiastes Solomon paints a tender, sentimental picture of the workings of the universe. As we've mentioned before, poetically he muses that there is a season for everything, and a time for every purpose under heaven (3:1). His statements are the stuff folk songs and greeting cards are made of, but the cold reality is that Solomon's words are written during a time of great personal anguish. He is in the throes of a severe mid-life crisis and, in Ecclesiastes 3, he spills his insides in frustration. Everywhere he turns he runs into God's restraining hand—God's plan, God's time. There is a time to be born and a time to die, and these are the Lord's alone to determine. A time to laugh and a time to cry . . . a time to build and a time to tear down (Ecclesiastes 33:1-8). For Jacob, there is a time to release Benjamin, and refusing to acknowledge that makes for a very lonely experience of resistance.

Ignoring the Obvious

Genesis 43:2 tells us that when Jacob and clan "had eaten all the grain they had brought from Egypt," the old man said to his sons, "Go back and buy us a little more food." Talk about ignoring the obvious! Jacob knows the requirements Joseph has laid out, that there can be no trade unless Benjamin accompanies his brothers to Egypt. But he chooses to act as if the rules don't exist. At this moment, he does not plan to be obedient.

Jacob is tough and bullheaded. No stranger to stubbornness, he is the man who, in Genesis 32, wrestled all night with the angel of the Lord, who in reality was Christ himself (32:24ff). It was a futile struggle. Now, years later, he hasn't any intention of acquiescing to the commands of a foreign official in a faraway land. He simply tells his sons to fetch more food, as if that were possible without his cooperation.

Jacob refuses to surrender. Perhaps one of the most difficult conclusions you and I will ever come to in our lives is to realize that God generally does not make provision for us until we're willing to give in to him in certain areas. For example, there is no provision of divine salvation until we're willing to surrender to Jesus Christ. There is no meaningful life until we're willing to throw in the towel and do things God's way—obeying his laws, communicating with him through prayer, learning the instructions and insights he has for us in his word. How often we are oblivious to his requirements and how easy it is to overlook the disobediences in our own lives. Then we wonder why God is not pouring out his provision and blessing upon us.

I think of how I fought leaving a Christian conference center I had directed, appealing to the board, resisting the change. But God in his sovereign plan was ready to give birth to a new ministry in my life. My pride kept me resisting what he was doing for many weeks. Oh, what peace we often forfeit, what needless pain we bear, all because we are drawing battle lines with God rather than obeying marching orders!

In his book *Growing through Mid-Life Crisis* John Sterner includes the following anecdote which sums it up well:

> As I get into middle age, I realize that I have not kept all of Jesus' requirements or even any com-

> pletely. I remember that little old lady . . . in a prayer meeting singing, "I surrender some," because she wanted to be honest with God. At times, my honest song would be, "I don't surrender a thing tonight, and I haven't for a long time; but keep hanging in there, God, and I just might" (Sterner 104-105).

"I surrender some," "I don't surrender a thing tonight . . . but keep hanging in there, God, and I just might"—if we're honest, those statements probably hit close to home for many of us. They describe how we relate to God much of the time. The challenge is for us to sink to our knees and, with the psalmist, implore of the Lord, "Search me, O God, and know my heart; test me and know my anxious thoughts. See if there is any offensive way in me, and lead me in the way everlasting" (139:23-24). Words such as these might pour from our hearts: "Lord, I renounce the things that are standing in the way of your blessing. I'm turning loose; I'm letting go. It's kind of scary, Lord, because I'm so used to running and directing things. Please take my hand in this darkness and lead me out into the light of your provision." It could be that a great outpouring of God's blessing upon your life awaits that step and is dependent upon your surrender.

Everyone in Jacob's family is affected because of his stubborn, unrelenting resistance. They're starving, yet he holds the key to abating their hunger if he'll only give in to the inevitable and let go of his baby boy. It's a situation in which the obvious cannot be ignored.

The Argument

Jacob's fourth-born son, Judah, speaks to his father. "The man warned us solemnly, 'You will not see my face again unless your brother is with you,' " he reminds Jacob (43:3). There is really no alternative to sending Benjamin. To do anything else means the mission will fail.

Although Reuben is the oldest son of Jacob, he fades

from the picture in influence and importance at this point. Judah becomes the great intercessor, and we'll cry with him over the next few painfully touching episodes. It is Judah who brings his father back to reality, his caring confrontation communicating concern for the primary issue. In essence he tells Jacob, "Dad, there's no choice. If Benjamin goes, we go. If Benjamin stays, we stay, and we die. Without him, we'll get no food and the 500-mile round trip will have been for nothing. Face facts: you can't get around the conditions in the contract." This time, son proves to be as stubborn as father.

Giving Up the Benjamins

Give us your *Benjamin.* That is what Judah requests of his father. It's an issue that, in some form or another, we ought to all consider. What is the *Benjamin* in your life? Maybe God right now has his finger on one thing in your life and it is the well-stopper, the spirit-quencher. It is keeping the living water from bubbling up in your soul; you feel like you're dwelling in a dry, parched land (Jeremiah 2:13). It is restraining the joyful reality that God is alive and that Jesus Christ dwells within. Perhaps it is a relationship, a job, a commitment, a desire, a habit. Whatever it is, it may be something God wants you to surrender to him. "Give me that *Benjamin,*" he begs, "and things will begin to really happen in your life." And still we stubbornly hang on.

It really makes me feel sad sometimes when I think of the times I've held on when I should have given up . . . to him. I wonder about the blessings I've missed, the provisions I've avoided. When I have turned things over to God, the results have been beyond belief, and I kick myself for not doing it more often. Case in point: for a long time I resisted spending personal time with the Lord in the study of his word and prayer. Oh, I was studying and I was praying, but only in connection with the Bible lessons I was preparing for others. I figured that was enough . . . but I was wrong. I cannot describe the blessings that have come from spending personal time with him on a daily basis—reading, praying, praising, worshiping. We grow too soon old and too late smart! I've missed so much intimate communion with God because I wasn't willing to act sooner.

Switching the Subject

For Jacob, the resistance begins to border on the ridiculous. He lashes out in anger, frustration, and fear. "Why did you bring this trouble on me by telling the man you had another brother?" he wails in protest (43:6). How easy it is for us to try to fog the issue and turn the beam of the spirit of God off of our lives! Jacob switches the subject from the immediate problem and provokes his sons with his unfair accusation. "It's your fault that this has happened! Why did you tell the man about Benjamin in the first place? You got us into this mess by spilling the beans! Good grief, who said you had to tell everything you knew?" For a moment, his strategy works.

What started as a debate between Jacob and Judah suddenly involves the whole crowd in a noisy family feud. Eight voices join their brother's in protesting their father's comments. "The man questioned us closely about ourselves and our family. . . . We simply answered his questions. How were we to know he would say, 'Bring your brother down here'?" (43:7). Little does Jacob know that if his sons had been less than honest, Joseph might have dealt far more severely with them.

The Intercessor

Judah steps in once more to break up the fray. "Send the boy along with me and we will go at once, so that we and you and our children may live and not die," he urges his father, again bringing the subject in focus (43:8). Then he makes a most amazing, unselfish promise. "I myself will guarantee his safety; you can hold me personally responsible for him. If I do not bring him back to you and set him here before you, I will bear the blame before you all my life" (43:9).

I believe Judah senses that his father is running out of arguments. Jacob's resistance, futile as it is, is beginning to weaken. The hooked fish has made its last run in the struggle against yielding to the inevitable. The fragrance of brokenness is beginning to show (Philippians 4:18; 2 Corinthians 2:15-16). Judah, seizing the moment, presses for the advantage, making an incredibly unselfish offer.

Judah vows to be responsible for Benjamin. He will bear the blame before Jacob if anything happens to him. Judah stops short of making the type of impetuous statement that Reuben does in Genesis 42:37, where he promises to hand over his own two sons for the kill if anything happens to baby brother. Not a spur-of-the-moment remark, Judah's statement is well thought out. He has weighed the consequences. He fully knows what he is doing, and he makes an offer Jacob truly cannot refuse.

Then Judah delivers the knock-out blow. "As it is," he tells it to his father straight, "if we had not delayed, we could have gone and returned twice" (43:10). "Dad, you've been sitting on your hands for the last three months. We could have been there and back by now! We are perishing in the pigpen of our own poverty because of your unwillingness to let go and submit. The time is now or never!"

Giving In to God—Genesis 43:11-14

> Then their father Israel said to them, "If it must be, then do this: Put some of the best products of the land in your bags and take them down to the man as a gift, a little balm and a little honey, some spices and myrrh, some pistachio nuts and almonds. Take double the amount of silver with you, for you must return the silver that was put back into the mouths of your sacks. Perhaps it was a mistake. Take your brother also and go back to the man at once. And

> may God Almighty grant you mercy before the man so that he will let your other brother and Benjamin come back with you. As for me, if I am bereaved, I am bereaved.

In *Growing through Mid-Life Crisis* John Sterner quotes an anonymous folk song which goes like this:

> Oh, life is a toil, and love is a trial;
> Beauty will fade and riches will flee.
> Pleasures, they dwindle, and prices, they double;
> And nothing is as I would wish it to be
> (Sterner 22).

As Genesis 43 continues, nothing is as Jacob wishes it to be, either. God is forcing his hand. The last thing Jacob wants to do is to send Benjamin to Egypt with his brothers, but he has no choice. He turns to his sons and says with resignation, "If it must be, then do this: Put some of the best products of the land in your bags and take them down to the man as a gift—a little balm and a little honey, some spices and myrrh, some pistachio nuts and almonds" (43:11).

"If it must be . . ." What glorious words of surrender! You can almost hear the strains of the hymn, "Just As I Am," in the background: "Just as I am, though tossed about/With many a conflict, many a doubt./Fightings and fears within and without,/O Lamb of God, I come! I come!" The human soul thirsts for independence. It desires to play the game its way—to protect its ego, to grant wishes to others rather than to receive what is graciously given. Surrender is a learned response, and Jacob is learning.

When Jacob makes the decision to let go of Benjamin and cooperate with God's program, we reach a pivotal point in our saga. Now the mindset of the leader of the children of Israel is one of submission not resistance, acquiescence not argumentation, obedience not rebellion, trust not doubt. Reconciliation can be accomplished in the face of resignation.

Characteristically, we see that Jacob still hasn't learned to cooperate without sending a gift, though. Years earlier, even after seeing a vision of God's angels and spending the night locked in conflict with the Lord himself in Genesis 32, Jacob still rounded up over 500 head of livestock as an impressive gift with which to appease his brother Esau when the pair met the following day (32:13-16). Not one of his presents proved necessary, because Esau came in peace (Genesis 33). Decades later, preparing to send his sons into an encounter with the hostile ruler of another land, Jacob still cannot resist taking out a little insurance for the trip, adding what gifts he can to sweeten the package.

Jacob also plays it safe by instructing his sons to carry double the amount of silver into Egypt than they had previously taken there. You never know—the fact that their silver had been returned earlier might have been a mistake (43:12). Then he utters the most difficult words of all: "Take your brother also and go back to the man at once" (43:13).

Necessary Losses

Jacob saves the worst till last. Take gifts . . . take silver . . . and then, with halting resignation, take Benjamin, he tells his sons. The words stick in his throat because, with Benjamin's departure, Jacob will face the trauma of being completely alone for one of the few times in his life. The struggle subsides and he casts himself upon the Lord.

You see, until this moment of surrender, Jacob has nearly always had at least one other special person with whom to share his life. First it was his mother, Rebekah. Then, after fleeing to Paddan-Aram and the home of his uncle, Rachel entered his life. Later, Joseph and Benjamin arrived. Now Rebekah is dead; Rachel is dead; it is even likely that Leah is dead. Joseph is apparently no more. Simeon is a hostage in Egypt. The nine other boys are leaving, and now even Benjamin must go. All that are left in Jacob's settlement are women and grandchildren, none of them his immediate relatives but only his extended family. He confronts the crucible of the empty-nest syndrome when he says of Benjamin, "Take him and go." And thus he faces what author Judith Viorst would later call, in a book by the same name, his "necessary losses."

We all face necessary losses in our lives. We are forced to choose, to leave, to let go. We change careers; our kids sprout wings and flutter from the nest; our parents pass away; our friends move to other cities. Losses are inevitable—facts of life in an inconstant world. Perhaps the most important time of losing occurs as we prepare to exit this world for eternity. We raise impotent hands to stop the process, but time waits for no one.

Each of us one day will be stripped of our supports and excuses, and will stand before the Lord himself. If we have accepted Christ as savior, we'll enter his presence eternally. If not, we'll be forever barred from God and condemned to the outer darkness. It's easy to put off making a decision for Jesus Christ while our spouses sit beside us, our kids run around us, our hobbies and occupations consume us. But someday all that will be gone. "It's just you and me," the Lord will tell us. Will we be ready? Will *you* be ready? Think about it now, while there is time.

A Final Blessing

At last Jacob reaches the point of surrender. He will give up his Benjamin to whatever the Lord has in mind. "And may God Almighty grant you mercy before the man so that he will let your other brother and Benjamin come back with you. As for me, if I am bereaved, I am bereaved," he says with finality to his departing sons (43:14).

When Jacob speaks of "God Almighty," he uses the Hebrew term *El Shaddai* referring to God as the keeper of the covenant, the breasted one, the sustaining one, the all-powerful one. It is into God's hands that the sons of Jacob commit themselves, and into which their father finally releases them. This, Jacob at last admits to himself.

"As for me, if I am bereaved, I am bereaved"—what words of submission those are! What will be, will be! Contrast this statement with the defiant complaint Jacob had made a few months before when the brothers first returned from Egypt. "Everything is against me!" he whined (42:36). That was resistance. The barricades were up, the warrior armed for the losing battle. Now we witness surrender. It's time to raise the white flag and allow the Lord to handle the situation according to his will.

Many, many others in scripture arrived at the point of surrender reached by Jacob in Genesis 42. When the Persians under Xerxes threatened to annihilate the Jewish population already captive within their empire, Queen Esther saw a God-given opportunity to influence the situation. Beloved of the king who had no idea she was a Jewess, Esther prepared to risk life and limb by entering into his presence without being summoned, and seeking to entreat him on behalf of her people. Before she leaped from the frying pan into the fire, however, she instructed her uncle, Mordecai, "Go gather together all the Jews who are in Susa, and fast for me. Do not eat or drink for three days, night or day. I and my maids will fast as you do. When this is done, I will go to the king, even though it is against the law. And if I perish, I perish" (Esther 4:16).

"And if I perish, I perish"—those are words of classic surrender, acceptance of whatever God intends. It is the same attitude displayed by Job. After tragically losing his possessions and his children, he exclaims:

> Naked I came from my mother's womb,
> and naked I will depart.
> The Lord gave and the Lord has taken away;
> may the name of the Lord be praised (Job 1:21).

No greater or more significant conquest takes place than the conquering of the human will by the king of kings. Like Esther and Job, Jacob is ready to face life alone if necessary, with God. And with that sort of surrender, comes peace. I'm sure that once Jacob acknowledges the wisdom of Judah's requests, and releases Benjamin to the hands of the Lord, he feels an enormous sense of relief. A burden is lifted. The blessings—whatever they might be—are free to come. What will be, will be. For Job, reaching the point of surrender where he could pray for his friends meant that the Lord restored his wealth twofold and granted him sons and daughters as before (Job 42:10). For Jacob, surrender will mean blessing as well, in ways he could never have anticipated.

A Royal Reception—Genesis 43:15-25

> So the men took the gifts and double the amount of silver, and Benjamin also. They hurried down to Egypt and presented themselves to Joseph. When Joseph saw Benjamin with them, he said to the steward of his house, "Take these men to my house, slaughter an animal and prepare dinner; they are to eat with me at noon."
>
> The man did as Joseph told him and took the men to Joseph's house. Now the men were frightened when they were taken to his house. They thought, "We were brought here because of the silver that was put back into our sacks the first time. He wants to attack us and overpower us and seize us as slaves and take our donkeys."
>
> So they went up to Joseph's steward and spoke to him at the entrance to the house. "Please, sir," they said, "we came down here the first time to buy food. But at the place where we stopped for the night we opened our sacks and each of us found his silver—the exact weight—in the mouth of his sack. So we have brought it back with us. We have also brought additional silver with us to buy food. We don't know who put our silver into our sacks."

> "It's all right," he said. "Don't be afraid. Your God and the God of your father has given you treasure in your sacks; I received your silver." Then he brought Simeon out to them.
>
> The steward took the men into Joseph's house, gave them water to wash their feet and provided fodder for their donkeys. They prepared their gifts for Joseph's arrival at noon, because they had heard that they were to eat there.

When I teach on the life of Joseph in my classes, I always tell my students to circle the word *hurried* in verse 15: "They hurried down to Egypt and presented themselves to Joseph." Why do they rush so? It is because time is of the essence. Thanks to Jacob's dillydallying, if their families are going to survive the famine, the brothers must make the round trip to Egypt and back in record time. Once entering the foreign land, they waste no time in presenting themselves to Joseph. There is not a moment to spare: if they hesitate, their wives and children will be lost.

When we arrive at the point of surrender, God often does things in a way we would never expect. Once Joseph spies Benjamin among the company of his brothers, he instructs his steward, "Take these men to my house, slaughter an animal and prepare dinner; they are to eat with me at noon" (43:16). The brothers probably assume they'll approach Joseph, introduce Benjamin, obtain Simeon's release, pay for the grain, and away they'll go. It will be a quick trip and everyone will be happy. Instead, Joseph, speaking to his steward, invites them home for lunch!

The fact that the noon meal is the next one on the agenda indicates that the brothers have traveled all night and arrived in Egypt in the morning. That's how it is when we're in a hurry to get to our destinations—we travel late to get there early. The brothers want to be sure to reach the food distribution center when it opens, before the long lines of hungry people begin to snake around the city blocks. Then a foreign official, at the command of the governor, says, "Come with me."

Guilt Works Overtime

How would you feel if you were in the brothers' position? Think about it. Picture yourself in the customs line at a middle eastern airport. You move slowly forward, watching the officers inspect the bags of others. Before you reach the head of the line, another man in an official-looking uniform approaches you, grasps your carryon bag, and purposefully says, "Come with me." What would you do? Panic would hit. You'd be terribly alarmed, even though you knew you were innocent of any wrongdoing. You'd inquire and you would probably protest: "What's this all about? I haven't done anything!"

Guilt is like that. Fear and guilt cause us even to be suspicious of small kindnesses and gentle actions. We detect ulterior motives where there are none. As Joseph's servant follows instructions and escorts the brothers to his master's home, verse 18 reveals that the men become frightened. Guilt and fear slowly build in intensity with each footstep. They haven't actually committed any crimes, but there is the matter of the returned silver to consider. Could it be that this has spurred the invitation to the ruler's home? Are they walking into a trap? Does the governor merely wish to lure them to an out-of-the-way spot where his henchmen will attack them, overpower them, enslave them?

"Please, sir," the frantic brothers pause at Joseph's doorstep and explain to his steward, "we came down here the first time to buy food. But at the place where we stopped for the night we opened our sacks and each of us found his silver—the exact weight—in the mouth of his sack. So we have brought it back with us to buy food. We don't know who put our silver in our sacks" (43:19-22). They're making sure to cover all the bases, supplying ample assurances of their innocence and honesty.

Anonymous Giving

The steward's response to the brothers' panicky explanations about the silver tells us a lot about his master. "It's all right," the servant reassuringly states. "Don't be afraid. Your God and the God of your father has given you treasure in your sacks; I received your silver" (43:23).

We know that it was Joseph who ordered that the silver be replaced in the saddlebags of his brothers. It was his decision, and he could easily have grabbed the glory for the giving. Yet he chooses not to. Instead, Joseph elects to remain anonymous. Because of this, the credit goes wholly to God. What a pleasure it is to give secretly and sacrificially to someone else, and let the Lord receive the honor. He knows everything that we do. Even a cup of water offered in his name does not go unbeknown to him (Matthew 10:42).

Perhaps Joseph has instructed the steward to say nothing of his involvement in the return of the silver to the brothers. Maybe the servant elects to remain silent because he has seen the kind of man his master is, and he knows that Joseph would want to remain an unknown benefactor. Surely the steward, like Potiphar and pharaoh before him, has taken notice of Joseph's character and close relationship with God.

Anticipation

Once he assures them not to be concerned about the replaced silver, the steward deals with the next thing on the brothers' worry list. He briefly withdraws from the room and returns shortly with Simeon (43:23). He then attends to the personal needs of the men, giving them water with which to wash up and food for their animals (43:24). He does everything he can to make them comfortable, graciously anticipating and caring for their every need.

After they've rinsed off the dirt and seen that the

donkeys are watered, the brothers begin to relax a bit and do a little anticipating of their own. Simeon is safe; their fears about the silver are quieted. The next thing to do is to unpack the gifts Jacob has sent and get ready for the meal to come when the governor gets home. I imagine they stretch out on some of Joseph's luxurious couches to wait till noon. Maybe the situation isn't so bad after all!

And what of Benjamin? As far as we know, he hasn't been out of Canaan before. I'd wager his eyes are as wide as saucers, soaking in the fabulous abode of his brother. He's just a country boy from Hebron, who's probably never known opulence like this existed. Can't you picture him gazing about the mansion in awe? All too soon, it seems, Joseph comes home to join the festivities.

Section Two of the Exam—Genesis 43:26-34

> When Joseph came home, they presented to him the gifts they had brought into the house, and they bowed down before him to the ground. He asked them how they were, and then he said, "How is your aged father you told me about? Is he still living?"
>
> They replied, "Your servant our father is still alive and well." And they bowed low to pay him honor.
>
> As he looked about and saw his brother Benjamin, his own mother's son, he asked, "Is this your youngest brother, the one you told me about?" And he said, "God be gracious to you, my son." Deeply moved at the sight of his brother, Joseph hurried out and looked for a place to weep. He went into his private room and wept there.
>
> After he had washed his face, he came out and, controlling himself, said, "Serve the food."
>
> They served him by himself, the brothers by themselves, and the Egyptians who ate with them

> by themselves, because Egyptians could not eat with Hebrews, for that is detestable to Egyptians. The men had been seated before him in the order of their ages, from the firstborn to the youngest; and they looked at each other in astonishment. When portions were served to them from Joseph's table, Benjamin's portion was five times as much as anyone else's. So they feasted and drank freely with him.

When Joseph walks in the door of his house, it marks the first time in over twenty-two years that all twelve brothers are together within the confines of a single room. With his entrance, the pieces of God's puzzle begin to fit even more closely than before. Verse 26 reveals that the brothers take the first chance they get to present him with the gifts they have brought, and then bow down before him "to the ground." What thoughts must have flickered through Joseph's mind at this sight—eleven men paying him homage, their actions a tangible fulfillment of the dream he had been given at age seventeen (37:7).

After asking the men how they are, Joseph's concern naturally shifts to his father. He poses the question, "How is your aged father you told me about? Is he still living?" (43:27).

"Your servant our father is still alive and well," the brothers reply, and they bow low once more to pay Joseph homage (43:28).

A Battle of the Emotions

And then, in perhaps the most emotional scene of all, Joseph's eyes scan the room. He glances at each rugged, sunburned face. Finally his gaze rests upon the more youthful countenance of Benjamin, his own mother's son. With supreme self-control, Joseph asks, "Is this your youngest brother, the one you told me about?" Charged with the electricity of the moment, his voice trembling with barely concealed emotions, he says to the younger man, "God be gracious to you, my son" (43:29).

Joseph's mind must suddenly fill with a flood of memories of Rachel, her gentleness, her tragic death giving birth to the man before him now. Benjamin, his only full brother, stands in his very presence. And yet there can be no contact, no acknowledgment of the relationship—at least not for the time being. The test is not yet complete. Overcome with emotion, Joseph rushes from the room into a private chamber, where he freely sheds tears of joy and heartache (43:30).

Perhaps some of you reading this have grown up with the notion, much as I did, that tough guys never cry. It isn't manly to show emotion. Real men never admit when they are hurt. As far as scripture goes, those ideas are completely false! Stirred by the pain of seeing his beloved friend Mary in anguish at the tomb of her brother Lazarus, Jesus himself shed tears of sorrow and compassion (John 11:33-35). Joseph weeps when his younger brother stands before him. Their reunion is so near and yet so far. The pain increases in intensity until he must pour out his heart through sobs and cries. There is nothing unmanly about it. Writes Robert Foster:

> The lack of "tears" in the heart and eyes of most men could be a signpost of a cold heart, unbroken spirit and unrepenting will.
>
> What God's Word has put together . . . don't try to tear asunder. We need sowing and reaping, weeping and shouting, passion and production, ardor and advance.
>
> When a man weeps, we say that he is broken down. True tears are the signs of brokenness. No more hardness or resistance . . . staggered by a sensitivity of sin, this is the heart of Godly religion.
>
> How easily we become hard, proud, "intellectually balanced" and soul-dry (Foster 58).

Joseph is far from "hard, proud, 'intellectually balanced' and soul-dry"! His sensitivity spurs his tears. He does not wish to continue testing his brothers, but there is no alternative.

Looking for Changes in Attitudes

Joseph washes his face, hoping to conceal the redness of his eyes. In control of his emotions after this brief release, he reenters the room where his brothers are waiting. "Serve the food," he commands (43:31).

Out march servants bearing platterfuls of delectable treats. Jacob's sons haven't seen a spread like this in years, if ever! Verse 32 tells us that Joseph is served first, alone. Next the servants wait upon his brothers, who eat by themselves. Lastly, the Egyptian guests, who also eat by themselves, receive their meals. This eating arrangement is followed because, as the text tells us, it is "detestable" for Egyptians to dine at the same table as Hebrews (43:32). There is no caste system involved here, merely an Egyptian tradition. Perhaps the segregation reflects the age-old animosity between Arabs and Jews, present since the days of Isaac and Ishmael.

Joseph has some surprises in store for his siblings at the banquet. Verse 33 tells us that the brothers find themselves seated according to their ages, from the oldest to the youngest. At this, they look at each other "in astonishment" (43:33). It is too much to expect this to be a mere coincidence! Maybe their confidence wavers a bit as they realize that something strange is going on, and that someone knows more about them than they had imagined.

Something even more unusual happens next. The brothers are served grand meals, but one is even grander than the rest. Each brother receives a plentiful portion of each delicious item on the menu, but Benjamin literally receives quintuple as much as anyone else (43:34).

No doubt Joseph pauses to observe his older brothers' response to this obviously preferential treatment. If he hears one snide remark, one jealous comment, then he will realize that they haven't changed a bit from the time they tossed him in the pit. The test will be over and the brothers will have failed.

But what do the brothers do when they see Benjamin served five times the amount they get? Verse 33 tells us that "they feasted and drank freely with him." They don't whine. They don't complain. They enjoy their meal without envying baby brother. They pass this part of the test with flying colors. However, there is more to come, as we shall see.

LESSONS

There are several lessons that Genesis 43 leaves for us to consider.

Lesson one: *God sometimes kindly uses natural circumstances to prompt us to be responsive to his will.* Underline the word *kindly.* The stress of the famine finally forces Jacob to fall in with the Lord's purpose, but it is stress allowed by God in an act of ultimate kindness. The Lord sees the coming joyous reunion between father and son, the salvation of the children of Israel, the resolution of the conflict between Joseph and his brothers. He knows these blessings are in store once Jacob submits. His will for his children is ever and always kind.

Lesson two: *it is wise to hear the appeals of others and then to be receptive to a change of heart.* The older we get, the more difficult it is to do this. "We've always done it this way," we protest. What we're really insisting is, "Don't confuse me with the facts; my mind is already made up!" But Jacob listens to Judah, and eventually releases Benjamin. It is a wise move.

Lesson three: *it is the pattern of human nature to want to cover our fears and guilt with gifts.* Thus Jacob "plays it safe" by sending what meager presents he can with his sons.

Lesson four: *fear and guilt misinterpret kindness.* We look for ulterior motives where there are none, much as the brothers suspect Joseph's invitation to lunch.

Lesson five: *we are often tested when we are unconscious of it being so.* The brothers have no idea that their attitudes are being examined by Joseph and God as they sit at the dinner table.

Lesson six: *Joseph's gentleness and faith in God affect the other members of his household.* Even his steward has noticed that his master is different, a godly man.

Lesson seven: *peace comes when we surrender our "Benjamins," whatever they might be.*

Surrendering the Benjamins

I can just picture Benjamin at the supper table, can't you? His eyes still bulge in amazement. He's never seen that much food! I know how he feels, too. Once Pearl and I were in the Pacific northwest with the president of an airline company and his wife. We were trying to work out a way to catch a free flight home, meaning that we'd travel on one of our friend's planes. We were not departing from a city on the company's regular route, so it would take some doing to manage this. Yet, as it turned out, the company was flying a chartered plane of American servicemen from Seattle to Dallas, and we were able to hitch a ride.

I'll never forget the look on the face of one of employees after the jet had landed to refuel in Seattle. My friend approached him and asked, "Can we go on that plane?"

"Yes, sir," the fellow replied, "you can go on your plane whenever you want to, sir." And we did!

Was I treated royally while sitting next to the company president! Instead of one bag of honey-roasted peanuts, I got five. The flight attendant offered me at least ten diet sodas, three square meals, and very nearly a partridge in a pear tree! It was all because of whom I knew.

Whatever small perks I experienced on the corporate jet in the presence of the president of the company pale in comparison to what awaits us in eternity if we're

Christians. Christ says in John 14:2, "In my Father's house are many mansions: if it were not so, I would have told you. I go to prepare a place for you" (KJV). Friends, he's been working on our heavenly residence for two thousand years. It's going to be something to see . . . but if you're going to have that privilege someday, you'll need to get to know Jesus Christ first. If you've never made his acquaintance, I urge you to delay no longer. He is here, waiting.

And I ask you, "What is your *Benjamin?*" Is it doubt about the claims of Christ? Is it a desire to do things your way? If you are a believer, is it something that keeps you from getting closer to Christ? Is it your job, a hobby, some person, a habit?

"I've tried, but I can't surrender," you say? Simply put, happiness is a choice. Change the "I can't" to "I won't," and you'll have a better description of your dilemma. Rebels at heart would rather resist, refuse, revolt, and, in the process, restrain the mighty hand of God from doing something beautiful in their lives. Don't be one of them! Be a Jacob. Be willing to let God work.

Questions for Study

1. Jacob finally surrenders to God as he permits Benjamin to accompany his brothers. What is your *Benjamin?* Is there an area of your life you've kept from the Lord, tried to deal with on your own, allowed to become more important than God? If so, what might you do about it?

2. How does Joseph's servant respond when the brothers explain about the silver that they found in their saddlebags after their first trip to Egypt? What does his answer tell us about Joseph's character?

3. What does Joseph do when he spies Benjamin (43:30)? What do his tears tell us about the expression of emotion through weeping?

4. How is Benjamin treated differently than his brothers at the dinner in Joseph's home? Why? What is the brothers' response to this preferential treatment: do they pass or fail the test?

5. Guilt and fear cause the brothers to become suspicious of the invitation to Joseph's house. The key is to confess the guilt and ask God to cleanse it. Maybe you are carrying around a burden of guilt for something you've done in the past. If so, take a few moments to reflect on the deed, then ask the Lord to forgive you and remove the guilt.

7

Passing the Test

Genesis 44

My secretary, Jan Terry, has been a valuable addition to our ministry for the several years she has been on staff. Her parents, members of our board of directors, are among our staunchest supporters. The entire family is very dear to Pearl and me, and it has been heartbreaking to witness the suffering Jan has endured in the time we have known her. She has graciously given me permission to share parts of her story with you.

The victim of a traumatic divorce some time ago, Jan tackled the chore of being a single parent to two children who had not yet reached their teens. She moved to Tyler in order to be close to her parents, who had retired there, and soon afterward came to work with us. Life was tough, but Jan possessed an inner strength that can only come straight from God. She is more than a three-round fighter; she is able to go the distance.

Jan's folks and those of us at the ministry tried to ease her burdens as well as we could. We took a special interest in her children, investing our time in their lives, trying to fill the void. And, to be honest, we knew it wasn't enough. We prayed that the Lord would, if it were his will, send a godly man to be a husband to Jan and a father to her children.

Years passed. One afternoon a huge hulk of a fellow stalked into our offices. He was deputy sheriff Walt Terry, and he carried a warrant for Jan's arrest. It was his way of asking her for a date! She accepted. One thing led to another, and eventually they stood before me at the altar while I pronounced them husband and wife.

Walt was a good man, a decent godly man. It would take time, but we felt that eventually he would establish strong relationships with his new stepson and stepdaughter. He had wide shoulders—broad enough to carry the troubles Jan had borne alone, strong enough to support her when she felt like falling, gentle enough to cradle her with loving sensitivity and kindness.

You'll notice I've used the past tense when writing of Walt. Just over ten months after their wedding day, Walt was thrown from a horse in a riding accident. His skull fractured, he died a few hours later. It seemed so unfair. "Why, God, why?" we cried in honest confusion. Why should Jan be put through another devastating ordeal? Why should she be forced to face still another trial?

And the answer came. Jan was no different from the rest of us. Trials are part of life. They pummel and pound us. Often they are tests permitted by the Lord to check our responses and to gauge our Christian growth. Sometimes we pass such exams with flying colors; at other times we fail them abysmally. One thing is certain: they'll always be there.

I think of David's words in Psalm 38. This poignant lament is a song of penitence for some sin in the king's life. What specifically David has done wrong, we do not know. We do know that he has reached the end of his ragged human rope. He has suffered immense hardship, betrayal, desertion, agonizing loneliness, excruciating physical pain. Psalm 38 reveals that he eventually looks up from the bottom of the abyss to reach for the only person left to him, the Lord himself. Writes the king:

> O Lord, do not rebuke me in your anger
> or discipline me in your wrath.

For your arrows have pierced me,
and your hand has come down upon me.
Because of your wrath there is no health in my body;
my bones have no soundness because of my sin.
My guilt has overwhelmed me
like a burden too heavy to bear.

My wounds fester and are loathsome
because of my sinful folly.
I am bowed down and brought very low;
all day long I go about mourning.
My back is filled with searing pain;
there is no health in my body.
I am feeble and utterly crushed;
I groan in anguish of heart.

All my longings lie open before you, O Lord;
my sighing is not hidden from you.
My heart pounds; my strength fails me;
even the light has gone from my eyes.
My friends and companions avoid me because of my wounds;
my neighbors stay far away.
Those who seek my life set their traps,
those who would harm me talk of my ruin;
all day long they plot deception. . . .

O Lord, do not forsake me;
be not far from me, O my God.
Come quickly to help me,
O Lord my Savior (Psalm 38:1-12; 21-22).

You name it, it has happened to David. His body and spirit are broken. His friends literally avoid him like the plague. It is more than he can handle and, like Jan's series of ordeals, it seems so unfair.

When Injustice Is Eminently Just

Oftentimes situations in our lives do seem incredibly unfair, by human standards. Surely Joseph deserved better than his captivity in the pit, his experience in the house of Potiphar, and his time in prison. What sort of justice, humanly speaking, was that?

As we delve into Genesis 44, we're going to watch Joseph's brothers being tested by circumstances completely out of their control. What happens to them may seem unjust, but as we step back from the passage and objectively examine the events, we'll recognize what God is trying to teach the brothers—and, by application, us. What seems unfair really isn't unfair at all in the end, by God's standards. The apostle James writes:

> Consider it all joy, my brethren, when you encounter various trials, knowing that the testing of your faith produces endurance. And let endurance have its perfect result, that you may be perfect and complete, lacking in nothing.
>
> But if any of you lacks wisdom, let him ask of God, who gives to all men generously and without reproach, and it will be given to him (James 1:2-4 NASB).

Humanly, it is downright impossible to consider encountering trials "all joy." We don't like being in trouble. We dread unexpected repair bills, car wrecks, skyrocketing insurance premiums, bad grades on our kids' report cards, demotions and salary cuts at work, layoffs, roaches in the cupboard or spiders in the attic. Yet life is just one thing after another. And each of these situations—every last one of them—only comes our way after it has been sifted through the father's filtering fingers. When we, as his children, find ourselves incapable of withstanding the stress, the answer is to look to the Lord for wisdom. This he promises to dish out in ready supply (James 1:4).

There is always a God-ordained reason for the things that happen to us, although, as we've discussed earlier, we may not be privileged to discover the *why* behind the *what*—at least not till we meet him face to face in eternity. Jacob has no idea why he is forced to surrender Benjamin after losing his beloved Joseph. It seems very unfair. The seizure of Simeon is nearly inexplicable from the standpoint of human justice. Seated at the royal banquet table in Joseph's home, the brothers have no inkling of why Benjamin is served five times the amount they are. They do not object, but surely it seems strange to them, and certainly it is not equable. Yet without meaning to seem callous or trite, it is true that often what appears to us to be unjust is eminently just, divinely fair, in God's plan. It's all part of his program. This we shall observe as we watch the events of Genesis 44 unfold, and see Judah and his brothers run through the wringer.

SETTING THE SNARE—GENESIS 44:1-5

> Now Joseph gave these instructions to the steward of his house: "Fill the men's sacks with as much food as they can carry, and put each man's silver in the mouth of his sack. Then put my cup, the silver one, in the mouth of the youngest one's sack, along with the silver for his grain." And he did as Joseph said.
>
> As morning dawned, the men were sent on their way with their donkeys. They had not gone far from the city when Joseph said to his steward, "Go after those men at once, and when you catch up with them, say to them, 'Why have you repaid good with evil? Isn't this the cup my master drinks from and also uses for divination? This is a wicked thing you have done.' "

This chapter could be entitled, "The Second Visit to Egypt." Later, during this second visit, the brothers will finally recognize the ruler of the land to be the one they sold into slavery, their own younger brother. So it will be with Christ's second coming, when he establishes his kingdom. In that day, those who did not recognize him the first time—those who rejected and crucified him—are going to gaze upon him with freshly-opened eyes. They will realize that the one whom they pierced and scourged, Jesus Christ, is truly the son of God (Zechariah 12:10).

Meanwhile, back in Egypt, the brothers make ready to depart. Their hurried visit is nearly over, and they plan to leave early the next morning. Time is of the essence; things will go faster if their bags are packed the night before, and this is what we see happening as Genesis 44 begins. On this occasion, as when the brothers prepared to leave Egypt the first time, Joseph instructs his steward to "fill the men's sacks with as much food as they can carry, and put each man's silver in the mouth of his sack" (44:1). They'll be getting all their money back. The grain they'll cart back home is free. Joseph will not be a man in debt to his own flesh and blood; rather, he will be the giver.

But this time Joseph gives his steward an unusual additional order. "Then put my cup, the silver one, in the mouth of the youngest one's sack, along with the silver for his grain," he says (44:2). As we shall see, it is the beginning of a classic frame-up, and the steward immediately obeys.

We read in verse 3 that "as morning dawned" the men set out for home. They've spent a comfortable night in the luxurious Egyptian apartments. They're well fed, well rested—full, happy, and anxious to see their families. Won't the people back home be impressed with their success? What heroes they'll be! They can't wait to tell the story of the Lord's goodness.

Since the brothers have not packed their saddlebags themselves, they haven't the slightest idea about the surprising cargo within. Evidently Benjamin doesn't notice that one of his bags bulges a bit more than the rest. None of them spot it. The entire group is heading for home without looking back. Soon they'll receive the shock of their lives, and will face the toughest of challenges to date.

THE PLAN

Verse 4 reveals that before the brothers have gone far from the city, Joseph turns again to his steward. "Go after those men at once," he instructs the servant, "and when you catch up with them, say to them, 'Why have you repaid good with evil? Isn't this the cup my master drinks from and also uses for divination? This is a wicked thing you have done' " (44:4-5).

The plot thickens and the test continues. Joseph orders his steward to pursue the brothers and to falsely accuse them of theft. It isn't fair, according to human standards, but from God's perspective it will reveal the men's hearts as nothing else can.

Notice that Joseph tells his servant to inform the brothers that the cup they've supposedly stolen is the one he uses for "divination" (44:5). Divination is a pagan practice of foretelling the future or obtaining secret knowledge; it is demonic in nature. There is no reason to believe that Joseph has become involved in satanic practices and actually uses this silver cup for divination. God has given Joseph great wisdom, and accurate visions of the future, through the dreams that he has sent. Joseph has the real thing; he doesn't need satanic substitutes.

Why does Joseph even bring up the subject of divination? The brothers have already noticed his uncanny ability to discern things about them. Remember, he placed them at the dinner table so they were seated according to age. They are aware that he is not a typical government bureaucrat. There has to be some explanation for his extraordinary knowledge. It would make sense to assume that he practices divination.

Besides, it is essential that Joseph's identity remain secret for a little while longer, so that the test might have its desired results. By referring to divination, the steward will toss the brothers another curve. If they are getting suspicious, it'll throw them completely off track. They'll have no reason to suspect that Joseph has anything but Egyptian blood flowing through his veins. He employs divination just like any other adviser to pharaoh. And so the steward departs, following the fresh trail of the eleven men and their loaded donkeys headed for Canaan.

Springing the Trap—Genesis 44:6-13

> When he caught up with them, he repeated these words to them. But they said to him, "Why does my lord say such things? Far be it from your servants to do anything like that! We even brought back to you from the land of Canaan the silver we found inside the mouths of our sacks. So why would we steal silver or gold from your master's house? If any of your servants is found to have it, he will die; and the rest of us will become my lord's slaves."
>
> "Very well, then," he said, "let it be as you say. Whoever is found to have it will become my slave; the rest of you will be free from blame."
>
> Each of them quickly lowered his sack to the ground and opened it. Then the steward proceeded to search, beginning with the oldest and ending with the youngest. And the cup was found in Benjamin's sack. At this, they tore their clothes. Then they all loaded their donkeys and returned to the city.

It probably isn't too hard for the steward to locate the brothers. When he catches up with them, they're probably rambling along. Glancing over their shoulders, they spot the pursuing servant. The sinking feeling in the pits of their stomachs is much like the wave of nausea that hits a speeding driver who glances in the rear-view mirror just in time to see the flashing red lights of an approaching police car. We're in for it, they think. And everything was going so smoothly!

Joseph's steward must be a consummate actor, because he surely gives an award-winning performance when he pulls alongside the brothers. Keeping a straight face, he repeats the accusations of his master, although he knows full well that he has been the one to plant the cup in Benjamin's saddlebag.

"Why does my lord say such things?" the brothers respond in amazement (44:7). "Far be it from your servants to do anything like that! We even brought back to you from the land of Canaan the silver we found inside the mouths of our sacks. So why would we steal silver or gold from your master's house?" (44:7-8). In other words: "We're honest! We're innocent! What have we to gain by such a theft?"

So certain are they of their innocence that the brothers next come out with a very solemn offer. Although scripture doesn't say so, I imagine the one who speaks up is Reuben. Fond of dramatics, he tends to overstate the case. "If any of your servants is found to have it [the cup], he will die," pledges a voice from the crowd, "and the rest of us will become my lord's slaves" (44:9). It's death to the thief and slavery for his unwitting accomplices!

Providing a Means of Escape

"Very well, then," replies the steward, "let it be as you say" (44:10). But his next words show that it really isn't going to be as they have said. The steward, realizing that the brothers are undergoing a test, changes the conditions a bit. "Whoever is found to have it [the cup]," he continues, "will become my slave; the rest of you will be free from blame" (44:10).

Why does the steward alter the alternatives? In this way he'll provide the men with an opportunity to forsake Benjamin. He knows where that cup is. He knows Benjamin is about to be found guilty on circumstantial evidence. Now the brothers will have the chance to escape, leaving Benjamin behind, much as they deserted Joseph twenty-two years earlier. They're in a stressful situation—one permitted by God to gauge how little or how much they've morally grown over the years. And, like so many of God's exams, it's an unexpected test. The brothers are completely unaware that they're being set up for a reason.

The search commences, the brothers quickly lowering their sacks to the ground. Starting with the sack of the oldest, Reuben, the steward opens each and sifts through the contents. He works from the oldest to the youngest. Simeon is next, then Levi, then Judah. The sacks of the sons of the handmaids are then examined. Dan, Naphtali, Gad, and Asher aren't known for their sterling characters, but their saddlebags, too, are free from incriminating evidence. Next it's Issachar's turn, then Zebulun, and finally Benjamin.

The men probably breathe a sigh of relief as the steward walks over to their youngest brother. Maybe they begin to tie up their sacks and prepare to hoist them atop their donkeys, because surely Benjamin hasn't stolen the cup. He wouldn't do something like that!

The steward strides over to Benjamin and slowly, painstakingly, unties his sack. There is the cup! He rises from his work, and the silver chalice, glistening in the midmorning sun, is cradled in his hand (44:12).

I imagine the brothers turn as white as bleached sheets at this sight. Perhaps a few of them gasp in horror. Benjamin can probably think of nothing but immediate and severe punishment. Sweat beads pop out on his brow, and he swallows hard, fighting the feelings of panic welling up inside. Maybe the brothers crowd around him, demanding, "Why did you do it?" Why, why, when the ruler's been so good to you?"

Perhaps Benjamin can only stammer in reply, "But I didn't take it. I don't know how it got in my sack. I promise you, I'm innocent!" Perhaps, though, he reacts as Jesus Christ did, keeping silent when falsely accused.

In Isaiah 53:7, it is prophesied of the messiah that he would be "oppressed and . . . afflicted," yet would "not open His mouth" (NASB). And Matthew 27 reveals that, centuries later, as Jesus stood before Pontius Pilate and the accusations of the Jewish chief priests and elders were hurled at him, "he made no answer" (27:12 NASB). "Do You not hear how many things they testify against You?" inquired Pilate, but still Christ refused to respond to the charges. His sheer holiness and utter innocence spoke for themselves (27:13-14 NASB). As for Benjamin, he is so devastated that words probably won't come. It doesn't really matter; they won't do any good, anyway.

Regardless of whether Benjamin speaks up on his own behalf or remains quiet, we can be sure that he is upset. It's his first time away from home, and the horrid reality is that, guilty or not, he may never see his family again.

Benjamin's brothers must also realize this awful truth, for verse 13 tells us that they tear their clothes, making a gesture of deep grief and mourning. Then they load their donkeys and accompany the steward to the city.

It is a long trip back. Every step is agonizing. They dread the thought of being taken into the presence of the man they've offended so deeply. Yey they go, and this is important. Remember, the steward has said that only the one found with the cup will be taken captive. Technically, the brothers could say, "So long, Benjamin. Good luck—you'll need it." But they don't. They are not about to abandon their youngest brother—not yet, at least. Instead, they return to the city, to the uncertain fate and the wrathful ruler awaiting them there.

Widening the Escape Clause—Genesis 44:14-17

> Joseph was still in the house when Judah and his brothers came in, and they threw themselves to the ground before him. Joseph said to them, "What is this you have done? Don't you know that a man like me can find things out by divination?"
>
> "What can we say to my lord?" Judah replied.

> "What can we say? How can we prove our innocence? God has uncovered your servants' guilt. We are now my lord's slaves—we ourselves and the one who was found to have the cup."
>
> But Joseph said, "Far be it from me to do such a thing! Only the man who was found to have the cup will become my slave. The rest of you, go back to your father in peace."

When the steward and the brothers arrive at Joseph's house, they find that he has not yet left for work. Naturally, he expects them and sits in anticipation of their arrival. At least they won't have to wait for the confrontation. When they walk into Joseph's presence, the brothers throw themselves on the ground in front of him (44:14), once more fulfilling the dreams of long ago. They are frozen in fear because of the harsh treatment Joseph has doled out in the past. They haven't been on friendly terms with this fellow throughout most of their acquaintance with him. What will he do now?

"What is this you have done?" demands Joseph. "Don't you know that a man like me can find things out by divination?" (44:15). Again he makes mention of the pagan practice. He wishes to avoid giving them the slightest hint that he is anything but an Egyptian.

Judah answers for the group, "What can we say to my lord? What can we say? How can we prove our innocence? God has uncovered your servants' guilt. We are now my lord's slaves—we ourselves and the one who was found to have the cup" (44:16). Not a word of protest at this statement issues from any of the brothers.

Have Jacob's sons changed? Indeed, they have. Judah steps into the arena of leadership and makes a serious, and most difficult, pledge. He knows that only Benjamin need remain in Egypt; he has heard the words of the steward to that effect. But he refuses to desert his baby brother. Freedom awaits, yet he and the others choose slavery over abandoning Benjamin.

Joseph is probably astonished at the changes in his brothers. Are these the same men who sold him down the river years ago? The loyalty they're showing is incredible! He decides to broaden the escape clause a bit, and tries to convince them to leave Benjamin to his fate.

"Far be it from me to do such a thing!" exclaims Joseph at Judah's insistence that they all remain as slaves. "Only the man who was found to have the cup will become my slave. The rest of you, go back to your father in peace" (44:17). He begs them to reconsider, opening wide the door for them to exit Egypt permanently. His offer probably sounds most attractive to them.

Think about it. These men have left starving families behind in Canaan. The grain they carry is the only hope for their father, wives, children. Remaining as Egyptian slaves will only ensure the suffering and deaths of their loved ones. Besides, there is Benjamin's family to think about. He'll be concerned about his own children, and won't mind if the brothers take off while they have the chance. That way they can rescue his brood as well. Surely the logical thing to do is to leave! However, the logical and natural thing to do isn't always the supernatural thing to do.

Passing the Test—Genesis 44:18-34

> Then Judah went up to him and said: "Please, my lord, let your servant speak a word to my lord. Do not be angry with your servant, though you are equal to Pharaoh himself. My lord asked his servants, "Do you have a father or a brother? And we answered, "We have an aged father, and there is a young son born to him in his old age. His brother is dead, and he is the only one of his mother's sons left, and his father loves him.'
>
> "Then you said to your servants, 'Bring him down to me so I can see him for myself.' And we said to my lord, 'The boy cannot leave his father; if he leaves him, his father will die.' But you told your

> servants, 'Unless your youngest brother comes down with you, you will not see my face again.' When we went back to your servant my father, we told him what my lord had said.
>
> "Then our father said, 'Go back and buy a little more food.' But we said, 'We cannot go down. Only if our youngest brother is with us will we go. We cannot see the man's face unless our youngest brother is with us.'
>
> "Your servant my father said to us, 'You know that my wife bore me two sons. One of them went away from me, and I said, "He has surely been torn to pieces." And I have not seen him since. If you take this one from me too and harm comes to him, you will bring my gray head down to the grave in misery.'
>
> "So now, if the boy is not with us when I go back to your servant my father and if my father, whose life is closely bound up with the boy's life, sees that the boy isn't there, he will die. Your servants will bring the gray head of our father down to the grave in sorrow. Your servant guaranteed the boy's safety to my father. I said, 'If I do not bring him back to you, I will bear the blame before you, my father, all my life!'
>
> "Now then, please let your servant remain here as my lord's slave in place of the boy, and let the boy return with his brothers. How can I go back to my father if the boy is not with me? No! Do not let me see the misery that would come upon my father."

As he did in convincing Jacob to allow Benjamin to journey to Egypt, Judah assumes control of the situation, continuing to act as spokesman for the brothers. He begs Joseph to let him speak (44:18). No doubt emotions swell within Judah as he makes his speech. The atmosphere crackles with tension and electricity. Judah doesn't understand why events have turned sour, but he does understand his responsibilities, and his gentle arguments culminate in one of the most beautiful, self-sacrificing statements of all scripture.

Judah begins his quest to dissuade Joseph from enslaving Benjamin by refreshing the ruler's memory, reminding him of his questions about their family back in Canaan (44:19). Tactfully, he does not mention anything about the accusations of spying that Joseph had made (42:9,14,16). Neither does he comment about Simeon's subsequent imprisonment.

Judah recalls that if the brothers were to be allowed to purchase more grain, it was Joseph's condition that they fetch their youngest brother from home and bring him to Egypt (44:23). As expected, this news was greeted negatively by Jacob, who reminded his sons of their family's sad history and his own personal tragedy with these words:

> You know that my wife bore me two sons. One of them went away from me, and I said, "He has surely been torn to pieces." And I have not seen him since. If you take this one from me too and harm comes to him, you will bring my gray head down to the grave in misery (44:27-29).

Imagine the agony Joseph feels at these words. Memories of his beloved parent flood his mind afresh. He realizes again how much Jacob loved him. The torment his father must have felt upon hearing of his apparent death saddens him immensely. And what Judah says next only compounds Joseph's amazement at the change in his siblings.

Bound Up in the Life of His Boy

"So now," continues Judah, "if the boy is not with us when I go back to your servant my father and if my father, whose life is closely bound up with the boy's life, sees that the boy isn't there, he will die" (44:30-31). What concern Judah shows for Jacob! Could this be the same man who, twenty-two years earlier, haggled with merchants and traded away his own brother for twenty shekels of silver? Could this be the same fellow who, along with the brothers, splattered blood on Joseph's fine cloak and deceived their father into thinking him dead? At that time he gave little thought to the effect his actions would have upon Jacob. Now it is another story, and Judah is tremendously solicitous about his aging father.

Why all the worry? It is because, as Judah says without a trace of jealousy, Jacob's life is "closely bound up with the boy's life" (44:30). There are no feelings of animosity, no envy, no sarcasm in these words. Those emotions are long gone and, as Judah stands before this foreign official, his only thoughts are for the welfare of his father.

"Bound up in the life of his boy"—what a remarkable statement that is about the relationship between a parent and child! May I ask you a probing question? Are you, like Jacob was with Benjamin, bound up in the lives of your sons and daughters? Do you possess the kind of love and compassion for your children that he did for his youngest boy? Are they of paramount importance in your life, next only to your relationships with the Lord and with your spouse? Do you commit quantity and quality time to their upbringing? Are you constructively involved in their lives? Do they know that you care, that you aren't afraid to admit when you are wrong, that you deeply desire that they grow up to be godly adults? Or is it another type of parent that they see—one who works late at the office night after night after night, one who misses their soccer games, one who forgets promises made, one who is more bound up in the rat race than in the human race?

In his bestseller, *Rx for Addiction*, physician W. Robert Gehring relates the sad and sordid tale of his personal battle with drug addiction. In the book, Gehring reveals that it was not the condemnation of peers or the cold reality of prison that finally made him desire to end his substance abuse. Instead, it was the birth of a tiny miracle, his daughter. Writes Gehring:

> Courtney Robin Gehring was born at 2:54 PM on March 7, 1979. I looked at her pretty little face; I saw the dimple in her chin (just like mine); I held her warm little body in my arms. . . . When I held Courtney in my arms for the first time, I felt a warmth, a closeness, a protectiveness that I had never experienced before. It was a euphoria far superior to that generated by any drug.
>
> . . . I persuaded the nursery personnel to push Courtney's warmer to a remote corner of the nursery—away from the other babies. "We need to talk in private," I joked.
>
> I sat silently on a stool and watched this new person for over an hour. Courtney was flailing her arms and legs—trying them out, as babies do. I studied her little fingers and toes, her protuberant tummy, her healthy pink cheeks. A thousand thoughts bombarded my consciousness. Future thoughts, past thoughts, baby thoughts, father thoughts.
>
> I started talking to her in a soft whisper. "Happy birthday, little honey. Welcome to our world. We've got problems, to be sure, but it's not a bad world. There's still war and crime and starvation, but that's none of your concern, because your daddy will protect you from all that.
>
> "I'll try to guide your life so that you'll see the beauty of our world. There are fuzzy little animals and sunsets and flowers. There's music and poetry and . . . well, I could just go on and on. You'll have all that, Courtney. I promise. I'll protect you."
>
> Tears were streaming down my cheeks as I lifted

> her from the warmer and pressed her tiny body against mine. "Your daddy has a problem right now, little honey. He's gotten into something that he can't get out of. He's in way over his head. There's a beast inside of him that's consuming him. But that's not your concern. Your daddy's strong. Because of you, your daddy will kill that beast, and that beast will never threaten us again. I promise. I'll protect you" (Gehring 160-161).

Thankfully, the beast within Robert Gehring was eventually slain. It did not prevent him from becoming bound up in the life of his daughter, from fulfilling his promises to her. Yet each of us ought to ask ourselves, "What beasts are there in my life wreaking havoc in my relationship with my children?" Maybe the wild animals of workaholism, overcommitment, self-absorption, or lack of interest, are ravaging our family lives. We're not called to be parttime parents, but fulltimers, seeing our children as precious commodities on loan to us from the Lord. Too soon, they'll be gone.

A Substitute Sacrifice

If Benjamin is forced to remain in Egypt, Judah fears that his father will suffer immensely, will perhaps even die. As he continues to speak to Joseph, he reveals the promise he made to Jacob before taking Benjamin from their homeland.

"Your servant guaranteed the boy's safety to my father," says Judah to Joseph. "I said, 'If I do not bring him back to you, I will bear the blame before you, my father, all my life!' " (44:32). In other words, "Sir, I've entered into a contract with my father involving this boy. I have an obligation to see that he safely returns home."

"Now then," continues Judah, "please let your servant remain here as my lord's slave in place of the boy, and let the boy return with his brothers. How can I go back to my father if the boy is not with me? No! Do not let me see the misery that would come upon my father" (44:33-34). On their first visit, the ruler kept Simeon and let the rest go. Can he do that again, only this time keeping Judah?

Judah offers himself in the place of Benjamin. He is willing to make the sacrifice for his brother and for his father. He presents himself as a substitute, knowing that if his offer is accepted he will never see his family again. In this unselfish action, he mirrors Jesus Christ, his greatest descendant.

In the agonizing experience of Christ's death on the cross, there was a period of time more awful than the rest of the dreadful ordeal. It was the time when he was totally separated from the father. It was the time when he was literally being made sin for us, bearing the punishment for our iniquities, severed from the presence of God with whom he had constantly fellowshiped (Matthew 27:46). Christ offered himself for us. In a lesser though still meaningful manner Judah essentially does the same thing for Benjamin.

What will be Joseph's response to the gesture? This we shall discover as we turn to Genesis 45, but not without first considering a few of the lessons of chapter 44.

LESSONS

Lesson one: *often trials and difficulties come into our lives without an explanation from the father.* We don't know the *why* behind the *what.* God isn't obligated to tell us why he permits what he does. Yet there is always a reason.

Lesson two: *silence is sometimes the better part of valor.* Scripture doesn't record that Benjamin rises to his own defense with speeches and arguments. I would guess that he is so totally devastated by circumstances that he doesn't utter a word. Instead, Judah is the one who speaks.

Lesson three: *the brothers have learned to accept responsibility for each other.* There is new commitment, caring, and compassion. Do we feel the same sort of loyalty toward our siblings, parents, children, spouses, and fellow Christians? Or are we just thinking about ourselves, our happiness, our fulfillment? My wife asked me the other day, "Do you think there'll ever come a day when we don't have responsibility for someone else?"

"Yes," I replied, "when we die." And that is the truth. The rubber of our Christian lives meets the road as we commit ourselves to care for others.

Lesson four: *Joseph's brothers display no traces of selfishness.* They're in the struggle together—one for all and all for one. They've definitely changed in twenty-two years.

Lesson five: this one comes in the form of a question. *As a parent, is your life bound up in the lives of your children?* Now is the time to answer that one.

Lesson six: *Judah's love for his father is so great that he is willing to lay down his life for his brother.* His is an amazing testimony. We, too, ought to cherish our heavenly father so greatly that we are willing to sacrifice ourselves in such a manner. "Greater love has no one than this, that one lay down his life for his friends," teaches Jesus in John 15:13 (NASB). That sort of sacrificial attitude can only bring glory to God in the very highest! And we're not just talking about physical death, but sacrifices of time, finances, talent. It begins at home and should extend to the world.

Last Words

I mentioned in the beginning of this chapter that we often do not know the reasons tough times strike us, and I told the story of my secretary, Jan. In this case, her heavenly father's reasons are becoming clear.

It's been two years since Walt's death, and Jan has become better—not bitter—in that time. She has grown tremendously in her knowledge and understanding of the Lord. She recognizes that Walt was a precious gift from God, hers to have for a short, but very special, time. The hurt she has experienced has left her able to minister effectively to others who grieve and who have lost. The opportunities to do so come often, as do chances for her to tell others about the sustaining love of Jesus Christ. She is an increasingly sensitive servant of the father. As we have ached with her loss, now we rejoice in her victory.

When I think of Jan, I think of an anonymous poem I once ran across, called "God's Handwriting."

He writes in characters too grand
For our short sight to understand;
We catch but broken strokes and try
To fathom all the mystery
Of withered hopes, of death, of life,
The endless war, the useless strife—
But there, with larger, clearer sight,
We shall see this—His way was right!

QUESTIONS FOR STUDY

1. Judah states that Jacob's life is "bound up closely" with that of Benjamin. In your own words, explain what this means. Are you bound up in the lives of your children? What are some practical ways such closeness can be achieved?

2. What offer does Judah make when pleading for Benjamin's freedom? What does his offer tell us about the ways in which he has changed over the years? How does Judah's willingness to sacrifice himself remind us of what Jesus Christ, his greatest descendant, did centuries later?

3. How does Benjamin probably respond when the steward falsely accuses him of theft? Is silence sometimes a godly response when we're falsely accused? Explain your answer.

4. The brothers' actions show that they have a sense of responsibility toward one another. As Christians, are we responsible for others and to others? How so?

5. We're often not privileged to know why God permits what he does in our lives. Are you undergoing a trial right now? If so, check your response. Is it making you bitter or better? Are you drawing closer to God, or pulling away from him to lick your wounds yourself?

PART THREE

The Triumph and Transition

8

Freedom of Forgiveness

Genesis 45

Heigh-ho, Silver! So went the introduction to The Lone Ranger Show. Hearts pounding in anticipation of the week's adventures of the Ranger and Tonto, we'd sit in the living room, enraptured, while the masked stranger rescued someone in distress.

Do you know why the Lone Ranger hid behind a false face? At one time he was just an ordinary Texas Ranger, riding on patrol with his unit, which his brother, Captain Dan Reed, commanded. A low-down scout betrayed the unit and led them into an ambush. The notorious Butch Cavendish gang, of which the scout was a member, bushwhacked the brave Rangers and apparently killed them all—all but one, that is. For one lone ranger survived the massacre. Nursed back to health by Tonto the Indian, the Ranger vowed to track down the Cavendish gang and avenge the deaths of his brother and other comrades. To spare his brother's widow and son from possible danger because of his derring-do, the Ranger decided it would be best to maintain the pretense that he had actually perished in the ambush. When Tonto buried the Rangers, he dug an extra grave, which would remain empty just so the charade could continue. Choosing to remain anonymous, the Lone Ranger never removed his mask, deciding that being officially "dead" wasn't so bad if it helped to fight crime. And thus the saga continued and the mask stayed on.

Face to Face

In the past few chapters of Genesis, we've seen that Joseph, too, conceals his identity. Unlike the Lone Ranger, his motives are less to protect his loved ones than to provide them with a challenge. Neither does he seek revenge—he is not out to "get even" for the way they bushwhacked him twenty-two years before. The test the brothers undergo is not designed to intimidate or senselessly torment. It is tailor-made to teach them some lessons, and to awaken them to fresh truths about themselves, their responsibilities, their God. Now, as we approach Genesis 45, the time arrives for Joseph to strip off the disguise and stand unmasked before his family.

Whenever I approach this passage of scripture, I cannot help but think of Paul's words in 1 Corinthians 13:12, where the apostle speaks of the future return of Jesus Christ: "For now we see in a mirror dimly, but then face to face: now I know in part, but then I shall know fully just as I also have been fully known" (NASB). The hymnwriter Carrie Breck so vividly captures this moment in the lyrics to "Face to Face":

> Face to face with Christ my Saviour,
> Face to face—what will it be—
> When with rapture I behold Him,
> Jesus Christ Who died for me?
>
> Only faintly now I see Him,
> With the darkling veil between;
> But a blessed day is coming,
> When His glory shall be seen.
>
> What rejoicing in His presence,
> When are banished grief and pain;
> When the crooked ways are straightened,
> And the dark things shall be plain.

Face to face! O blissful moment!
Face to face—to see and know;
Face to face with my Redeemer,
Jesus Christ Who loves me so.

Three Cs to Consider

When Joseph does shortly lift the veil and disclose himself to his estranged brothers, it will be a most remarkable and unexpected revelation. I wonder how many of us, sitting here, reading these words, long to receive that sort of fresh revelation from God. We want him to become real to us in some way. Perhaps you have never felt that he was there. Or maybe you can wistfully think back to childhood days when, during vacation Bible school, camp, or Sunday school, you made a decision to receive Christ. He seemed so real to you then, so vital, so alive . . . and now perhaps he seems distant. Heaven seems made of brass, not gold; life is a struggle, not a victory—and God is far, far away.

It doesn't have to be that way, you know. Before we delve into the drama of Genesis 45, may I give you some points to ponder on just how God can become fresh, new, and powerfully real in your life? I call these the three Cs.

First there is *conversion*. Maybe you have never come into a personal relationship with Jesus Christ. You are searching; you long to know God. The truth is that the Lord is waiting to reveal himself to you at this very moment, just as Joseph waits to reveal himself to his family. "Behold, I stand at the door and knock," Jesus informs John in the book of Revelation, "if any one hears My voice and opens the door, I will come in to him and will dine with him, and he with Me" (3:20 NASB). Joseph looks first for a proper response from his brothers before giving away his identity. He wants to see new loyalty and changed attitudes. In offering his salvation, God doesn't ask for either of these. All he desires is that you open your heart and in faith invite Christ to be your savior. That's it. Then you're in his fold forever (John 10:27-29).

Those who are Christians may need to consider *confession*. Maybe you do. Maybe you're out of fellowship with God. You haven't spent much time with him in quite awhile. Your priorities have become fouled up. There's sin in your life and you know it, yet you're unwilling to deal with it. There will be no sense of his presence, his reality. God may even seem as cold and distant as before you received Christ as savior. Until you come before the Lord with a heart that is pliable and willing to follow the guidelines of 1 John 1:9, then your Christian growth will be severely stunted. There we read: "If we confess our sins, He is faithful and righteous to forgive us our sins and to cleanse us from all unrighteousness" (NASB).

Finally, you might need to think about *commitment*. Maybe you've walked with the Lord some time. Perhaps there are obvious evidences in your life that you know him personally, and that his hand is directing you. But he is asking for something more. He wants to know, "Will you surrender?" Will you give up whatever it is that keeps you from fully desiring to do his will? Will you completely commit yourself to him? If so, you're guaranteed to receive a fresh revelation of God's grace, power, and goodness.

Besides, once you make that commitment, he guarantees never to leave you in the lurch! As God reassures the prophet Isaiah, "So do not fear, for I am with you; do not be dismayed, for I am your God. I will strengthen you and help you; I will uphold you with my righteous right hand" (41:10; see also 2 Corinthians 12:9).

Before the Unveiling

We recall that before Joseph rips aside the curtain of illusion and discloses himself to his brothers, he looks for proper responses from them. These Joseph observes as they refuse to abandon Benjamin, although he is apparently guilty of theft. Genesis 44 closes with Judah's touching plea on behalf of his younger brother and father. Won't the ruler allow him to take the place of Benjamin, and serve as a slave instead? Benjamin's loss would destroy his elderly father! Surely the governor will be merciful (44:33-34).

Judah's willingness to sacrifice himself for his brother indicates that change has swept over the men in twenty-two years. Now love, unity, solidarity are present, where before bitter competition and seething resentment were there. Because they are not the same type of men who threw him in the pit long ago, Joseph is ready to shatter the facade and reveal himself. Let's turn to chapter 45, and watch as he does just that.

Shredding the Veil—Genesis 45:1-3

> Then Joseph could no longer control himself before all his attendants, and he cried out, "Have everyone leave my presence!" So there was no one with Joseph when he made himself known to his brothers. And he wept so loudly that the Egyptians heard him, and Pharaoh's household heard about it.
>
> Joseph said to his brothers, "I am Joseph! Is my father still living?" But his brothers were not able to answer him, because they were terrified at his presence.

Seared to the bone by Judah's poignant pleas, Joseph is overcome with emotion. His elder brother's spirit of contrition and brokenness plays upon Joseph's heartstrings. His hands probably begin to shake, his voice perhaps trembles, his face likely grows red with the heat of narrowly restrained tears. Finding that he cannot control himself any longer in front of his Egyptian attendants, he orders them from the room. "Have everyone leave my presence!" he commands (45:1). And Joseph is left alone with his brothers.

Why the privacy? This is family business. No outsiders are necessary. Joseph doesn't wish to embarrass his brothers by making his revelation public. The news will read soon enough, but the tender, private details of what is about to take place need not be witnessed by the merely curious, only the directly involved.

I'm sure the brothers gape in disbelief at what happens next. The man who moments before demanded that Benjamin remain in custody suddenly begins to weep violently. Tears literally cascade from Joseph's eyes, and sobs issue forth with such volume that the Egyptians in other parts of his vast home hear them plainly. Within moments, the news of Joseph's emotional outburst even reaches the household of pharaoh himself (45:2).

By thinking of what Joseph has been through, his tears become even more understandable to us. For over twenty years he has been in a foreign society, forced to learn a new language and adopt a strange culture. He's been much like a missionary serving abroad who has not been allowed to come home on furlough in two decades. The two visits of Joseph's brothers have given him brief glimpses of his past life. He has longed to speak with them, brother to brother. He's controlled himself till all the questions about their integrity have been answered, and, now that they have been, the pent-up emotions flood forth.

It's been said that tears are windows of the soul. Joseph's tears are like those shed at the funeral of a dear believer. We know the loved one has gone to be in the presence of Christ, but we pour out our grief because we miss him or her so deeply. We cry that way at weddings, too. As a father, I know what it is to let go of a child who's given me a peck of heartache and a bushel of matchless joy. You can't help but heave heavy sobs that are a mixture of happiness and sorrow, for it is painful to let go. We also cry at moments of reunion, as we are able to embrace relatives and friends we haven't seen in years. Joseph is ready for reconciliation, revelation, and reunion; the tears flow freely as he succumbs to the emotion of the moment and gives vent to feelings locked inside for twenty-two years.

Joseph, his vision surely blurred somewhat by salty tears, looks in the direction of his family. "I am Joseph!" he cries, and then he seeks reassurance about Jacob's welfare: "Is my father still living?" (45:3). Eyes and face glistening with wetness, his breath choked by sobs, he can say no more than these simple words.

Freely Forgiving

The faces of the brothers pale even more than before. Scripture states that they cannot answer him because they are "terrified at his presence" (45:3). You can imagine why! It's one thing to stand before the prime minister to pharaoh when you've been caught red-handed with incriminating evidence. It's quite another thing to find out that the official is really the brother whom you sold into slavery long ago, and who certainly, considering human nature, should be festering with so much bitterness and resentment that he's ready—and able—to have them executed. They'd laughed at his dreams, after all. They treated him like dirt, refusing even to speak a decent word to him. Overcome with hatred, they even shredded his cloak and hurled him into a well. Surely he seeks revenge!

But Joseph isn't like that. Neither was Jesus Christ. Joseph knows all about his brothers; Christ, on the other hand, proved his divinity by knowing all about everyone he encountered while walking upon the earth, God clothed in human flesh. In many instances in scripture, we read about displays of such supernatural knowledge.

In John 4, the apostle writes of a Samaritan woman who came to a well in the blazing heat of midday. There she met Jesus Christ, who asked for a drink of water and then offered her the "living water" of spiritual truth (4:14). In convicting the sinner of her need of a savior, Christ revealed details about the woman's life that he could only have known because he is God incarnate. He told her that she had had five husbands and currently, not bothering to marry, dwelt with a live-in lover (4:18).

They conversed further, and the woman indicated

that she looked for the coming of the savior promised the Jews. "I know that Messiah is coming (He who is called Christ)," she stated, "when that One comes, He will declare all things to us" (4:25 NASB).

Imagine her surprise when Jesus answered, "I who speak to you am He" (4:26 NASB). Picture your own shock if someone came up to you and said, "I am Jesus Christ, returning to claim my kingdom"!

Despite a sordid and shady past, the woman at the well was not condemned by Christ for her behavior. Completely cognizant of her indiscretions, he nevertheless approached her in gentleness, compassion, and forgiveness. So, too, does Joseph approach his brothers. They are struck speechless when he tells them who he is. And although they have wronged him immensely in years gone by, he comes to them this day with free forgiveness and flowing compassion.

You Sold, but God Sent—Genesis 45:4-8

> Then Joseph said to his brothers, "Come close to me." When they had done so, he said, "I am your brother Joseph, the one you sold into Egypt! And now, do not be distressed and do not be angry with yourselves for selling me here, because it was to save lives that God sent me ahead of you. For two years now there has been famine in the land, and for the next five years there will not be plowing and reaping. But God sent me ahead of you to preserve for you a remnant on earth and to save your lives by a great deliverance.
>
> "So then, it was not you who sent me here, but God. He made me father to Pharaoh, lord of his entire household and ruler of all Egypt."

Have you ever had one of those days when nothing seems to go right? The past ten or so hours have definitely made for one of those days for Joseph's brothers. How happy they were that morning, speeding through the wilderness as quickly as their donkeys would carry them, probably singing loud hosannas in praise and thanksgiving to the Lord for meeting the needs of their families. Some two hours later they're pulled to the side of the trail by Joseph's steward, snagged with circumstantial evidence, hauled back to the house of a hostile Egyptian. And now that fellow turns out to be none other than long-lost Joseph! It is more than they can handle. They shrink back from his tearful show of emotion.

Noticing his brothers' stunned silence and mounting terror, Joseph gently urges them, "Come close to me" (45:4). When they do this, he repeats his earlier message, with a few added details: "I am your brother Joseph, the one you sold into Egypt!" (45:4). Positive recognition dawns as the dumbfounded brothers study the ruler's countenance and notice the family characteristics—the lines of the face, the set of the jaw, the shape of the eyes. They continue to be gripped with fear.

"And now, do not be distressed," says Joseph reassuringly, "and do not be angry with yourselves for selling me here, because it was to save lives that God sent me ahead of you" (45:5). Joseph tells the brothers not to worry. He's not bitter. He's not resentful. He is fully aware that God has had a purpose in everything that has happened. Joseph can be victorious at this moment and can look his brothers square in the face, assuring them of his unconditional love, because he knows that God has placed him in Egypt for a reason. His brothers may have *sold* him, but God was the one who *sent* him. It was all part of a divine plan to save their very lives.

The Problem of Dealing with Problem People

For most of his life, Joseph has had to deal with problem people. First it was his brothers, then the slave traders, Potiphar, Mrs. Potiphar, pharaoh's cupbearer, and so on. How easy it would have been for him to succumb to anger, then allow that anger to turn to hatred over the years. But Joseph doesn't fall into that trap, because he possesses the ability to look beyond the horizontal, seeing the problem people as gifts from God designed to mold him into the man the Lord wants him to be.

Had Joseph remained in Canaan, he would have grown up in the tense atmosphere of a feuding family rife with jealousy. How much peace, how much time, to truly get to know God would he have had? He would have been constantly defending himself to his brothers. And had it not been for the seductive wiles of Mrs. Potiphar, Joseph might still be a slave in the house of his one-time master. Things do work together for good to those who love the Lord, and Joseph knows that. Even the problem people have a purpose.

As with Joseph, there are probably at least a few problem people in your life. You don't think of these folks as gifts from God. Or if you do see them as gifts, you'd really like to give them back! The key is to start looking at every individual who comes into your life as a sacred trust, established by the Lord, to affect you in some way.

Perhaps such a person is there to teach you patience, to elicit compassion, to encourage your gift of hospitality, to provide you with an opportunity to share the gospel. Whatever Tom, Dick, or Harry is currently causing you trouble, realize that he is there by sovereign intervention, and that there are some things God wants you to learn from this person's presence. Granted, some people make us want to learn our lessons quickly, so the Lord will send them on their way! But when we adopt an attitude of seeing things from a vertical perspective, it becomes easier to forgive and to love the human instruments God uses to shape us. It is when we are able to recognize that those things that men do to us have been permitted by a loving father for the ultimate accomplishment of his purpose, then we are ready to forgive the offenses of others. For Joseph, the attitude, "You sold me; God sent me," makes it possible for him to honestly love his brothers and to deal compassionately with them

Spelling It Out

Joseph goes on to explain just how the brothers' selling him into slavery will actually save their lives. "For two years now there has been famine in the land, and for the next five years there will not be plowing and reaping" (45:6). Pharaoh's dreams (41:1-7) will be fulfilled. Five long years of the seven-year famine remain. If they think things are tough now, all they need to do is hang on and it will get worse.

"But God sent me ahead of you to preserve for you a remnant on earth and to save your lives by a great deliverance," continues Joseph (45:7). The deliverance he's talking about is that which will come over the next five years. If Jacob and clan remain in Canaan, they'll die of starvation, but God has provided an escape clause. Why? So that a remnant—twelve tribes who will become the Hebrew nation—will be preserved. We know that God's ultimate reason for this rescue is to salvage the race into which Jesus Christ would one day be born.

Again Joseph reiterates his acknowledgment of God's guiding hand in all the circumstances that have gone before: "So then, it was not you who sent me here, but God. He made me father to Pharaoh, lord of his entire household and ruler of all Egypt" (45:8). God sent him; God established him as second-in-command to pharaoh and ruler over all Egypt. God's sovereign control has been evident in Joseph's life throughout. Because of this, Joseph is able to look beyond events and approach his brothers with the tremendous sense of freedom and forgiveness we see in Genesis 45.

Forgiveness Is not an Option

Forgiving those who have wronged us or injured our loved ones is one of the most difficult things we must do.

Notice that I say *must*, for, as Jesus states in Mark 11:25, "And whenever you stand praying, forgive, if you have anything against anyone; so that your Father also who is in heaven may forgive you your transgressions" (NASB). Essentially, if we as Christians do not forgive others, our relationships with God will be broken. We won't lose our salvation, but the sweet fellowship that is possible with him will be lost, buried under the ocean of bitterness that engulfs us. We won't feel free to communicate with the Lord. He'll seem distant—but only because we have been the ones to move away from his will through our unwillingness to be charitable to others.

In *The Family Album*, Arthur and Nancy DeMoss include a story that aptly describes the spiritual consequences of failure to forgive. It seems while Leonardo da Vinci labored on his masterpiece, *The Last Supper*, he became angry with another man. They quarreled, da Vinci hurling bitter accusations and threats at the other fellow. Returning to his canvas, the artist attempted to paint the face of Jesus, but found himself unable to do so. So upset was he that he could not compose himself for the painstaking work. Finally, he set down his brushes, sealed his paint pots, and went to search for the man with whom he had argued. He apologized, asking for forgiveness, which his antagonist graciously gave. Only then was Leonardo able to return to his workshop and complete the face of the savior (DeMoss 111).

Da Vinci had first to forgive the other man in his heart. Then he had to seek out the fellow and ask forgiveness for the wrongs he himself had wrought in the meantime. It wasn't easy. God never promises that forgiveness will be painless, but he makes it clear that it is essential.

The late Corrie ten Boom modeled forgiveness as perhaps no other twentieth-century personality. As we've mentioned earlier, she suffered intensely during her time at the Ravensbruck concentration camp. A few weeks after the Allied victory celebration began, Corrie learned the name of the man who had betrayed her family to the Gestapo. How should she react to him? Could she forgive him? A copy of the letter she eventually wrote to him is included in C.C. Carlson's tribute, *Corrie ten Boom: Her Life, Her Faith.* That letter, dated June 19, 1945, is reprinted below:

> Dear Sir,
>
> Today I hear that most probably you were the one who betrayed me. I went through ten months of concentration camp. My father died after ten days, my sister after ten months of imprisonment.
>
> What you meant to be harmful God used for my good. I have become closer to Him. A severe punishment is awaiting you. I have prayed for you that the Lord will accept you if you will turn to Him. Think about the fact that the Lord Jesus also carried your sins on the cross. If you accept that and will be His child, you will be saved forever.
>
> I have forgiven you everything; God will forgive you everything also, if you ask Him. He loves you, and He, Himself, has sent His son to earth to forgive you your sins, that is, to bear punishment for you and me. From your side an answer must be given. When He says, "Come to me, give your heart" then your answer must be "Yes, Lord, I will. Make me your child."
>
> If you have difficulty praying, ask then if God will give you His Spirit; He works the faith in your heart. Never doubt the love of the Lord Jesus. He stands with His arms wide open to receive you.
>
> I hope that the hard road that you now have to go will bring you to your eternal Savior (Carlson 127-128).

That is forgiveness of the highest order. "You sold me; God sent me," exclaims Joseph. "What you meant to be harmful God used for my good," writes Corrie ten Boom. What a testimony it is to these individuals that they are remembered as gracious forgivers, not bloodthirsty avengers.

So how are you doing? How will you be remembered? Is there someone out there whom you find difficult to pardon? I urge you to keep your forgiveness up-to-date. The apostles made sure they did. Although young John Mark failed miserably in his first missionary journey, deserting Paul and Barnabas in the thick of things (Acts 13:13), Paul later forgave him. "Get Mark and bring him with you," writes the elder apostle in his last letter to Timothy, "because he is helpful to me in my ministry" (2 Timothy 4:11). Early on, the apostle Peter had his share of difficulties with Paul (Galatians 2:11), and yet both men got their hearts right with each other. "Bear in mind that our Lord's patience means salvation, just as our dear brother Paul also wrote you with the wisdom that God gave him," Peter exhorts his readers in 2 Peter 3:15. These men kept their forgiveness up-to-date. Have you? (See also Matthew 5:23-24.)

"I can't do it. I can't forgive so-and-so for what he's done to me!" you say. Forgiving another is often easier said than done, but it is not impossible. It is an act of love, the tangible demonstration of a decision to love the other person. The power behind such love can only be God himself. As Walter Wangerin writes in *As for Me and My House:*

> This is our human predicament: we are able to sin infinitely against one another, but we are able to forgive only finitely. Left to ourselves alone, forgiveness will run out long before the sinning does.
>
> . . . But if forgiveness is a tool, it is also a power tool whose power comes from a source other than ourselves. We may use it; we may carefully and self-consciously apply it . . . but Jesus Christ empowers it. He is the true source of its transfiguring

love. And the love of the Son of God is infinite (Wangerin 82).

Getting On with the Program—Genesis 45:9-15

> "Now hurry back to my father and say to him, 'This is what your son Joseph says: God has made me lord of all Egypt. Come down to me; don't delay. You shall live in the region of Goshen and be near me—you, your children and grandchildren, your flocks and herds, and all you have. I will provide for you there, because five years of famine are still to come. Otherwise you and your household and all who belong to you will become destitute.'
>
> "You can see for yourselves, and so can my brother Benjamin, that it is really I who am speaking to you. Tell my father about all the honor accorded me in Egypt and about everything you have seen. And bring my father down here quickly."
>
> Then he threw his arms around his brother Benjamin and wept, and Benjamin embraced him, weeping. And he kissed all his brothers and wept over them. Afterward his brothers talked with him.

Joseph continues to speak to his brothers. He has explained the situation to them. It is time to get on with God's program. "Now hurry back to my father," Joseph instructs the others, "and say to him, 'This is what your son Joseph says: God has made me lord of all Egypt. Come down to me; don't delay' " (45:9). Joseph realizes how long it took the brothers to make their return trip to Egypt. He is aware that provisions in Jacob's settlement are exhausted, and so there is a sense of urgency to his words. Time is crucial. They must fetch Jacob posthaste, or else it will be too late.

Once the brothers return with the patriarch and their families, an incredible treat awaits them. They will dwell, promises Joseph, "in the region of Goshen," where they will be near him (45:10). There is room enough for all. Goshen is located in the northeastern section of the country, in the area of the Nile Delta, and is a tremendously lush, rich region. It is fertile land, excellent for grazing, perfectly suited to the rural lifestyle of Joseph's family. Once they've settled there, Joseph tells his brothers, "I will provide for you there. . . . Otherwise you and your household and all who belong to you will become destitute" (45:11).

The Ravens of Provision

"I will provide for you." Joseph tells his brothers that this is the last trip south they have to make to purchase grain. If they accept his offer, he'll handle their food supply from now on. It will be specially delivered to Goshen. Yet they do have an alternative; they can choose to reject his proposal. Of course, that will mean destitution at best, starvation at worst. But the choice is still there . . . and theirs.

In 1 Kings 17, the prophet Elijah had a similar choice to make. God revealed to Elijah that no rain would fall in the land of Israel for three-and-one-half years, and the prophet faithfully reported the news to King Ahab (17:1). Then the Lord instructed Elijah to journey to the brook Cherith, east of the Jordan River. There the prophet would find ample water in the brook, and ravens, commanded by God, would provide food for him (17:2-4). Elijah had two alternatives: return to his home in Gilead and suffer through the drought, or go to the brook Cherith and experience the Lord's provision. Though he might rather have remained in the familiar surroundings of his home town, Elijah chose the latter and set out for Cherith, where he enjoyed food and drink supplied straight from God (17:5-6).

Elijah's experience illustrates a principle worth noting. That is, we are the most happy and the most blessed when we find ourselves exactly where God wants us. It may not be a place of our own choosing—or of our preference—but in the long run we'll be far more content being within the will of God than outside that will.

What about you and me? When our circumstances become rough, when it seems we're constantly running uphill into the wind, it may be that we are not where God would have us to be. He is sending the ravens of provision elsewhere, but we're not open to his direction. We're refusing to go where he wants us to go, or we've hastily left the place where he has arranged to meet our needs. I'm not saying that every time things get difficult, it's because we're dwelling away from the will of God. But sometimes that is true.

In a short time in our story of Joseph and family, Jacob will have a choice to make. He can try to hang on for dear life in Canaan; but there will be no provision there, because the "ravens" are flying to Egypt. Or he can pack up the tents, load up the donkeys, and make headway for Goshen, which is precisely where God wants him.

Reunited . . . and It Feels So Good

As Joseph continues to speak to his brothers, they must be somewhat skeptical about his generous offer. "You can see for yourselves, and so can my brother Benjamin, that it is really I who am speaking to you," Joseph says convincingly (45:12). Why does he single out Benjamin? It is only natural. Joseph's love for his full brother is very intense. Their relationship had always been a special one.

Again, Joseph urges his brothers to hurry back to Canaan and bring Jacob to Egypt quickly (45:13). Perhaps he heaves a sigh when all has been said, looks once more at his family. Then the dam breaks. He can stand it no longer. Having made the revelation, it is now time for constructive reconciliation.

Verse 14 tells us that Joseph throws his arms around Benjamin and embraces him. Again the tears flow freely, and Benjamin answers his elder brother's actions with embraces and sobs of his own (45:14). It is surprising that Benjamin has lasted this long without breaking down. In the past twenty-four hours, his eyes have soaked in the unaccustomed grandeur of Egypt, and he's been treated with five times the honor of anyone else in his family. With morning's light comes accusation—he is caught with stolen property and branded a criminal. He returns to the ruler's home fearing enslavement and possible execution, then all the uncertainty evaporates as he beholds the brother he considered dead. Only God could have engineered something so wonderful, and Benjamin's outburst probably contains as many tears of relief as tears of joy.

Once Joseph is reunited with Benjamin, he moves toward his other brothers, kissing each, weeping with each (45:15). It is an enormously moving scene, and then, scripture reveals, his brothers talk with him (45:15). Oh, how I wish I had a record of that conversation! Of what must they speak after the sobbing subsides and the tears are wiped away? I would guess that the twelve brothers discuss the events of the past twenty-two years. Joseph needs to know all that has happened to his family back in Canaan, and the brothers are certainly curious about his elevation to power. Probably Joseph traces the steps of his dramatic rise to the position of prime minister. Surely the brothers inform him about their wives and children back home. And then the conversation must turn to more recent events. Maybe the brothers ask Joseph why he has allowed them to undergo such testing, and he explains, showing them the reasons why. Perhaps during this time also, he convinces them that he has long since learned to trust God, and truly has forgiven them for what happened when he was seventeen.

The day will come when God, like Joseph, unrolls the canvas and reveals to us the big pictures of our own lives. Then we'll understand why we had to endure the events that have occurred in our lives. We'll be able to talk with him and explore the alternatives of the past. I have no doubt that when the revelation is over, we'll be able to say to the Lord, "You were right. You did exactly what was best for me and, if I'd had your knowledge, I'd have chosen precisely the same path for myself that you did. Thank you, Lord." It will likely be in eternity when we confront the truth face to face. But that day will come, not unlike it does for Joseph's brothers in Genesis 45.

Orders from the Oval Office—Genesis 45:16-20

> When the news reached Pharaoh's palace that Joseph's brothers had come, Pharaoh and all his officials were pleased. Pharaoh said to Joseph, "Tell your brothers, 'Do this: Load your animals and return to the land of Canaan, and bring your father and your families back to me. I will give you the best of the land of Egypt and you can enjoy the fat of the land.'
>
> "You are also directed to tell them, 'Do this: Take some carts from Egypt for your children and your wives, and get your father and come. Never mind about your belongings, because the best of all Egypt will be yours.' "

At the close of Ephesians 3, Paul depicts the Lord as "Him who is able to do exceeding abundantly beyond all that we ask or think" (3:20 NASB). Exceeding abundantly . . . beyond all we ask or think . . . how well these phrases describe the way God acts! When his hand is in a situation, we'll recognize it, because events will occur that are beyond our wildest dreams. It may be that we'll tangibly feel his comforting presence as we grieve over a loss. Perhaps our financial needs will be miraculously met in some way. Or, as Joseph and family experience in Genesis 45:16-20, maybe unimaginable provision will be made from an unexpected source.

In the case of Joseph and clan, that source is pharaoh himself. The brothers could never have imagined that they'd enter Egypt begging to buy food, and leave the country in a style befitting royalty. It is too good to be true, but it is true, nevertheless. Verses 16 and 17 tell us that the news of the brothers' presence in Egypt rapidly reaches pharaoh, pleasing the king and his officials. Without hesitation, pharaoh instructs Joseph, "Tell your brothers, 'Do this: Load your animals and return to the land of Canaan, and bring your father and your families back to me. I will give you the best of the land of Egypt and you can enjoy the fat of the land" (45:17).

This is what Joseph has already promised his brothers (45:9-11), but it's nice to have pharaoh's stamp of approval on the deal. Why is the king so eager to invite Joseph's entire family into the land? He owes Joseph a lot for the last nine years of leadership the Hebrew has contributed. Egypt is the only country in the world capable of surviving the economic crunch, and it's all because of the policies Joseph has implemented. No doubt pharaoh feels indebted to Joseph, and the least he can do is provide for his top man's family.

The king continues to exercise royal prerogative, issuing an executive order for Joseph to relay to his brothers: "You are also directed to tell them, 'Do this: Take some carts from Egypt for your children and your wives, and get your father and come. Never mind about your belongings, because the best of all Egypt will be yours' " (45:19-20). The brothers won't just be ambling home on donkeys laden with grain, they'll be escorted by a fleet of carts large enough to convey their families to their new residence. The King James and New American Standard versions of the Bible translate the word *carts* as "wagons." These weren't tiny vegetable carts the brothers would be towing home, but huge, sturdy wagons.

Jacob, the wives, and children aren't even going to need to pack their clothes for the trip, because once they make it to Egypt, the very best the country has to offer will be theirs, absolutely free. It reminds me of what awaits us in heaven. If you're a Christian, you ought to be looking forward to the hereafter. God expects us, like

Jacob and family, to be willing to leave behind our earthly belongings to go to our permanent home. Dying isn't hard when we're living for what's over there; death becomes difficult when what we've lived for is earthbound and temporary. If we've treasured things such as houses, children, careers, money, and possessions, then dying means leaving behind what is most important to us instead of journeying to a place we've longed for. Yet, since our departure is inevitable, isn't it better to get our priorities straight in the here-and-now, rather than waiting till we're at the edge of the hereafter? Heaven is something to look forward to with excitement and anticipation!

STUBBORNNESS, SURRENDER, SATISFACTION—GENESIS 45:21-28

> So all the sons of Israel did this. Joseph gave them carts, as Pharaoh had commanded, and he also gave them provisions for their journey. To each of them he gave new clothing, but to Benjamin he gave three hundred shekels of silver and five sets of clothes. And this is what he sent to his father: ten donkeys loaded with the best things of Egypt, and ten female donkeys loaded with grain and bread and other provisions for his journey. Then he sent his brothers away, and as they were leaving he said to them, "Don't quarrel on the way!"
>
> So they went up out of Egypt and came to their father Jacob in the land of Canaan. They told him, "Joseph is still alive! In fact, he is ruler of all Egypt." Jacob was stunned; he did not believe them. But when they told him everything Joseph had said to them, and when he saw the carts Joseph had sent to carry him back, the spirit of their father Jacob revived. And Israel said, "I'm convinced! My son Joseph is still alive. I will go and see him before I die."

Joseph obeys pharaoh's instructions, and the brothers are soon equipped to exit Egypt in grand style. The wagons are hitched up; provisions for the trip are packed; it's time to head home (45:21). Before they depart, Joseph gives his brothers some going-away presents. All except Benjamin receive a set of fine clothes, probably far better than these sheepherders have ever worn! Benjamin, however, receives not one but five sets of clothes plus some cash, three hundred shekels of silver (45:22). And as before, there are no murmurs of jealousy from the rest of the brothers.

Joseph also sends gifts along for Jacob, ordering that ten donkeys be laden with the best things of Egypt and ten female donkeys be loaded with grain and bread (45:23). Seeing is believing and, after spotting that sizable caravan, even the old patriarch will have no doubt that it really is his son Joseph awaiting him in Egypt.

"Don't quarrel on the way!" Joseph calls after his brothers as the wagon train moves out (45:24). He knows his brothers well, and he wants no recriminations about the past to delay their return.

The Direct Approach

However they conduct themselves along the way, when the brothers arrive in Canaan, they evidently decide to give Jacob the direct approach. They'll spare him the details of their guilt for the moment—those will come later, after Jacob experiences the initial shock of learning that Joseph lives.

"Joseph is still alive!" exclaim the sons to their father. "In fact, he is ruler of all Egypt" (45:26). Upon hearing this, verse 26 reveals that Jacob is stunned and incredulous. Joseph, alive? How could this be?

Put yourself in Jacob's sandals a moment. Weak with hunger, he drags himself from his tent when he hears shouts that a caravan approaches. Frantically he makes a head count of the riders . . . eleven! Yes, there are eleven men! Benjamin is there; Simeon is there; God be praised! They've all come home.

So relieved is Jacob when he greets his eleven sons

that the thought of number twelve is a completely foreign one. The idea that Joseph is alive hasn't crossed his mind in years. The news leaves him speechless and astonished. But then the brothers begin to explain. They tell him what Joseph had said to them in Egypt (45:27). Can't you just hear them?

"Father, we want to tell you a story. Some of it isn't too pretty, but it's all working together for good. Joseph really is alive, and he wants us to join him in Egypt. He's a hero there—you'll be so proud of him. He wants you and the rest of us to come quickly and travel light. We'll be given everything we need once we get there. The king of the land even says so!" Their words—plus the fact that twenty loaded donkeys were stopped outside his tent (45:27)—at last cause Jacob to believe.

The Three Ss

"I'm convinced," says the patriarch. "My son Joseph is still alive. I will go and see him before I die" (45:28). What a road Jacob has traveled in these past few chapters. His journey of trust is perhaps best reflected in three of his statements. These illustrate what I call the three Ss—stages of submission to God's purpose.

In Genesis 42:36, Jacob rails at his sons, "You have deprived me of my children. Joseph is no more and Simeon is no more, and now you want to take Benjamin! Everything is against me!" His words are the epitome of *stubbornness.*

Surrender is best seen when Jacob finally relinquishes his grasp on Benjamin and allows him to accompany his brothers to Egypt. "As for me, if I am bereaved, I am bereaved," sighs Jacob with resignation in Genesis 43:14, as he lets Benjamin go. What will be will be—God's will be done.

From stubborn lack of cooperation to submissive surrender journeys Jacob. Then, and only then, does he find *satisfaction.* "I'm convinced! My son Joseph is still alive. I will go and see him before I die," cries the patriarch with joy and thanksgiving in Genesis 45:28. How good and gracious God is! It is time to celebrate! It is time to go and be with Joseph!

Yet before we read of that touching reunion, let's briefly consider the lessons of Genesis 45.

LESSONS

Lesson one: *remember the three Cs: conversion, confession, and commitment.* If your life with the Lord seems dry and stale, it may be because one of these areas needs attention. Joseph reveals himself to his brothers only after their confession—their repentance and acknowledgment of guilt. Perhaps God is waiting for you to take such a step before he reveals himself to you in a fresh, new, vital way.

Lesson two: *when we realize that God is in control of people and circumstances, we're freed to forgive the instruments he uses to accomplish his purposes.* If others have injured us, it is only because he has permitted it, and we are free to forgive those who have done us wrong. In fact, we must forgive them!

Lesson three: *acknowledging that God is the author of our circumstances enables us to have wisdom to properly relate to our situations.* It helps to remember that, in the midst of the melee, he is looking for the proper responses from us.

Lesson four: *if things are consistently difficult for us over a long period of time, it may be that God is sending the ravens of provision elsewhere.* Perhaps we're in Canaan when we should be in Egypt. Examine your circumstances and see if this might be true.

Lesson five: *Joseph manifests compassion and concern for his family. We should do no less, no matter what sort of nuts grow on our family tree! By the way, the caring should extend to our brothers and sisters in Christ, also.*

Lesson six: *Jacob begins to see the big picture of God's*

overall plan for him and his family, as he learns that the entire dozen of his sons are safe. "I am convinced" is the expression of a joyful heart realizing what the Lord is doing.

Lesson seven: *God is able to do exceeding abundantly, beyond anything we'd ask or think.* Just ask Jacob.

Lesson eight: *Joseph is deeply touched by the change he sees in his brothers.* Spiritual growth in our friends and family members should affect us as well.

The Father and Child Reunion

As we leave Jacob eagerly anticipating the reunion with his beloved Joseph, I cannot help but think of the day when we Christians, the bride of Christ, will be united with our bridegroom. It is coming—perhaps sooner than we expect. What better words to close this chapter with than those performed by gospel singer Sandi Patti? In the lyrics to "We Shall Behold Him," we are reminded that one day we'll exchange the temporary ills of human life for the permanent joy of heavenly residence in the presence of our Lord.

> The sky shall unfold
> Preparing His entrance
> The stars shall applaud Him
> With thunders of praise
> The sweet light in His eyes
> Shall enhance those awaiting
> And we shall behold Him
> Then face to face
>
> Oh, we shall behold him
> We shall behold Him
> Face to face in all His glory
> Oh, we shall behold Him
> Yes, we shall behold Him
> Face to face our Savior and Lord

(Dottie Rambo, "We Shall Behold Him,"
copyright John T. Benson Pub.)

QUESTIONS FOR STUDY

1. How can the three Cs of conversion, confession, and commitment help us to have a closer relationship with the Lord?

2. The brothers are amazed to learn that the official they've dealt with is really Joseph, just as the woman at the well in Samaria was astonished to learn that the man she spoke with was the messiah. How do Joseph and Jesus reveal themselves in these situations? Are they gentle or harsh? Condemning or forgiving?

3. Joseph has had to deal with problem people most of his life, just as we do. Why do you think God allows these folks to come into our lives? What does Joseph's example teach us about how to deal with them?

4. God makes provision for Elijah at the brook Cherith; he arranges for Jacob's needs to be met in Egypt. Both men must leave familiar surroundings in order to experience the Lord's provision. What lessons can we learn from these episodes?

5. Why is it important to keep our forgiveness up to date? If we, as Christians, are not willing to forgive others, what happens to our fellowship with God? (See Mark 11:25.)

9

Trust and Obey

Genesis 46 and 47

Last October I was driving into Tyler with a friend from our church at Hide-A-Way Lake. Our destination was the medical center. The church office had received a phone call that was both expected and dreaded: an accident victim had slipped into the presence of the Lord. My buddy asked if he might ride into town to offer his assistance and express his sorrow to the newly-widowed woman we'd find waiting for us in the hospital corridors. Perhaps because of the sadness of the moment, we used the time en route to the medical center to offer words of encouragement to each other.

"This is a book I thought you'd enjoy," he said, shoving a small volume into my hand. "It's full of poems that are folksy and simple, but that really speak to your heart." And so I received my introduction to poet Edgar Guest, via his book *Just Folks.* He is now one of my favorites.

The following poem, found in *Just Folks,* and titled "Fishing Nooks," especially reminds me of Jacob as Genesis 46 begins.

> "Men will grow weary," said the Lord,
> "Of working for their bed and board.

They'll weary of the money chase
And want to find a resting place
Where hum of wheel is never heard
And no one speaks an angry word,
And selfishness and greed and pride
And petty motives don't abide.
They'll need a place where they can go
To wash their souls as white as snow.
They will be better men and true
If they can play a day or two."

The Lord then made the brooks to flow
And fashioned rivers here below,
And many lakes; for water seems
Best suited for a mortal's dreams.
He placed about them willow trees
And sent the birds that sing the best
Among the foliage to nest.
He filled each pond and stream and lake
With fish for man to come and take;
Then stretched a velvet carpet deep
On which a weary soul could sleep.

It seemed to me the Good Lord knew
That man would want something to do
When worn and wearied with the stress
Of battling hard for world success.
When sick at heart of all the strife
And pettiness of daily life,
He knew he'd need, from time to time,
To cleanse himself of city grime,
And he would want some place to be
Where hate and greed he'd never see.
And so on lakes and streams and brooks
The Good Lord fashioned fishing nooks.

We all need time to get away from the rat race, pause, and refresh ourselves. Jacob is no exception. His life has been tough—a constant struggle of one sort or the other. "My years have been few and difficult," he later confides to pharaoh (47:9), and indeed they have been. When young, he battled to win his father's favor and antagonized his hotheaded brother in the process. After stealing Esau's blessing, he was forced to flee for his life, never again to see his mother Rebekah. He labored twenty years for the ungrateful and deceitful father-in-law in whose land he had taken refuge. After leaving Laban to return to Canaan, his hip was permanently crippled in an appointment with God, and he faced a potentially dangerous confrontation with Esau the next day. Not long afterward, he watched with heartache as some of his sons proved themselves ill-tempered, cruel, and unworthy in the incident at Shechem, and he also buried his beloved wife Rachel. Years later, his favorite boy was ripped from his arms at age seventeen, the victim, apparently, of a hideous death in the jaws of a wild animal. Twenty-two years following that tragedy, the stomachs of his grandchildren shriveled with the pain of hunger as a severe famine blanketed his homeland.

No, life has not been easy for Jacob. Yet now, as he faces his final years, it appears that the Lord has fashioned what Edgar Guest would call a "fishing nook" just for him. He is going to Egypt, to rejoin his son Joseph, there to live out the rest of his days in peaceful reflection and relaxation. Coming down the home stretch, Jacob will be cared for, not careworn, during the seventeen years that are left of his life.

We've seen the old man come so far—from stages of stubbornness and surrender to satisfaction. As Genesis 46 opens, we watch as he and his budding nation pile into the sturdy wagons pharaoh has sent and set out for the land of Egypt. Around seventy-five strong, their exodus will surely affect the economy of the area about Hebron. They'll be missed. No mournful occasion, this scene is one of great thanksgiving. I've no doubt the company breaks into song as they edge their way out of Hebron—maybe a psalm like the well-loved hymn, "Trust and Obey":

When we walk with the Lord
In the light of His Word
What a glory He sheds on our way!
While we do His good will
He abides with us still,
And with all who will trust and obey.

The Problem

Whatever songs and shouts of praise resound from the mouths of the Israelites, there is a problem with their departure for Egypt. Perhaps only Jacob has misgivings about the journey, for he is the one most likely to have heard stories of what happened to his great-uncle Lot and his grandfather Abraham when they went to Egypt. It's likely he learned these lessons as a small child while sitting on his mother's lap. The theme of the childhood stories was clear: Egypt was to be avoided at all costs. Bad things happened when God's people went there.

Jacob would have known that it was in Egypt that Uncle Lot was seduced by the lure of money, power, and the good life. Lot was never the same after returning to Canaan. His experiences in the opulence of Egypt caused him to choose to live in the lush, attractive, well-watered plains of the Jordan. The region reminded him of the country of pharaoh. There he settled nearby, then actually moved into the city of Sodom. We know the rest of the sordid story. When God's judgment rained fire and brimstone upon Sodom and Gomorrah because of their citizens' blatant sexual perversions, Lot, his wife, and two of his daughters had to be led out by rescuing angels. Most of Lot's family remained behind to perish in the flames. Mrs. Lot couldn't resist looking back at what she was leaving and was instantaneously killed, her flesh turning to salt. It was a time of tragic loss—which might have been avoided had Lot's eyes not been enticed by the glitter and glitz of Egypt years before (Genesis 13:10-11; 19:1-29).

While Abraham learned his lessons more thoroughly than his nephew did, he too experienced his share of hard knocks while in the land of Egypt. Upon entering the country, he became fearful for his life and convinced his wife Sarah to lie about their relationship. Assuming that she was Abraham's sister, pharaoh snatched Sarah for his harem. God intervened to prevent any sexual misconduct from occurring, but the whole fiasco left a bad taste in Abraham's mouth. He was forced to leave the land red-faced, rebuked by a pagan king for his deceit. It was a thoroughly embarrassing, humiliating ordeal (Genesis 12:10-20).

As he prepares to exit the promised land, Jacob surely remembers the stories of his grandfather and uncle. Like Jacob, Lot and Abraham had fled Canaan for the richness of Egypt because of famine. In so doing, they had marched right out of the will of God . . . and had suffered the consequences. Is Jacob making the same terrible error? Does God really want him to go to the land of Egypt? Make no mistake—Jacob's heart is in Egypt already. He strongly desires to cross the border. After all, Joseph is on the other side! But is that where the Lord would have him to go? As you can see, it is quite a dilemma. Let's take a look at Genesis 46 and see how the problem is solved.

Making Sure—Genesis 46:1-7

> So Israel set out with all that was his, and when he reached Beersheba, he offered sacrifices to the God of his father Isaac.
>
> And God spoke to Israel in a vision at night and said, "Jacob! Jacob!"
>
> "Here I am," he replied.
>
> "I am God, the God of your father," he said. "Do

> not be afraid to go down to Egypt, for I will make you into a great nation there. I will go down to Egypt with you, and I will surely bring you back again. And Joseph's own hand will close your eyes."
>
> Then Jacob left Beersheba, and Israel's sons took their father Jacob and their children and their wives in the carts that Pharaoh had sent to transport him. They also took with them their livestock and the possessions they had acquired in Canaan, and Jacob and all his offspring went to Egypt. He took with him to Egypt his sons and grandsons and his daughters and granddaughters—all his offspring.

When we truly seek to know God's will in a situation, he is faithful to make it known to us. Most likely we'll find the riches of his wisdom as we peruse his word. Perhaps circumstances will develop that will leave us no alternative except to make certain choices. Maybe the answer to a problem will come to us as we faithfully pray. The point is, if we are open to his leading, we shall know, in time, what he wants us to do and where he wants us to go (John 10:4,27).

As we've discussed, Jacob has to find out if he is doing the right thing in leading his family out of the destitution of Canaan into the plenty of Egypt. Scripture tells us that at Beersheba, some forty miles south of Hebron, he stops and offers sacrifices to the Lord (46:1). Why does Jacob choose this location? For one, he is familiar with the area, as it was at this place that he lived with Isaac, Rebekah, and Esau. The region is filled with memories; here Esau sold Jacob his birthright for a mess of stew. Perhaps more important, this stopover provides Jacob with a final glimpse of home. Beersheba is not far from the southern boundary of the land, and is one of the last places the Israelites will pass through before they cross the border of Egypt. Before he takes an uncertain, possibly irrevocable, step in entering Egypt, Jacob must ascertain that leaving is what he should do. This is his last opportunity to make sure.

The Desires of Our Hearts

I admire Jacob's wisdom and self-control in laying the decision before the Lord as he does. If you had asked him in Hebron what would satisfy him emotionally, what would fill his heart, what would make him positively ecstatic, he would have probably replied something like, "All I want is to see my boy Joseph before I die. This alone would make me the happiest man around." Emotionally, he's ready to ride into Egypt. His heart is there. His son is there! Yet he's learned what we all should: when we respond to circumstances on a purely emotional level, and we do not prayerfully and objectively consider things from God's perspective, we're inviting trouble. And sometimes, it's big trouble!

Psalm 37 says, "Delight yourself in the Lord; and He will give you the desires of your heart" (37:4 NASB). The verse is often misinterpreted to mean that as long as we trust the Lord, we'll receive every material thing we want, but this is not the case.

Just as God will not give us all our physical wants, so also we mustn't assume that our emotional wants are necessarily within the boundaries of his will. As parents, we're terrific at pointing out that principle to our kids. If they fall head over heels for a boyfriend or girlfriend whose suitability we question, we're quick to caution, "Now, you be sure to pray about this. Don't become so emotionally involved with him (or her) that you'll make a decision you'll regret for the rest of your life." Despite our inclination to point out the dangers of rash decisions to our children, often we plunge into similar sorts of rapid-fire mistakes ourselves—changing jobs, churches, or spouses because we feel unfulfilled. We figure God wants us to be happy, so anything goes. But Psalm 37 doesn't say that.

What the psalm does say is this: if we are delighting ourselves in the Lord, then we will honestly want the things he wants for us. What we desire for ourselves will be what he desires for us. He will work on our hearts, molding, shaping, snipping, prodding, poking, so that his wishes and our wants will be in harmony. We'll be able to say to him, "Thy will be done," and we will mean it.

Jacob's heart is in Egypt. His body is in Canaan, and it's going to stay there until he is convinced of God's plan and purpose. It's time to approach the master in prayer.

At the Altar

Night falls after Jacob offers sacrifices to the Lord at Beersheba. In the midst of the blackness, the voice of God rings out from the heavens, calling "Jacob! Jacob!" (46:2).

"Here I am," the old man immediately answers (46:2). Remember that decades earlier, as Jacob fled the anger of Esau and prepared to leave Canaan for the home of his uncle in Paddan-Aram, God met him at the top of a ladder in a vision at Bethel. Then the Lord promised Jacob that he would be with him, would keep him, would bring him back into the promised land (Genesis 28:15). Everything came true. Now, as Jacob is ready to leave the land and live out the remaining years of his existence in a foreign country, God appears once more to offer reassurance and counsel.

Notice that God calls Jacob by name in verse 2. What a wonderful thing it is to read scripture and realize that he knows each of us by name as well! "What are you doing here, Elijah?" he questions his prophet (1 Kings 19:9). "Samuel! Samuel!" he calls to his servant (1 Samuel 3:10). We are his beloved children—not groups or numbers, but names and individuals distinctly catalogued in his memory.

Jacob hears and recognizes his master's voice. Oh yes, God comes to us in times when we're thirsting for his will. We won't hear voices out of heaven, but we'll hear his voice as we read his word. If we're in fellowship with the Lord, we'll be amazed at how scripture comes alive to speak to the reader about critical decisions. The wisdom of the word is able to protect us from making miserable mistakes and from straying from God's perfect will. Our job is to listen, learn, and live within the protective custody of his plan for us.

The Protection and Provision of Providence

"I am God, the God of your father," the Lord continues speaking in Jacob's vision. "Do not be afraid to go down to Egypt, for I will make you into a great nation there" (46:3). Jacob's provision will no longer be found in Canaan, but in Egypt. Even though he doesn't understand it fully, by leaving the promised land, Jacob is lining up with God's purpose. It is the beginning of the fulfillment of the Lord's promise to Abraham in Genesis 15:13-14, where God informed the patriarch:

> Know for certain that your descendants will be strangers in a country not their own, and they will be enslaved and mistreated four hundred years. But I will punish the nation they serve as slaves, and afterward they will come out with great possessions.

The "country not their own" is Egypt. Abraham's descendants are those in Jacob's extended family, and all who will be born after them. God is going to provide for Jacob and family. He is going to protect them; he always does. He is the same Lord who, back in Genesis 15:1, tells a quivering Abraham who has miraculously rescued Lot from five enemy kings, "Do not fear . . . I am a shield to you; Your reward shall be very great" (NASB). He is the same God who sent an angel of mercy to tell the apostle Paul, whose vessel was thrashed about by the violent waves of a turbulent storm, "Do not be afraid,

Paul; you must stand before Caesar; and behold, God has granted you all those who are sailing with you" (Acts 27:24 NASB). Jacob! Jacob! It's all right to go to Egypt. Your sons, daughters, grandsons, granddaughters, will flourish there. They'll form an immense nation, a special people! Get a move on! You've got a green light from God to proceed.

Not only will God provide for Jacob and the children of Israel in Egypt, but Jacob will never be alone, either. "I will go down to Egypt with you," says the Lord, "and I will surely bring you back again. And Joseph's own hand will close your eyes" (46:4). The Lord will be with Jacob. Joseph will be there, too. How comforting God's words must be to the elderly man. But there is another message in the statement. The over two hundred miles which Jacob has left to go to reach the land of Egypt will be his final long journey alive. It's to be a one-way trip, physically. He'll die in the foreign land, but Joseph will be at his side, gently closing the lids of his eyes as their life and luster fade in death. Jacob's body will be brought back to Hebron for burial, but he will never set foot in the promised land again as long as he lives.

Resuming the Journey

I imagine with dawn's early light, Jacob is anxious to move. He realizes he will probably die in Egypt, but at least it will be in the arms of his beloved son. Verse 5 tells us that Jacob, his sons, and their wives and children climb back into the wagons and resume the trip. We also read that they take with them "their livestock and the possessions they had acquired in Canaan" (46:6).

Didn't pharaoh instruct Joseph that his family should bring nothing into their new land? Hadn't he made it clear that the Israelites would be the guests of the government, that their needs would be fully met with the best Egypt had to offer? Indeed, he did, but Jacob chooses to bring his possessions and animals anyway. Perhaps he still believes he must do something to earn his way; maybe he wants to avoid feeling like a charity case; it might be that some of the possessions he's acquired in his years in Canaan have become special, and he's sentimental. Whatever the case, he's on his way, and all his offspring are along for the ride (46:7).

THE FAMILY RECORD—GENESIS 46:8-27

> These are the names of the Israelites (Jacob and his descendants) who went to Egypt:
> Reuben the firstborn of Jacob.
> The sons of Reuben:
> Hanoch, Pallu, Hezron and Carmi.
> The sons of Simeon:
> Jemuel, Jamin, Ohad, Jakin, Zohar and Shaul the son of a Canaanite woman.
> The sons of Levi:
> Gershon, Kohath and Merari.
> The sons of Judah:
> Er, Onan, Shelah, Perez and Zerah (but Er and Onan had died in the land of Canaan).
> The sons of Perez:
> Hezron and Hamul.
> The sons of Issachar:
> Tola, Puah, Jashub and Shimron.
> The sons of Zebulun:
> Sered, Elon and Jahleel.
> These were the sons Leah bore to Jacob in Paddan-Aram, besides his daughter Dinah. These sons and daughters of his were thirty-three in all.
> The sons of Gad:
> Zephon, Haggi, Shuni, Ezbon, Eri, Arodi and Areli.
> The sons of Asher:
> Imnah, Ishvah, Ishvi and Beriah.
> Their sister was Serah.
> The sons of Beriah:
> Heber and Malkiel.
> These were the children born to Jacob by Zilpah,

> whom Laban had given to his daughter Leah—sixteen in all.
>
> The sons of Jacob's wife Rachel:
>
> Joseph and Benjamin. In Egypt, Manasseh and Ephraim were born to Joseph by Asenath daughter of Potiphera, priest of On.
>
> The sons of Benjamin:
>
> Bela, Beker, Ashbel, Gera, Nasman, Ehi, Rosh, Muppim, Huppim and Ard.
>
> These were the sons of Rachel who were born to Jacob—fourteen in all.
>
> The son of Dan:
>
> Hushim.
>
> The sons of Naphtali:
>
> Jahziel, Guni, Jezer and Shillem.
>
> These were the sons born to Jacob by Bilhah, whom Laban had given his daughter Rachel—seven in all.
>
> All those who went to Egypt with Jacob—those who were his direct descendants, not counting his sons' wives—numbered sixty-six persons. With the two sons who had been born to Joseph in Egypt, the members of Jacob's family, which went to Egypt, were seventy in all.

Like the passenger list of any tour, cruise, or airline flight, the Bible includes a detailed record of the family members who accompany Jacob into the land of Egypt. It's tempting to skip over verses 8-25 of Genesis 46—computer printouts of the names of travelers are not the stuff of morning devotions and silent meditations. But it would be a mistake to ignore God's specific record keeping in this (or any) section of scripture. He had a purpose in prompting Moses, the author of Genesis, to list the names of the children of Israel who journeyed to Egypt to join Joseph.

Verses 8-12 list the offspring of the first four of Leah's sons: Reuben, Simeon, Levi, and Judah. The four oldest of Jacob's sons have produced eighteen boys in all, not to mention Judah's two grandsons, Hezron and Hamul (46:12). Two of the eighteen have already died, however. As verse 12 reveals, Judah's life has been touched by tragedy.

Er and Onan, the first- and second-born sons of Judah, are not alive to witness the wonderful family reunion about to happen in Egypt. I often wonder how their deaths affected Judah. In the last few chapters of Genesis, he has emerged as a self-sacrificing intercessor. He has shown himself willing to become a substitute, offering to endure Benjamin's punishment. He is seen as a sensitive, compassionate, caring individual, well deserving of the name given him, which means "praise" (Genesis 29:35). How tenderhearted, how unselfish, how tuned in to God, would Judah have been had he not suffered the tragic loss of two boys? Before the deaths of Er and Onan, he was more than willing to sell Joseph into slavery. With the tempering forces of time and tragedy, he has become a different man.

Like Judah, when we experience hurts in our life, we can be sure that the Lord will give us a chance to be triumphant in our circumstances. He'll provide us with opportunities to use our personal tragedies to minister to others. For example, if we suffer the loss of a spouse, we will be able to understand the torment of another who is separated from a loved one through death or divorce. If the empty-nest syndrome hits as our kids marry or go off to college, we'll be able to console others in the same situation. If our finances take a nosedive during an economic downturn, we'll be able to comfort the person who's lost everything through a bad investment. When life hands us lemons, God is perfectly capable of making lemonade with them, if only we'll respond properly in the squeeze and allow him to! Judging by the fruit we see in his life, evidently Judah has done just that.

Scripture continues its passenger list by naming the seven sons of Issachar and Zebulun. With the mention of

Jacob's daughter Dinah, the names of the children and grandchildren of Leah (thirty-three in all) are concluded (46:15). How gracious of the Lord to honor Leah, the unloved wife, by listing her children first in the text. Not only that but, as the names resume, we see that the children of Zilpah, Leah's handmaid, are given next. These seven sons of Gad and four sons, one daughter, and two grandsons of Asher, were technically considered the offspring of Leah, according to custom. And so we see that Leah's side of the marriage triangle that she was forced into with Jacob and Rachel has produced some forty-nine members of the family tree. While not blessed with marital bliss, Leah could at least claim to have the most offspring.

In comparison to Leah's, as we approach Rachel's side of the family record, we almost need to start subtracting. There are so few. As we already know, Joseph is the father of only two sons: Manasseh and Ephraim (46:20). Benjamin, on the other hand, has been more prolific, siring ten boys (46:21).

The sons and grandsons of Rachel's handmaid, Bilhah, are mentioned next (46:23-24), bringing the head count on Rachel's side of the family to twenty-one. And so it is that, in the company of sixty-six sons, daughters, and grandchildren, plus an assortment of daughters-in-law, Jacob journeys into Egypt. There Joseph, Manasseh, Ephraim, and Jacob himself will bring the number to a nice, round seventy.

Why is God so specific in enumerating the children of Israel? It is because they are supposed to remain a separate people, not intermarrying with other nationalities, forming a special nation all their own. Each generation will be able to trace its roots to the original passenger list of Genesis 46. It will be four hundred years before the children of Israel, then under the leadership of Moses, make the mass exodus from Egypt. The remarkable thing about the return trip to Canaan is that, although over sixty went in to Egypt in the first place, over six hundred thousand eventually emerge (Exodus 12:37), and that's counting only the men.

Father and Son—Genesis 46:28-34

> Now Jacob sent Judah ahead of him to Joseph to get directions to Goshen. When they arrived in the region of Goshen, Joseph had his chariot made ready and went to Goshen to meet his father Israel. As soon as Joseph appeared before him, he threw his arms around his father and wept for a long time.
>
> Israel said to Joseph, "Now I am ready to die, since I have seen for myself that you are still alive."
>
> Then Joseph said to his brothers and to his father's household, "I will go up and speak to Pharaoh and will say to him, 'My brothers and my father's household, who were living in the land of Canaan, have come to me. The men are shepherds; they tend livestock, and they have brought along their flocks and herds and everything they own.' When Pharaoh calls you in and asks, "What is your occupation?' you should answer, 'Your servants have tended livestock from our boyhood on, just as our fathers did.' Then you will be allowed to settle in the region of Goshen, for all shepherds are detestable to the Egyptians."

As the wagon train rolls into Egypt, Jacob sends Judah ahead to find out directions to Goshen. The fact that Judah is chosen for this task illustrates how Jacob has begun to depend upon him, to lean on him because in recent years he has proved to be such an effective servant. It's exciting how God can turn our lives around if only we let him!

I imagine that as soon as Judah arrives at the nearest watering hole and asks the way to Goshen, Joseph gets wind of it. Undoubtedly he drops everything and orders his servants to bring around his chariot. Then, as rapidly as flying horses' hooves will carry him, he makes tracks for the land of Goshen, some seventy-five miles away from his home in Memphis. His father and brothers are already there when Joseph drives his royal chariot into the region (46:28-29).

What an emotional scene follows! Verse 29 tells us that when Joseph appears before Jacob, he throws his arms around his dear father. Sobs gush forth again, and the weeping goes on for a long time (46:29). Finally, words are spoken.

"Now I am ready to die," says Jacob tenderly to the son he has missed so much, "since I have seen for myself that you are still alive" (46:30). Catching a glimpse of Joseph is enough. Jacob is now ready to enter his eternal home. The touching scene foreshadows a later one, recorded in Luke 2. There an old man named Simeon cradles a baby in his arms; the child is none other than the infant Jesus Christ. Simeon has waited all his life to see his savior, and at last his eyes behold the messiah. "Now Lord, Thou dost let Thy bond-servant depart/In peace according to Thy Word," he exclaims (Luke 2:29 NASB). Satisfaction—how sweet it is!

Just imagine what thoughts pierce Jacob's mind and wrench his heart during these moments of reunion with Joseph. Twenty-two years of sadness are washed away. Now the dreams Joseph had while still a lad are fulfilled. It must be with a mingling of regret and joy that Jacob embraces his son. The years of separation cannot be retrieved, but perhaps he will yet have time to spend with his boy. If not, it is enough that he has seen him.

Instructions

Following the touching moments with his father, Joseph turns to his brothers and considers the business at hand. The family must be presented to pharaoh, and the manner in which they address him is important. Joseph has surveyed the land of Egypt, and the region of Goshen—where he intends for his relatives to settle—is ideal for ranching. The fact that Egyptians do not like to mix and mingle with shepherds and the fact that Goshen is not a favorite region of pharaoh (Unger 420) mean the Israelites are likely to be left alone if they settle there. It is an ideal spot to build a nation in relative isolation. Yet pharaoh might have other ideas. Perhaps he'll want Joseph's family to dwell in his capital. The brothers' answers will determine their fate.

Joseph reveals his game plan to the family. First he will approach pharaoh and inform him of his relatives' arrival. Then he will explain that the clan members make their living by tending livestock, and have brought along their flocks and herds (46:31-32). The brothers are to reiterate this, and the information should prompt pharaoh to allow them to settle in Goshen (46:34). There they'll be able to stay together—close enough to Joseph, yet far enough away from the influence of Egyptian society to remain a separate people. As we come to Genesis 47, we'll see if Joseph's strategy works.

Presentation at the White House—Genesis 47:1-12

> Joseph went and told Pharaoh, "My father and brothers, with their flocks and herds and everything they own, have come from the land of Canaan and are now in Goshen." He chose five of his brothers and presented them before Pharaoh.
>
> Pharaoh asked the brothers, "What is your occupation?"
>
> "Your servants are shepherds," they replied to Pharaoh, "just as our fathers were." They also said to him, "We have come to live here awhile, because the famine is severe in Canaan and your servants' flocks have no pasture. So now, please let your servants settle in Goshen."
>
> Pharaoh said to Joseph, "Your father and your brothers have come to you, and the land of Egypt is before you; settle your father and your brothers in the best part of the land. Let them live in Goshen. And if you know of any among them with special

> ability, put them in charge of my own livestock."
>
> Then Joseph brought his father Jacob in and presented him before Pharaoh. After Jacob blessed Pharaoh, Pharaoh asked him, "How old are you?"
>
> And Jacob said to Pharaoh, "The years of my pilgrimage are a hundred and thirty. My years have been few and difficult, and they do not equal the years of the pilgrimage of my fathers." Then Jacob blessed Pharaoh and went out from his presence.
>
> So Joseph settled his father and his brothers in Egypt and gave them property in the best part of the land, the district of Rameses, as Pharaoh directed. Joseph also provided his father and his brothers and all his father's household with food, according to the number of their children.

Joseph, accompanied by some, perhaps all, of his brothers and Jacob, returns to the capital city of Memphis. There he makes a progress report to pharaoh, informing the ruler, "My father and brothers, with their flocks and herds and everything they own, have come from the land of Canaan and are now in Goshen" (47:1).

Verse 2 reveals that Joseph next selects five of his brothers and presents them to pharaoh. It is an honor as great as being invited to Buckingham Palace for an audience with the queen. The text doesn't specify which brothers are chosen, but I would guess that he picks the four oldest: Reuben, Simeon, Levi, and Judah, plus Benjamin. "What is your occupation?" questions pharaoh of the five (47:3).

"Your servants are shepherds, just as our fathers were," reply the brothers, carefully following Joseph's earlier directions (47:3; see 46:34). "We have come to live here awhile, because the famine is severe in Canaan and your servants' flocks have no pasture," they continue. "So now, please let your servants settle in Goshen" (47:4). They come right out with the subject of Goshen—no hemming or hawing here! The brothers are ready to resolve the matter. They're tired, emotionally and physically drained, and they'd like to get on with their lives in the new land. Besides, Goshen is the perfect place to resume their ranching operation.

Pharaoh no doubt peers into the faces of the brothers as they speak, but then he turns to Joseph to render his decision. "Your father and your brothers have come to you, and the land of Egypt is before you; settle your father and your brothers in the best part of the land. Let them live in Goshen" (47:5-6). The request is allowed, evidence once more of pharaoh's deep, abiding respect for Joseph, and his attitude of gratitude concerning all that his second-in-command has done. Obviously thinking of Joseph's tremendous skill and ability, pharaoh voices the thought that maybe such talent runs in the family. "And if you know," he says to Joseph concerning the brothers, "of any among them with special ability, put them in charge of my own livestock" (47:8). Not only may Joseph's people stay rent free in one of the lushest regions of Egypt, but if any among them is qualified, he can have a civil service job working for the government, tending pharaoh's flocks and herds!

Blessings and Passages

The next order of business is for Joseph to bring Jacob before the ruler, and this he does. Imagine the old man as he enters the presence of the king. I like to think of him riding in a palace wheelchair, pushed along by his proud son. Maybe he just shuffles in, clinging to Joseph. Or maybe he walks alone, haltingly, leaning upon his staff. Certainly he limps slightly from the wound in his thigh received in the wrestling match of long ago. He stops at the throne of pharaoh, and scripture tells us that he blesses the ruler (47:7).

Why does this patriarch of God's chosen people bless the pagan king of a foreign land? It is because Jacob is immensely grateful for all that pharaoh has done for his son Joseph. He is deeply appreciative of the ruler's willingness to allow his family to settle in Egypt. He is a man whose heart is filled with gratitude, and he very humbly blesses pharaoh for the part the king has had in making life so beautiful for Joseph, and for the whole family.

"How old are you?" asks pharaoh (47:8), his question reflecting a respectful curiosity.

"The years of my pilgrimage are a hundred and thirty," answers Jacob. "My years have been few and difficult, and they do not equal the years of the pilgrimage of my fathers" (47:9). Archaeological finds suggest that such a reply followed the court etiquette of the day. In other words, it was proper for any visitor before pharaoh to humbly admit that his years had been few and difficult. But in Jacob's case, court protocol reflects reality. His life has been harsh; his age has not equaled that of either Isaac, Abraham, or great-grandfather Terah.

Again Jacob blesses pharaoh, and takes leave of the ruler. The entire scene shows us that the family patriarch is turning over the business end of things to his sons. It is an inevitable rite of passage that each of us will one day experience. We will find the roles we've assumed in dealing with our children reversing. They will become the nine-to-fivers while we will slowly relinquish our authority. Jacob speaks not a word of family business to pharaoh. This is left to his sons, particularly Joseph.

As we continue in Genesis 47, we read that Joseph does settle his family in Goshen, and gives them "property in the best part of the land, the district of Rameses, as Pharaoh directed" (47:11). Rameses is a city located in Goshen, some twenty-five miles south of the Mediterranean. It is in the midst of the Nile Delta region, and is also only some seventy-five miles north of Memphis, where Joseph is headquartered. They will be comfortably close to him.

Joseph doesn't stop with setting up his relatives with a fine piece of real estate. Verse 12 tells us that he also provides everyone with food. No favorites are played in this process; each brother receives provisions according to the number of children he has. And so life in Egypt begins for the children of Israel.

Drastic Measures—Genesis 47:13-26

> There was no food, however, in the whole region because the famine was severe; both Egypt and Canaan wasted away because of the famine. Joseph collected all the money that was to be found in Egypt and Canaan in payment for the grain they were buying, and he brought it to Pharaoh's palace. When the money of the people of Egypt and Canaan was gone, all Egypt came to Joseph and said, "Give us food. Why should we die before your eyes? Our money is used up."
>
> "Then bring your livestock," said Joseph. "I will sell you food in exchange for your livestock, since your money is gone." So they brought their livestock to Joseph, and he gave them food in exchange for their horses, their sheep and goats, their cattle and donkeys. And he brought them through that year with food in exchange for all their livestock.
>
> When that year was over, they came to him the following year and said, "We cannot hide from our lord the fact that since our money is gone and our livestock belongs to you, there is nothing left for our lord except our bodies and our land. Why should we perish before your eyes, we and our land as well? Buy us and our land in exchange for food, and we with our land will be in bondage to Pharaoh. Give us seed so that we may live and not die, and that the land may not become desolate."
>
> So Joseph bought all the land in Egypt for Pharaoh. The Egyptians, one and all, sold their fields, because the famine was too severe for them. The land became Pharaoh's, and Joseph reduced the people to servitude, from one end of Egypt to the

> other. However, he did not buy the land of the priests, because they received a regular allotment from Pharaoh and had food enough from the allotment Pharaoh gave them. That is why they did not sell their land.
>
> Joseph said to the people, "Now that I have bought you and your land today for Pharaoh, here is seed for you so you can plant the ground. But when the crop comes in, give a fifth of it to Pharaoh. The other four-fifths you may keep as seed for the fields and as food for yourselves and your households and your children."
>
> "You have saved our lives," they said. "May we find favor in the eyes of our lord; we will be in bondage to Pharaoh."
>
> So Joseph established it as a law concerning land in Egypt—still in force today—that a fifth of the produce belongs to Pharaoh. It was only the land of the priests that did not become Pharaoh's.

Once his family is settled in Goshen, Joseph finds he must direct his attention toward other urgent matters. The land of Egypt is in the midst of the remaining five years of economic disaster, and the situation is desperate. Verse 13 tells us that both Egypt and Canaan are wasting away because of the severity of the famine. Had Jacob and his sons stubbornly remained in Hebron, they'd be knocking on death's door by now. Instead, they dwell in safety and plenty, for Joseph has scheduled grain appropriations to be transported north to Rameses on a regular basis. He is taking care of his own.

Dwindling Resources

The rest of the country is not so fortunate. The citizens have emptied their pockets and depleted all their cash. Money does little to fill an empty stomach, so they have freely used all their financial resources to purchase grain from Joseph (47:14). Now their savings are exhausted and they are frantic. Verse 15 reveals that they approach Joseph and beg of him, "Give us food. Why should we die before your eyes? Our money is used up."

"Then bring your livestock," Joseph replies (47:16), offering to accept their cattle, sheep, goats, horses, and donkeys in exchange for food. The Egyptians gladly agree to these conditions, and the transactions are completed. The citizens have enough food to make it through another year (47:16-17).

Perhaps you are wondering if the Egyptians truly agree gladly to trade away their livestock. I believe that they do. When a man must choose between feeding a starving family and feeding animals, there is really no alternative except to sacrifice the livestock. The flocks and herds are nothing more than an additional burden during a time of crisis, and Joseph is helping the people by releasing them from the extra responsibility. It is actually a relief for the people to sell their beasts.

How can I be so sure? It's because we experienced much the same thing at our ministry a few years ago. We had been given nineteen horses to be used at the camping facilities we hoped to obtain. The Lord hadn't seen fit to provide us with a permanent camp, and the horses were a constant drain on our finances. In order to be effective stewards of God's money, at the direction of our board we sold the animals. It was a conservation move, an it helped us survive financially. Especially in retrospect, I am glad we sold the horses. Although it was a difficult decision, it was the right thing to do, and it has truly been a relief.

Another year of famine passes quickly, and the people of Egypt again come to Joseph clamoring for food. "We cannot hide from our lord the fact that since our money is gone and our livestock belongs to you, there is nothing for our lord except our bodies and our land," the Egyptians reason. "Why should we perish before your eyes—we and our land as well? Buy us and our land in exchange for food, and we with our land will be in bondage to Pharaoh. Give us seed so that we may live and not die, and that the land may not become desolate," they plead (47:18-19). And Joseph complies (47:20-21).

Working to Make It Work

Notice, the people come up with the idea of selling their real estate and themselves to pharaoh in exchange for food. It is not Joseph's brainstorm, although he probably thinks it a good plan. The citizens have no choice, and so Joseph purchases their land and alters their status to that of servants of the king. This he does for every Egyptian except the priests, who receive a regular stipend from pharaoh and are not lacking for provisions (47:22).

Also notice, the people do not ask merely to be given food. Instead, they request seed in exchange for their land and service. They want to work; they want to make the land productive again. They're not asking the government to subsidize their lives with handouts; they're asking for the chance to help themselves. It is a matter of dignity. Joseph recognizes this and sells them seed according to the conditions they have suggested. When the crops are harvested, the people are directed to give a fifth of the produce to pharaoh. The rest they may keep as food for their families and seed for future planting seasons (47:23-24).

These Egyptians continue to amaze me. They didn't complain when Joseph sold them grain at the beginning of the famine. They don't grumble now when they have to surrender land, livestock, and themselves. Their attitude is so drastically different from many today. Through state and federal subsistence programs, we're making it very easy for people to be able to exist in America without lifting a finger, and this I can tell you from personal experience.

Only a short time ago we were interviewing candidates for a bookkeeping position in our office. One woman had excellent references and substantial experience. When I asked if she'd be interested in the job, she replied, "Mr. Anderson, I have to be honest with you. The salary has to be X number of dollars [she named a figure], or it isn't worth it for me to work for you because my unemployment is this much [another figure]." I was shocked that the amount she collected on unemployment was more than we were able to offer her at the time! So we didn't hire her and, naturally, that was fine with her because it was easier and more financially rewarding for her to stay at home.

The "welfare syndrome" in a nutshell is this: we pay to make it possible for people to do nothing. Please don't misinterpret what I'm saying. I am not suggesting that every assistance program be cut off, but perhaps we ought to take a long, hard look at what's happening in America. It is frightening to contemplate how soft we as a nation have become, while other countries around the world know what it's like to sacrifice in order to survive. We seem more concerned with standards of living than with standing on our own two feet! Our attitudes are not biblical. We demand, "Give me, give me, give me," rather than asking, "What can I give, how can I sacrifice, where can I conserve?"

Joseph handles five years of economic crisis in an incredible way—no giveaways, no free rides. He even institutes a tax on production throughout the land of Egypt, and it works. It remains in effect at the time Moses pens Genesis, centuries later (47:26). And nobody complains. The people approach Joseph with heartfelt gratitude. "You have saved our lives," they exclaim (47:25). They're not stupid; they're just men and women who have survived a devastating crisis—pride intact, dignity preserved.

Last Wishes and Worship—Genesis 47:27-31

> Now the Israelites settled in Egypt in the region of Goshen. They acquired property there and were fruitful and increased greatly in number.
>
> Jacob lived in Egypt seventeen years, and the

> years of his life were a hundred and forty-seven. When the time drew near for Israel to die, he called his son Joseph and said to him, "If I have found favor in your eyes, put your hand under my thigh and promise that you will show me kindness and faithfulness. Do not bury me in Egypt, but when I rest with my fathers, carry me out of Egypt and bury me where they are buried."
>
> "I will do as you say," he said.
>
> "Swear to me," he said. Then Joseph swore to him, and Israel worshiped as he leaned on the top of his staff.

Thanks to Joseph, Jacob and family remain free from the economic hardships experienced in the rest of Egypt. Verse 27 states that the Israelites acquire property in Goshen and increase greatly in number. They literally multiply, and provide us with a beautiful picture of life flourishing in the center of God's will.

Seventeen years pass, and Jacob reaches the ripe old age of 147. He's survived five years of famine and has enjoyed twelve prosperous years in the new land. He realizes that he is failing, however, and that the time of his physical demise is near. He is not afraid to die, but there are preparations to make before the funeral, and he begins to deal with these at the close of Genesis 47.

First, there is the matter of his burial. Jacob calls Joseph to his side. "Do not bury me in Egypt," he asks his favorite son, "but when I rest with my fathers, carry me out of Egypt and bury me where they are buried" (47:29-30). It's been nice while it lasted, but in the end, Egypt is not home. Jacob desires to be laid to rest in more familiar surroundings: beside the graves of Abraham and Isaac. Leah is there, too. God had promised Jacob that he would return to Canaan, albeit after Joseph had "closed his eyes" (46:4). The elderly patriarch just wants to make sure his son understands instructions.

Joseph immediately agrees to his father's request.

"Swear to me," Jacob insists, earlier having asked Joseph to place his hand on his thigh while vowing to fulfill these last wishes (47:31; see 29). And this the obedient son does. The chapter closes with a picture of Jacob, leaning on his staff, worshiping God.

This chapter ends as it began, with an act of worship. In Genesis 46:1, Jacob detours by Beersheba and sacrifices to God in an attempt to discern his will about leaving Canaan. Now, as he reaches the end of his earthly days, he worships again. It's been seventeen years of fruitfulness, joy, and prosperity in the company of his favorite son. Ironically, Joseph spent only the first seventeen years of his own life with Jacob, and they are able only to spend the final seventeen of Jacob's earthly pilgrimage together. But it is enough. It is sufficient. And Jacob is getting ready to go out in a blaze of glory.

LESSONS

Eight lessons emerge from these two chapters of scripture. Let's examine them briefly.

Lesson one: *Jacob wants to be certain that he is in the center of God's will before leaving Canaan.* When we're getting ready to make decisions, it's essential to consult our heavenly father first.

Lesson two: *the Lord responds to our fears through his word.* When we find ourselves quaking in our boots, we are able to turn to the promises of the word of God and know that he will speak to us there.

Lesson three: *the Lord gives the best to those who leave the choice to him.* It is far better for Jacob to follow God's leading into Egypt than stubbornly to refuse to budge from Canaan. It's best to let the choice be his, in all matters.

Lesson four: *what peace and blessing come when we surrender to God's eternal purposes!* Jacob spends seventeen glorious years completely in the center of God's will and, as his life draws to a close, he feels fully satisfied.

Lesson five: *Joseph cares for his father in the latter's old age.* We have the same sort of responsibility toward our own parents.

Lesson six: *as in the early years of the famine, there are no government giveaway programs in Joseph's economic agenda for the nation of Egypt.*

Lesson seven: *if we're Christians, we'll come face to face with the Lord and echo the words the citizens of Egypt exclaim to Joseph, "You have saved our lives!"* Amen to that one!

Lesson eight: the passage we've studied begins and concludes with scenes of worship. *Do we begin and end major events of our lives seeking God's will and praising him as Jacob did? Do we begin and end our days with prayer and praise?* Test your hearts on that one, and look at your schedules. God wants to hear from you.

Leaning on the Staff

As Genesis 46 closes, I can picture white-headed old Jacob leaning against his staff, can't you? As he clutches his wooden support, anticipating his final journey home, he probably peers intently into Joseph's eyes, and then scans the lush countryside where he has dwelt. Thoughts of the one true God—the God who keeps his promises, the God who never changes—comfortably cross his mind. And I can almost hear him singing these words of praise:

> There's a land that is fairer than day,
> And by faith we can see it afar;
> For the Father waits over the way,
> To prepare us a dwelling place there.
>
> *Refrain* In the sweet by and by
> We shall meet on that beautiful shore
> In the sweet by and by
> We shall meet on that beautiful shore.

We shall sing on that beautiful shore
The melodious songs of the blest,
And our spirits shall sorrow no more,
Not a sigh for the blessing of rest.

To our bountiful Father above
We will offer our tribute of praise.
For the glorious gift of His love
And the blessings that hallow our days.
(S.F. Bennett and J.P. Webster,
"Sweet By and By")

Questions for Study

1. Why does Jacob stop at Beersheba before leaving the land of Canaan? What does his action tell us about the need to consult the Lord before taking important steps?

2. In your own words, explain the meaning of Psalm 37:4: "Delight yourself in the Lord; and He will give you the desires of your heart" (NASB).

3. What is reassuring to us about the fact that God calls Jacob by name in verse 2?

4. Judah's life has been touched by tragedy; he has suffered the loss of two sons. In what ways may our own attitudes, outlooks, and actions change after we too are touched by tragedy?

5. In your opinion, is Joseph unjust in requiring the Egyptians to purchase food during the crisis? Why or why not?

10

Nearing the Finishing Line

Genesis 48

But age, with his stealing steps, Hath claw'd me in his clutch," sings Shakespeare's clown in *Hamlet* (V.i, 79-80). "I don't feel old. I feel like a young guy that something happened to," writes author Mickey Spillane. Both Shakespeare and Spillane have a point: old age sneaks up on us while we remain, to a large extent, blissfully unaware of its encroachment. Yes, there are the usual wrinkles, gray hairs, paunch . . . but nothing major. Then comes the awful day when we realize we're no longer on top of the mountain, but slipping down the other side.

I recall the first time I felt old. It was earlier this year (so I can still remember it). One morning I couldn't see well enough to find my glasses, I forgot where I was planning to go, and I didn't hear the phone ring. At age fifty-four, I'm reaching the stage where, to paraphrase Dana Robbins, actions are starting to creak louder than words. And I'm starting to think that growing old isn't necessarily a pleasant experience. In fact, it can be downright traumatic.

I guess my acceptance of maturity is helped by the fact that other people think I'm getting up there. Evidently the American Association of Retired Persons figures I'm their kind of guy, because my AARP card came in the mail the other day. Three or four days after the card arrived, the postman delivered the AARP catalogue to our door, so it was a double trauma. I flipped the book open to see what retired persons read, and the first thing I saw was a page of coupons for discounts on moisture retention cream and deep-heating rub. I'm too young to be old!

Of course, I'm not the only one to have felt that way. Even some of the great men of scripture bewailed the aches and pains of aging. In the book of Ecclesiastes, for example, Solomon describes old age as a stretch of great physical infirmity. As he puts it, it's the time . . .

> when the keepers of the house tremble,
>   and the strong men stoop,
> when the grinders cease because they are few,
>   and those looking through the windows grow dim;
> when the doors to the street are closed
>   and the sound of grinding fades;
> when men rise up at the sound of birds,
>   but all their songs grow faint;
> when men are afraid of heights
>   and of dangers in the streets;
> when the almond tree blossoms
>   and the grasshopper drags himself along
>   and desire no longer is stirred.
>
> (Ecclesiastes12:3-5)

If Solomon's allusions seem vague, look more closely. The "keepers of the house" to which he refers are the arms and legs. Old people become weak, it's hard to keep a steady hand, and often it's difficult to walk without a cane. The "strong men" that "stoop" are the shoulders. Just look at your eighty-year-old relative and see if her shoulders aren't bent a bit. The "grinders" that "cease" are the teeth, and you don't have to be a dentist to know that the bridge over troubled waters is something many old folks wear in their mouths! The eyes are described as "those looking through the windows" which "grow dim." Have you ever met an octogenarian with 20/20 vision? They are few and far between. Instead they corner the market in bifocals and large-print Bibles.

Our hearing is affected as we age, also. Many sounds seem muffled, distant, as if the "doors to the street are closed," and it seems even loud noises, like the "sound of grinding," fade. Curiously, although much environmental noise congeals into an indistinguishable hum, the elderly sometimes become sharply sensitive to small sounds. It becomes more difficult to sleep. The chirping of crickets pierces the auditory fog with annoying clarity, and men even "rise up at the sound of birds," awakening at the least warble from the throat of a songbird outside.

The eyesight falters, the hearing fades . . . and the voice also gives way as we age. Many a church choir director patiently puts up with a dear little old lady whose clear soprano voice has become a crackly ghost of its former glory.

Old age is also a time of increasing fear—fear of "heights and of dangers in the streets." It's difficult to climb a ladder. It can be terrifying to take a nighttime walk or go for a drive after dark. Muggers and thieves prey upon the elderly, yes, but at the heart of the matter is a loss of confidence in one's ability to cope. A young man, assured of his capacity to defend himself, swaggers anywhere. An old man, fully cognizant of his frailties, has to be more careful.

Our appearances change as we age, too. Solomon uses the white blooms of the almond tree to symbolize the white hair that sprouts upon the head of the elderly. Like grasshoppers—thin, delicate, fragile—very old people drag themselves along. And, perhaps worst of all, "desire no longer is stirred." Food doesn't taste as good any more, and we aren't able to eat as much of it. Sex and other sensual pleasures simply aren't as important. That is what it is to grow old.

With the Finish Line in View

In Ecclesiastes, Solomon also writes that old age is when "man goes to his eternal home and mourners go about the streets" (12:5). As we open to Genesis 48, Jacob is there. He is 147 years old. Life has been tough, and he is worn out. The last seventeen years have been joyous ones for him, though. He's been in the center of God's will in Egypt. All twelve of his sons live near him—most in his immediate camp. His clan has increased as babies have been born to his grandsons, granddaughters, and their spouses. Surely Joseph's two sons, Manasseh and Ephraim, have brought special happiness into his life, too, as they have visited him, and he has watched them grow into young manhood.

At the close of chapter 47, we left Jacob leaning against his staff, worshiping. He makes a final request of Joseph, and this is that his body be returned to Canaan for burial. Now, as the curtain opens on Genesis 48, Jacob's health has worsened; indeed, he clings to a slender thread of life. His time is near, very near, and he slowly, yet inexorably, approaches the finish line.

At the Bedside of a Dying Father—Genesis 48:1-7

> Some time later Joseph was told, "Your father is ill." So he took his two sons Manasseh and Ephraim along with him. When Jacob was told, "Your son Joseph has come to you," Israel rallied his strength and sat up on the bed.
>
> Jacob said to Joseph, "God Almighty appeared to me at Luz in the land of Canaan, and there he blessed me and said to me, 'I am going to make you fruitful and will increase your numbers. I will make you a community of peoples, and I will give

> this land as an everlasting possession to your descendants after you.'
>
> "Now then, your two sons born to you in Egypt before I came to you here will be reckoned as mine; Ephraim and Manasseh will be mine, just as Reuben and Simeon are mine. Any children born to you after them will be yours; in the territory they inherit they will be reckoned under the names of their brothers. As I was returning from Paddan, to my sorrow Rachel died in the land of Canaan while we were still on the way, a little distance from Ephrath. So I buried her there beside the road to Ephrath" (that is, Bethlehem).

Anticipating the Phone Call

When terminally ill loved ones teeter on the brink, our own lives come to a standstill. We wait as if in suspended animation for death, or remission, or perhaps recovery. Obligations may force us to be kept busy with the routine demands of life, but our minds and hearts are elsewhere. We think of the hospital bed, the IV tubes, the heart monitor, and we think of the fragile loved one so close to going to his eternal home. I know these feelings well.

My own dad passed away last spring following a lengthy bout with cancer. Through the years that he struggled with the disease, he—and we, his family—faced crisis after crisis. Miraculously, he survived years longer than expected. But eventually the doctors took him off all medication, and we became players drafted into an incredibly slow-paced, anguish-filled waiting game. For months, each time the phone rang, Pearl and I answered with the thought that this could be it. Every time we lifted the receiver, we wondered if it would be my mother calling to give us the dreaded news. Finally, one day, it was. Mom simply said, "He's gone."

This is how Joseph feels as Genesis 48 commences. We are not sure exactly how much time elapses between the close of Genesis 47 and the opening of 48, but it is clear that Jacob's condition has deteriorated markedly since we last saw him. Unable to neglect his administrative duties for too long, Joseph has had to return to Memphis and the office. As Pearl and I greeted each phone call with trepidation during the final months and weeks of my dad's illness, undoubtedly Joseph watches the horizon every day for a sign of a messenger riding to inform him that Jacob is nearing the end. One day, the message comes. "Your father is ill," Joseph is told (48:1). Immediately, he rounds up Manasseh and Ephraim and together they head for Goshen.

Rallying for the Finale

Many times even desperately ill people will experience a short burst of energy in the days before they succumb to the inevitable. Perhaps it is the coming of a special friend or family member that spurs the temporary show of strength. One instance in which I have found this to be true vividly stands out in my memory.

During the first year Don Anderson Ministries was in operation, I had the privilege of meeting a very precious couple, and of presenting the gospel to them. The husband became a Christian. A few years later, he was stricken with cancer. I visited him from time to time as the disease made its awful progression. One day word came that he had lapsed into a coma and that the end was extremely close. Circumstances were such that I was able to be in their city, so I made a trip to the hospital. The wife greeted me with this news, "He's been in a coma for seventeen hours and hasn't said anything. The doctors don't give him much time now."

She and I walked into the hospital room, and she leaned over toward her husband and whispered in his ear, "Don is here to see you." Surprisingly, he opened his eyes, sat up in bed, and said in a weak, joking voice, "Let's have a party!" We talked for a few moments and prayed together. Within twenty-four hours he was home with the Lord.

Much the same thing happens to Jacob when he gets wind that Joseph and his boys have arrived. Genesis 48:2 tells us that when he is told, "Your son Joseph has come to you," he rallies his strength and sits up on the bed. It is a final act of willpower.

The Past Flashing By

Something else that happens as death looms imminent is that the significant events of our lives parade through our consciousness. The past becomes vividly real; episodes long forgotten emerge with clarity from the recesses of our memories. Many extremely ill people have told me that this is true.

As Jacob nears the end, he begins to remember. He reminisces about three particularly important events that he has experienced during his many years. When Joseph first enters his father's sickroom, Jacob speaks to him, saying, "God Almighty appeared to me at Luz in the land of Canaan, and there he blessed me and said to me, 'I am going to make you fruitful and will increase your numbers. I will make you a community of peoples, and I will give this land as an everlasting possession to your descendants after you' " (48:4).

The first event that Jacob recalls is the meeting with God at the top of the stairs. It took place at the end of the day when Jacob fled from Beersheba and set out for Paddan-Aram to escape Esau, whose birthright he had stolen. He fell asleep at Luz (later called Bethel) and there had the vision we sing about as "Jacob's Ladder." Even before Jacob left home, his father Isaac bestowed this blessing:

> May God Almighty bless you and make you fruitful and increase your numbers until you become a community of peoples. May he give you and your

> descendants the blessing of Abraham, so that you may take possession of the land where you now live as an alien, the land God gave to Abraham (Genesis 28:3-4).

God, from the top of the stairway in Jacob's dream, later voiced these promises to the sleeping fugitive at Bethel:

> I will give you and your descendants the land on which you are lying. Your descendants will be like the dust of the earth, and you will spread out to the west and to the east, to the north and to the south. All peoples on earth will be blessed through you and your offspring. I am with you and will watch over you wherever you go, and I will bring you back to this land. I will not leave you until I have done what I have promised you (Genesis 28:13-15).

God's meaning at Bethel was clear. It would be Jacob who would inherit the promises first given to his grandfather Abraham in Genesis 12. He would be the father of a mighty nation, through whom all the "peoples on earth will be blessed" by the coming of a special descendant, Jesus Christ. And thus Jacob would figure prominently in God's plan for the world.

Jacob's vision of the Lord at the top of the stairs is important to him because it was the time in which these promises were officially given. Yet there is still another reason why the memory is of such great significance to the dying man. Jacob's dream at Bethel marked the first time he met God directly. It can be called the moment of his conversion, his coming to know the Lord as his creator, sustainer, and savior. It was his first real encounter with the living Lord. We know that it affected him, because the next day he built a crude altar at the spot and poured oil on it as an act of worship (Genesis 28:18).

Notice that when Jacob describes his memory to Joseph in Genesis 48, he speaks of the promised land in

God's covenant with him as "an everlasting possession." Isaac had not described the land as an everlasting possession in his blessing. Neither had God called it an everlasting possession at Bethel, although he had promised to give the land to Jacob and his descendants. It was earlier, in speaking with Abraham, that the Lord decreed that the promised land would belong to the Hebrew nation forever and ever.

In Genesis 17:8, we read God's words to Abraham, the first of the patriarchs, "The whole land of Canaan, where you are now an alien, I will give as an everlasting possession to you and your descendants after you; and I will be their God." Apparently, Jacob had learned of the eternal nature of the Lord's gift of the land as he sat at his grandfather's knee. It is a promise he holds dear as he faces his final hours. Neither should we overlook its importance. Reading Jacob's dying statement removes any doubt as to who is morally and biblically right in the modern Arab-Israeli conflict. The land by deed and title belongs eternally to the descendants of Abraham. Knowing this should make our choice of sides a foregone conclusion.

Notice also that when speaking to Joseph, Jacob calls the Lord "God Almighty," or *El Shaddai*, the all-powerful one. He is a God who is able and faithful to keep all his promises. It is this concept of the living father that Jacob chooses to share with his son on his deathbed. This is the God whom he knows, praises, and loves. This is the God in whom he desires Joseph to fully trust.

The Double Portion . . .

"Now then," Jacob continues to address his son, "your two sons born to you in Egypt before I came to you here will be reckoned as mine; Ephraim and Manasseh will be mine, just as Reuben and Simeon are mine" (48:5). Things become a bit technical here. Basically, Jacob is telling Joseph that he desires to adopt the two boys in his place. It was custom that when the patriarch of a clan died, the oldest son received a double portion of the inheritance. Instead of granting that double portion to his eldest son, Reuben, Jacob is transferring the honor to Joseph. As Joseph's offspring, Ephraim and Manasseh will receive a share of the family inheritance equal to that of each of Jacob's other sons. And so, the distribution of the double portion will go through the line of Joseph.

The question naturally arises, "Why not Reuben? Why is he bypassed as the rights of the firstborn are doled out?" It is because of an incident from his past—one that Jacob cannot forget, one that reflects a serious flaw in Reuben's character. We'll receive the explanation in the next chapter.

Eventually, the sons of Jacob will form twelve tribes composed of their descendants, and these twelve tribes will grow into the nation of Israel. Because their grandfather recognizes their status and essentially adopts them, Ephraim and Manasseh will each head tribes of their own, just as the other sons of Jacob. Thus, in the genealogy of the Hebrew people, Jacob's best-loved wife Rachel becomes the matriarch of three tribes: those of Ephraim, Manasseh, and Benjamin.

. . . And the Choices It Demands

Joseph's sons are probably in their early twenties in Genesis 48. They've grown up watching their father's heroics in saving Egypt from disaster. Don't you imagine they've dreamed from time to time of following in his footsteps? Don't you think they've entertained notions of entering government service? I think so. I think they enjoyed living in the prime minister's mansion. I think they loved the attention their father received. I think they felt Egypt was home. But now, thanks to Jacob and the Lord's leading, they are faced with a choice.

By being technically adopted by Jacob, Ephraim and Manasseh must switch loyalties. Egypt cannot be their country; Israel must be. They might remain in the land of Egypt for the rest of their lives, but at the heart of it all they will be Jews, not Egyptians. They have basically the same options Moses did, of whom it is written in Hebrews 11:24-25, "By faith Moses, when he had grown up, refused to be called the son of Pharaoh's daughter, choosing rather to endure ill-treatment with the people of God, than to enjoy the passing pleasures of sin" (NASB).

By faith, Moses makes the right choice, the godly choice. He'll suffer with the Hebrews rather than swing with the Egyptians, because the consequences are eternal. Judging from Joseph's example, Ephraim and Manasseh will make the right choice, too. They'll mirror their father in depending upon the Lord, and in seeing beyond the circumstances. So should we all.

The order in which Jacob refers to his grandsons is worth noting. Consistently, he says Ephraim's name first, although Manasseh is the oldest. Jacob's wording is not a slip of the tongue. He is preparing Joseph, and the boys, for the painful reality of what is to follow. As we'll observe shortly, he'll be saying some things that are going to hurt. He'll even make Joseph rather angry. But it really won't matter, because at the heart of it all the issue is, as Jacob has learned, the necessity of doing God's will.

A Sorrow that Shouldn't Have Been

As pictures of his life continue to sweep across his mind, Jacob recalls a second significant event from his past. Remember, the first episode of importance that he mentions is his confrontation with God at Bethel. The next poignant menory is revealed in verse 7, as Jacob recalls, "As I was returning from Paddan, to my sorrow Rachel died in the land of Canaan while we were still on the way, a little distance from Ephrath. So I buried her there beside the road to Ephrath [Bethlehem]" (48:7).

It is perhaps the greatest sorrow of his life that springs to Jacob's mind as he lies upon his own deathbed. Bidding farewell to his beloved Rachel in a remote section of the Judean wilderness was one of the most difficult things he had to do. Watching her die bringing Benjamin into the world wrenched his heart and left him grief-stricken, emotionally devastated. The agony of the moment has only slightly diminished with the passage of time. Sheldon Vanauken, writing of the aftermath of the death of his own beloved wife Davy, captures the essence of Jacob's grief over Rachel with these words:

> The loss of Davy, after the intense sharing and closeness of the years, the loss and grief was, quite simply, the most immense thing I had ever known. . . . I was having to bear the unbearable. If I must bear it, though, I *would* bear it—find the whole meaning of it, taste the whole of it. I was driven by an unswerving determination to plumb the depths as well as to know the Davy I loved: to understand why she had lived and died, to learn from sorrow whatever it had to teach. It was a kind of faithfulness to her. I would not *run* away from grief; I would not try to hold on to it when—if, unbelievably—it passed (Vanauken 187-188).

For Jacob, grief over the death of Rachel is a cloud that has never fully vanished from the horizon of his emotions. Its tragedy lingers for him. Yet the greatest tragedy of all may well be the fact that, for Jacob, Rachel's death was a sorrow that shouldn't have been.

Let me explain. It is a principle that much pain occurs in our lives because we love the things we shouldn't. For example, a bank balance may become so important to us that when the stock market slides, our happiness does too. A golf game may replace more significant things in our affections, and we cannot deal with it if ill health impairs us from playing. The desire for social status may begin to dictate our actions and attitudes; then, how devastating it is when we find we aren't invited to the party of the year. Simply put, we are asking for trouble when we love the things we shouldn't.

In loving Rachel, I believe that Jacob misplaced his affections. It can be argued that she was never the woman God intended him to have. Instead, her sister Leah was the wife the Lord had in mind. My reasoning follows.

For one, there was no evidence that Jacob prayed about his choice of a wife. He caught a glimpse of Rachel and it was love at first sight. He became emotionally involved with her before he really knew her and, in order to win her, committed himself to seven years' hard labor without a backward glance. That was sorrow number one. Surely Laban would have gladly handed over the less attractive Leah without making any demands. He'd have been happy to play father of the bride and give Leah away.

Second, while Laban's trickery in substituting Leah for Rachel on her younger sister's wedding night cannot be excused, the fact remains that God permitted it to happen. He allowed the marriage to be consummated. He could easily have prevented the fiasco, just as he kept pharaoh from touching Sarah years before (Genesis 12:17). Instead, God chose to permit Leah to become Jacob's first wife, and the significance of that cannot be overlooked. Neither can the fact that nowhere in the Bible is polygamy sanctioned. Always, the union of one man and one woman—particularly the first marriage—is extolled (Genesis 2:18,24). Jacob's early morning discovery that Leah shared his bed would not have been shocking had he expected her there in the first place. Another painful episode would have been avoided.

As we look at the history of their marriage, we see that it was Rachel, not her sister, who caused Jacob a great deal of trouble, too. She moaned and cried and complained, although understandably, about her barrenness. She was the first of the wives to offer her handmaid to Jacob, thus making the love triangle a foursome.

When Leah followed suit it became a quintet—and what peace could there be in Jacob's household with four women sharing the same man? It was also Rachel who, as Jacob and his entourage prepared hastily to leave Haran, stole Laban's household idols and hid them. It's likely that the loss of his idols, more so than the loss of his daughters and hardworking son-in-law, provoked Laban heatedly to pursue the escapees (Genesis 31:19,30). It was a thoroughly avoidable threat.

But perhaps the best argument in scripture that Rachel was not the woman God intended for Jacob lies in the fact that neither of her children became the one through whom the messiah is descended. That honor belonged to Judah, a son of Leah. True, God greatly used Rachel's boy Joseph to work out his plan for the nation of Israel. And it's also true that Joseph, more than any of the other brothers, consistently displayed godly qualities throughout his life. Nevertheless, it is through the line of Judah that the savior eventually comes.

How ironic it is that the greatest sorrow of Jacob's life is one that was wholly avoidable. He loved a woman he shouldn't have loved, and because of it he knew suffering and sorrow he need never have known. God took their love and allowed it to produce someone very special: Joseph. But even he was virtually raised by Leah, not by his natural mother.

I'm sure Joseph has heard the story of his mother's death many times before, but old people repeat themselves. They tell the same stories over and over again. This is what Jacob is doing as he recalls upon his deathbed with painful intensity a sorrow that needn't have been, a sorrow he will carry to the grave.

A Grandfather's Goodbye—Genesis 48:8-14

> When Israel saw the sons of Joseph, he asked, "Who are these?"
>
> "They are the sons God has given me here," Joseph said to his father.

> Then Israel said, "Bring them to me so I may bless them."
>
> Now Israel's eyes were failing because of old age, and he could hardly see. So Joseph brought his sons close to him, and his father kissed them and embraced them.
>
> Israel said to Joseph, "I never expected to see your face again, and now God has allowed me to see your children too."
>
> Then Joseph removed them from Israel's knees and bowed down with his face to the ground. And Joseph took both of them, Ephraim on his right toward Israel's left hand and Manasseh on his left toward Israel's right hand, and brought them close to him. But Israel reached out his right hand and put it on Ephraim's head, though he was the younger, and crossing his arms, he put his left hand on Manasseh's head, even though Manasseh was the firstborn.

Having spoken a good deal, Jacob perhaps rests a moment. As his eyes leave Joseph's face, he notices two shadowy forms in the background. "Who are these?" he asks of Joseph (48:8).

"They are the sons God has given me here," replies Joseph (48:9). As always, Joseph gives the credit and glory to God. What an attitude! Remember that when he addressed the brothers after dropping the charade and revealing his identity, he explained, "But God sent me before you" (45:7). Later, in speaking of his position of prominence, he puts it this way, "God has made me lord of all Egypt" (45:9). "God has given . . . God sent . . . God has made me lord of all Egypt"—these statements reflect the heart of a man fully attuned to the master. Joseph sees the Lord's hand in each of the major events of his life. And how touching it is that he would speak of his own sons as gifts from God. Don't you imagine that Rachel, as she cradled him in her arms or bounced him upon her knee, said much the same thing? "Joseph, you are my special boy. I wasn't able to have babies for so long, then God gave you to me. You are a wonderful gift from him." Now, as his own children come before their dying grandfather, Joseph shows us that he sees his boys as precious gifts from the Lord.

It's not that Jacob cannot recognize Ephraim and Manasseh, either. They undoubtedly have visited their grandfather many times over the past seventeen years. Time was precious, and there was much lost that had to be made up for. Yet, on his deathbed, Jacob's eyes are failing him, as verse 10 reveals. He cannot clearly see the boys, and his question, "Who are these?" is understandable.

Beyond Our Expectations

Because of his father's faltering eyesight, Joseph brings his sons close to the old man's side. Jacob kisses and embraces the boys (48:10). Turning to Joseph, the grateful grandfather gently says, "I never expected to see your face again, and now God has allowed me to see your children too" (48:11). Stubbornness, submission, satisfaction . . . how good God is when we trust him to work his will in our lives!

Yes, God can take our traumas, trials, and heartaches, and turn them into positive things. The key is surrender. It's giving up the *Benjamins* that we spoke of in chapter 6 (Genesis 43). And when surrender comes, the Lord is ever surprising his people with added blessings beyond their expectations.

I remember a small incident that happened at our ministry's Colorado family camp a year ago that illustrates this principle well. Fellowship is an integral part of each of our camps. We urge our staffers to mix and mingle with the guests, to get to know them as individuals, so that we'll be able to effectively minister to their needs. One particular morning I decided I'd had enough mixing and mingling for the moment. I was swamped with work: studies to write, books to read, manuscripts to review. I figured I'd hide out in my room and work instead of going down to the river for an afternoon raft ride with some of the guests. I felt uneasy with this decision, since my work had gone smoothly the night before and I wasn't all that behind on things. So when afternoon came, I reluctantly shut my books, folded my papers, capped my pen, and wandered down to the river. That was my act of surrender—doing what God would have me to do in spending time with the campers. Wouldn't you know it? When I stepped onto the raft at riverside, one of the guides turned out to be a student from my Willow Bend class in Dallas! I had no idea that young man was in Colorado for the summer, working for the company of outfitters from whom we'd rented the rafts. He and I were able to reminisce about the class and some of the folks who had attended, and it was a special time—a moment of blessing that I would have missed out on completely had I not been willing to surrender my treasured time. The Lord is so good, and often when we least expect it.

In Jacob's case, for over two decades he did not entertain the notion that Joseph still lived. In the last seventeen years he has miraculously been reunited with his long-lost son, and has experienced the additional blessing of watching two dear grandsons grow up. No wonder his heart is bursting with praise as he prepares to go home to the father!

The Blessing Begins

Verse 12 tells us that Joseph removes his sons from beside his father's knees and he bows before Jacob, his face to the ground. Then he positions Ephraim on his right side, across from Jacob's left hand, and Manasseh on his left, opposite Jacob's right hand (48:13). Joseph's reasoning is easy to understand. Manasseh is the older of the two boys, and he should receive the blessing of the firstborn. This blessing Jacob would normally bestow with his right hand. Joseph's intentions are perfectly pure. He knows his father cannot see too well, and so he simplifies things by lining up his sons as he deems proper. But Jacob has a surprise in store for his son and grandsons.

Instead of reaching out to Manasseh with his right hand, Jacob crosses his arms. He places his left hand on Manasseh's head and his right atop the head of Ephraim (48:14). It is a move that Joseph and the boys do not comprehend, at least at first. The explanation eventually comes.

Unanticipated Actions—Genesis 48:15-22

Then he blessed Joseph and said,
"May the God before whom my fathers
Abraham and Isaac walked,
the God who has been my Shepherd
all my life to this day,
the Angel who has delivered me from all harm
—may he bless these boys.
May they be called by my name
and the names of my fathers
Abraham and Isaac,
and may they increase greatly
upon the earth."

When Joseph saw his father placing his right hand on Ephraim's head he was displeased; so he took hold of his father's hand to move it from Ephraim's head to Manasseh's head. Joseph said to him, "No, my father, this one is the firstborn; put your right hand on his head."

But his father refused and said, "I know, my son, I know. He too will become a people, and he too will become great. Nevertheless, his younger brother will be greater than he, and his descendants will become a group of nations."

He blessed them that day and said,
"In your name will Israel pronounce this
blessing:
'May God make you like Ephraim and
Manasseh.' "
So he put Ephraim ahead of Manasseh.

> Then Israel said to Joseph, "I am about to die, but God will be with you and take you back to the land of your fathers. And to you, as one who is over your brothers, I give the ridge of land I took from the Amorites with my sword and my bow."

As he crosses his arms to place his right hand upon the head of his younger grandson, I wonder what thoughts flicker through Jacob's mind. Does he remember dressing in animal skins to trick his own aged father into handing over the birthright and bestowing the blessing upon him? Whether he does or not, Jacob is not about to play the fool in Genesis 48. He knows what he is doing in choosing Ephraim over his older brother.

The Bible is full of instances in which the younger brother is selected instead of the older. Scripturally, it was Seth instead of Cain, Shem instead of Japheth, Abraham instead of Nahor or Haran, Isaac instead of Ishmael, Jacob instead of Esau. Now it is Ephraim instead of Manasseh.

THE GOD OF ABRAHAM, PRAISE!

Jacob then speaks the words of blessing. He begins this way: "May the God before whom my fathers Abraham and Isaac walked, the God who has been my Shepherd all my life to this day . . ." (48:15). And thus Jacob acknowledges the Lord as the one who has shepherded him. God has led him, guided him, returned him to the fold when he has gone astray, much as he did for David, who also was perhaps in his old age when he penned the words of Psalm 23:

> The Lord is my shepherd, I shall not want.
>
> He maketh me to lie down in green pastures: he leadeth me beside the still waters.
>
> He restoreth my soul: he leadeth me in the paths of righteousness for his name's sake.
>
> Yea, though I walk through the valley of the shadow of death, I will fear no evil: for thou art

> with me; thy rod and thy staff they comfort me.
>
> Thou preparest a table before me in the presence of mine enemies: thou anointest my head with oil; my cup runneth over.
>
> Surely goodness and mercy shall follow me all the days of my life: and I will dwell in the house of the Lord for ever (KJV).

Jacob also calls the Lord "the Angel who has delivered me from all harm" (48:16). In his words we see the third significant event of his life that he recalls as the hours wane. Event number one was his conversion at Bethel; number two was the death of Rachel; number three was his experience wrestling with the angel of the Lord—God himself clothed in flesh, an appearance of the preincarnate Christ—at Peniel, recorded in Genesis 32 (32:24ff). Why does he make mention of the all-night wrestling match? Remember that Jacob hung on to the angel with such stubborn intensity and resistance that God had to injure him on the thigh. The Lord had to touch Jacob physically before he could touch him spiritually. Sometimes this is the way God has to deal with us in order to get our attention. Jacob perhaps wishes to remind Joseph, and especially his boys, of this for they have many years left and it is a lesson worth learning early.

The old patriarch goes on, voicing three desires concerning God's dealings with Ephraim and Manasseh, saying of the Lord, "May he bless these boys. May they be called by my name and the names of my fathers Abraham and Isaac, and may they increase greatly upon the earth" (48:16). Jacob's wishes for his grandsons are that God would bless them, that they would be known as sons of Abraham, and that they would multiply, having children and grandchildren of their own.

The Agony of Misunderstanding

As the blessing takes place, Joseph is disturbed. Verse 17 reveals that he is displeased, and actually grasps his father's right hand in order to move it from the head of Ephraim to that of Manasseh. "No, my father," he exclaims, "this one is the firstborn; put your right hand on his head" (48:18). Maybe Jacob cannot see what he is doing. Maybe in his senility, he has forgotten which boy is the oldest. Whatever the case, his actions exasperate Joseph and, as in the episode with the cupbearer in prison, he tries to take things into his own hands. His expectations and anticipation frustrate him in the face of present reality.

Joseph attempts to manipulate the situation, but Jacob knows full well what he is doing. "I know, my son, I know," he says quietly to Joseph (48:19), even as he refuses to budge his right hand.

What we see here is the agony of misunderstanding. Make no mistake, Joseph is angry at what is happening. His temper only flares, however, because he does not understand. Do you know what might be said here, what perhaps needs to be said here? "Joseph, the God who sent you into Egypt, the God who delivered you from prison in his time and in his way, the God who made you lord of the land, the God who gave you these sons, is going to bless these boys in his own way. It isn't going to be how you expect." Instead, Jacob simply replies, "I know, son, I know." Things will be different than Joseph anticipates. The younger will exceed the older.

Have Thine Own Way, Lord: the Higher Way

It is an untarnishable truth that the happiest people in the world are those who are letting God have his way in their lives. Often circumstances and situations will arise that we'd like to change. We'll try to change them . . . sometimes we will change them. But other times what is happening to us is within the will of God, and we'll find ourselves involved in a losing battle as we kick against the goads. As we've mentioned before, all the whys of our lives won't be answered until eternity. What we can—indeed, what we must—cling to is the belief that God knows what he is doing. "For my thoughts are not your thoughts, neither are your ways my ways. . . . As the heavens are higher than the earth, so are my ways higher than your ways and my thoughts than your thoughts," says the Lord in Isaiah 55:8-9. He means it.

Life won't necessarily be easy. I think of my oldest daughter Donna and her husband Mark. Coming from a home with five children, Donna desired a large family, and so did Mark. They'd be super parents, but the Lord hasn't permitted it yet. They've struggled with infertility for years, and have tried every medical route with which they feel comfortable. Still, nothing. They've even written a manuscript about their problems with infertility, and the name they've given it speaks volumes of their trust in their heavenly father's wisdom. The book is called *The Higher Way,* and, for them at the moment, infertility is God's higher way.

In the meantime, Mark and Donna are happy. They use their gifts working with the young people in our youth groups and camps. They constructively invest themselves in the lives of others. It gets tough, especially as grandchildren continue to arrive in our family. But Mark and Donna have chosen the higher way—the path of accepting their situation, of leaning on the Lord when things get rough, of submitting to his plan and purpose in their lives.

We, too, can find fulfillment in the higher way if we're simply willing to trust God and allow him to work. As he watches his father bestow the blessings on his boys in a manner he would not choose, Joseph faces the same option. He could become unhappy and resentful. He is fifty-six years old, and could easily spend the remainder of his years in bitterness if he refuses to accept the fact that his father has the prerogative to bestow the patriarchal blessings as the Lord leads him. Evidently, Joseph respects his father's wishes in the matter, for he says nothing more. He utters no more protests . . . and Ephraim is chosen over his brother.

Still, Joseph is surprised at the turn events have taken.

And Ephraim and Manasseh are surprised as well. It's an awkward situation. Perhaps sensing this, Jacob offers these words of comfort concerning Manasseh's future: "He too will become a people, and he too will become great" (48:19). "Nevertheless," Jacob continues, "his younger brother will be greater than he, and his descendants will become a group of nations" (48:19). That is the way it is going to be.

Jacob continues blessing the boys with these words: "In your name will Israel pronounce this blessing: 'May God make you like Ephraim and Manasseh' " (48:20). And so the episode of benediction ends.

Turning the Ifs to Whens

Jacob turns to Joseph and speaks again, changing the subject. "I am about to die," says the patriarch, "but God will be with you and take you back to the land of your fathers" (48:21). Although Joseph's earthly father is about to depart, his heavenly father will never desert him. God will be with Joseph and will eventually return him to the land of Canaan.

What is perhaps most beautiful about the dying man's words in verse 21 is that there are no ifs—only whens. It is a declaration of purpose, concerning not *if* God will return Joseph to the land, but *when* he will do so. There is no doubt in Jacob's mind that Joseph will again enter the land and eventually he does, although it is after his death that his bones are permanently conveyed there during the exodus (Joshua 24:32).

As Christians, we exercise faith when we turn our ifs to whens also. Faith is not saying, "If God provides," but, "When God provides." It is, as Hebrews 11:1 states, "Being sure of what we hope for and certain of what we do not see." The fulfillment of the Lord's promises comes in his time. But rest assured, fulfillment is a certainty, not a mere possibility.

"And to you, as one who is over his brothers," continues Jacob, confirming Joseph's predominance in the family, "I give the ridge of land I took from the Amorites with my sword and my bow" (48:22). We are not certain which piece of land Jacob refers to, although evidently he has conquered a section in a skirmish of some sort. His final bequest in this portion of scripture suggests that he expects Joseph actually to dwell in Canaan again. This does not happen, although Joseph returns there to bury his father. With the words of verse 22, the curtain drops on the tender moments between a favored son, his beloved dying parent, and two precious grandsons.

LESSONS

There is so much to be learned from the interchange between Joseph and Jacob in Genesis 48. Let's look at some of the lessons.

Lesson one: *Joseph displays caring concern for his father in the hour of his infirmity and approaching death.* He manifests what you and I have the responsibility to do in our own families.

Lesson two: *Jacob has obviously grown spiritually through the many experiences he has had.* What a beautiful passage is Genesis 48, because we see him reach the final stages of his life a transformed man, totally ready to pull up the tent stakes and go to his heavenly home.

Lesson three: *Jacob rests in the presence and promises of God as he recounts the covenant the Lord has made with him.* He fully depends on God's faithfulness. What a way to get ready to die!

Lesson four: *as the end approaches, Jacob is filled with gratitude concerning the past. He is not bitter, but better, for all that has happened.* He offers us another lesson in how to live and how to die, as he speaks fondly of God as the one who has shepherded him throughout.

Lesson five: *the love in Jacob's heart is evident as he gives his farewell address to Joseph, Ephraim, and Ma-*

nasseh. He does not conceal his feelings, but makes sure that there is no doubt about his affections in his final hours.

Lesson six: *children are gifts from the Lord.* Joseph calls his sons the children whom God has given him, and how right he is.

Lesson seven: *God is ever surprising his children with added blessings beyond their expectations.* Jacob expresses joy in verse 11, when he exclaims over the fact that he not only has been able to see Joseph, but also his grandsons.

Lesson eight: *God's will is accomplished in the crossing of Jacob's hands as he pronounces the blessing.* The Lord's purpose often involves situations and circumstances we do not understand, or even like, but there is a reason. We must be careful not to put our own wills and desires ahead of God's will for our lives.

Lesson nine: *we begin to demonstrate faith when all our ifs are changed to whens.*

Lesson ten: *friends and loved ones die and leave us, but God will never leave or forsake us.* We can count completely on him to remain a constant in our lives.

Preparing to Die

In Genesis 48 and in the chapter that follows, we witness Jacob tying up the loose ends of his life as he prepares to meet his maker. Many of us will be in his position some day, gradually loosening our grips on the strings of life down here. Some of us will linger, as does Jacob. Some will die suddenly, rapidly, unexpectedly—victims of auto accidents, heart attacks, strokes, drowning. And probably most of us will go home to be with the father only partially prepared. Oh, our last wills and testaments will be in order. Directions for the disposal of our properties will be given. Guardians for our children will be named. But we might just be leaving a whole lot of unfinished business behind, anyway.

What I'm referring to is what Paul Powell writes about in *When the Hurt Won't Go Away.* Reflecting upon the inevitability of his death, Powell says:

> Each time I think about my own death, I ask myself three kinds of questions to help me do that:
>
> "Am I right in my relationship with God?"
>
> "Am I right in my relationship with my family, with my friends, with my co-workers? Are there any relationships I need to reconcile? Are there words I need to say?"
>
> "Am I investing myself in things that will last for eternity?"
>
> The more I look to the life to come, the more nobly it makes me want to live the life I now have (Powell 141).

The questions Powell poses are worth considering, and worth considering well. Like Jacob, before we die, are we going to wrap up the loose ends, speak to those we need to speak with, reconcile ourselves with our relatives, patch up quarrels, hand out apologies as necessary, and, most important, call upon the God we know we need as savior? Or, are we going to wait till it's too late? I've preached at many a service where the dearly departed left behind a passel of unresolved issues. Believe me, a funeral offers cold comfort to the family and friends of a person who waited too long. Don't let it be you.

QUESTIONS FOR STUDY

1. What three significant events from his life does Jacob recall as he prepares to die? If you found out the Lord intended to call you home tomorrow, what do you think you'd be recalling?

2. Do you agree that Rachel's death was a sorrow that needn't have been for Jacob? What can happen when we love too intensely the things and the people we shouldn't?

3. How does Joseph react at first when Jacob chooses to bless Ephraim over Manasseh? What lessons about God's sovereignty can we learn from the fact that, in this case, the younger son is chosen over the older?

4. Read Isaiah 58:8-9. Is there a situation in your life in which God is calling you to follow a "higher way"? What is it?

5. God is able to do exceeding abundantly, above anything we'd ask or think. How has Jacob been blessed beyond his wildest dreams these last seventeen years of his life?

11

Going Out a Winner

Genesis 49

The might have beens—how often they rise up to plague us as we become older. Some men and women reach their sixties or seventies, and their missions in life become bewailing the past, groaning about what might have been. I can't tell you how many retired folks I've counseled who've muttered one of the hundreds of if onlys, too. You know them: "If only I'd spent more time with my children . . . changed careers . . . been kinder to my spouse . . . made that move when the company asked me to . . . nagged my husband less . . . gone to church more." Facing the final years of life causes us to evaluate honestly what's gone before. Frankly, few are the men and women who have no regrets. Most of us wind up wishing we'd done some things differently.

It does no good to wallow in the might have beens and the if onlys. As we age, we ought to learn that there is no use crying over spilled milk. The mistakes of the past belong back there where they happened: in the past. What we could have been or could have done shouldn't concern us. What we need to care about is what we still can be and still can do—even as we prepare for death itself. And yet we seldom do.

Perhaps one of the reasons is we never quite accept

the reality of our own mortality. Despite the truth of George Bernard Shaw's wry sentiment, "The statistics on death are quite impressive. One out of one people die," we figure there'll always be time. I can't tell you the number of men and women I've talked with whose medical conditions have been diagnosed as terminal, and who have expressed a desire to make a last contribution of some sort. Maybe they want to spend a day alone with the son with whom they've often disagreed. Maybe they want to apologize to a relative they've wronged. Perhaps they want to change their will to fund a camp or college scholarship, or they want to donate money to a church or charity. It could be that they want to tell a non-believing golf buddy about the love of Jesus Christ. Whatever the final wishes, more often than not the funeral bells toll before the deed is ever done.

So if you're alive today, get busy! You don't have forever. One day it will be too late. You'll be facing your final hours, lingering in a hospital bed, lying in a rest home, or strapped to a stretcher in an ambulance pulling away from the site of an accident.

Tying Up the Loose Ends

As Genesis 49 opens, we find Jacob preparing to die. In our last episode, knowing the end was near, the patriarch had Joseph officially assume Reuben's position in the family. Jacob also adopted Joseph's two sons, Manasseh and Ephraim, as his own, naming Ephraim, the younger, as the one to receive the blessing traditionally bestowed upon the firstborn. With these actions, Jacob began tying up the loose ends, but before he closes his eyes forever, there are a few more cords to bind. Jacob must say farewell to the rest of his sons, and impart a father's final words of wisdom and blessing.

Here is a man at the end of a life that has been filled with heartache and suffering. At times there have been tremendous blessings and insight but, by and large, Jacob's years have been splattered with sorrow. He's been getting his act together with the Lord for decades. On his deathbed we do not read of his whining about what might have been. He's not going to leave important words unsaid or significant actions untaken, either. He's going out a winner. He's finishing strong. Let's watch Jacob make his phenomenal exit in a finale that is grand indeed. He shows us all how to die.

The Twelve Tribes—Genesis 49:1-2

> Then Jacob called for his sons and said, "Gather around so I can tell you what will happen to you in days to come.
>
> "Assemble and listen, sons of Jacob;
> listen to your father Israel."

Sensing his time is near, Jacob rallies his strength and calls for his sons, saying, "Gather around so I can tell you what will happen to you in days to come" (49:1). He'll be making prophetic statements, revealing to each man the future of his descendants. We see unfolding before us the establishment of Israel as a nation composed of twelve tribes who will one day inherit the promised land (Genesis 49:28; Joshua 14:1-5). Each of Jacob's sons, except Levi, will be the forerunner of one of these land-possessing tribes.

Joseph's situation is special. The tribe of Joseph will actually be composed of two tribes: those formed by the descendants of his two sons, Ephraim and Manasseh. The tribes of Ephraim and Manasseh, along with the tribe of Reuben, the tribe of Simeon, the tribe of Judah, and so on, will eventually occupy specific sections of the holy land.

Jacob's son Levi will also head a tribe, but Levi's descendants will be priests. They'll be scattered about, owning no area of land themselves. Technically, we might say that there are actually thirteen tribes that form the nation of Israel. But only members of the tribes of Reuben, Simeon, Judah, Issachar, Zebulun, Dan, Gad,

Asher, Naphtali, Ephraim, Manasseh, and Benjamin actually inherit property in Canaan.

The formation of the twelve tribes is part of God's plan, just as is the fact that the next several generations of Jacob's heirs will remain in Egypt, strangers in a strange land. What we'll read about in Genesis 49 is merely one of the first steps in the development of the nation.

Picture the scene. Jacob's twelve sons are gathered together, maybe huddled in a corner of the tent. The last medical reports on their father haven't been too good. He's slipping away. They whisper to one another about his condition, and about how strange life will be without him. Jacob hears the low rumbling of hushed voices in the background, and realizes that his first summons has brought the men into his chambers. He calls his boys to come closer, so that they might hear the last words he has for them.

"Assemble and listen, sons of Jacob; listen to your father Israel," Jacob instructs them (49:2). Notice, he refers to himself as Israel. It was the name given to him by the angel of the Lord after they wrestled at Peniel. It means "God's fighter" and it will be the name by which God's nation is known. I don't imagine Jacob is whispering these words as he summons his sons. Tough fighter that he is—and that his name implies—I believe his voice is steady and strong. He's not allowing himself to indulge in self-pity. He's saying what needs to be said, and his final words are going to come across loud and clear.

The Sons of Leah—Genesis 49:3-15

> "Reuben, you are my firstborn,
> my might, the first sign of my strength,
> excelling in honor, excelling in power.
> Turbulent as the waters, you will no longer excel,
> for you went up onto your father's bed,
> onto my couch and defiled it.

"Simeon and Levi are brothers—
their swords are weapons of violence.
Let me not enter their council,
let me not join their assembly,
for they have killed men in their anger
and hamstrung oxen as they pleased.
Cursed be their anger, so fierce,
and their fury, so cruel!
I will scatter them in Jacob
and disperse them in Israel.

"Judah, your brothers will praise you;
your hand will be on the neck of your enemies;
your father's sons will bow down to you.
You are a lion's cub, O Judah;
you return from the prey, my son.
Like a lion he crouches and lies down,
like a lioness—who dares to rouse him?
The scepter will not depart from Judah,
nor the ruler's staff from between his feet,
until he comes to whom it belongs
and the obedience of the nations is his.
He will tether his donkeys to a vine,
his colt to the choicest branch;
he will wash his garments in wine,
his robes in the blood of grapes.
His eyes will be darker than wine,
his teeth whiter than milk.

"Zebulun will live by the seashore
and become a haven for ships;
his border will extend toward Sidon.

"Issachar is a rawboned donkey
lying down between two saddlebags.
When he sees how good is his resting place
and how pleasant is his land,
he will bend his shoulder to the
burden
and submit to forced labor."

Reuben: What Should Have Been and Never Was

Looking at his sons as intently as his blurred vision allows, Jacob begins his farewell remarks. He first addresses the sons of Leah, then the sons of the handmaids, and finally the sons of his dear Rachel. Reuben is first, and there are serious words to be said.

"Reuben, you are my firstborn, my might, the first sign of my strength, excelling in honor, excelling in power," begins Jacob, at first painting a flattering portrait of his eldest boy (49:3). But there is more, as Jacob continues. "Turbulent as the waters," says father to son, "you will no longer excel, for you went up onto your father's bed, onto my couch and defiled it" (49:4). There had to be a reason why Jacob replaced Reuben with Joseph as his chief heir in chapter 48. This is it. Reuben, who should have been excelling in power, honor, and strength, showed himself to be a rash and immoral adult. He should have been consistent, reliable, dependable, but instead he was as unstable as water, impatient, impetuous, unsettled—a river overflowing its banks without regard to the consequences.

We've witnessed Reuben's dramatics. We've seen him overdo things, such as in Genesis 42:37 where he offers his two sons as sacrifices if Benjamin doesn't return from Egypt. But what he did in a moment of moral weakness overshadows all other acts of impetuosity. As Jacob reminds him, he went up onto his father's bed. He slept with one of his father's concubines.

It was Bilhah, Rachel's handmaid, with whom Reuben had his affair. Mention of the cheap seduction is made in 1 Chronicles 5:1-2. For this rash act, this momentary satisfaction of desire, Reuben loses his birthright and forfeits his position as firstborn of his father. I imagine Reuben reminds his father of brother Esau, who so lightly valued his own birthright that he sold it for a pot of stew (Genesis 27:25-34). Regardless, because of Reuben's instability and immorality, Jacob chooses to deal with Joseph, Ephraim, and Manasseh instead.

The Reasons for the Attraction

It makes you wonder why, doesn't it? Why did Reuben chance his father's disfavor by sleeping with Bilhah? And why did the concubine of the clan's patriarch risk Jacob's displeasure by lying with his son? While there's no excuse for the behavior of Reuben and Bilhah, there are reasons behind their sin. We can understand why the affair took place, even if we, like Jacob, must condemn the incident.

Consider the atmosphere in which Reuben had been raised. He'd grown up watching four women compete for the attentions and affection of his father. He'd seen the bickering and recognized its causes. He'd even been involved in the struggle of his mother to lay claim upon Jacob sexually. The incident occurred one day when Reuben, then a young boy, returned from the fields with a couple of mandrake plants in his hands. Superstition held that mandrake fruit possessed aphrodisiac qualities and promoted fertility. When Rachel, still childless, spied the fruit Reuben carried, she cried to Leah, "Please give me some of your son's mandrakes" (Genesis 30:14).

Leah replied, "Wasn't it enough that you took away my husband? Will you take my son's mandrakes too?" (30:15).

"Very well," countered Rachel, speaking of Jacob, "he can sleep with you tonight in return for your son's mandrakes" (30:15). And that evening Jacob returned from the fields to find Leah ready and waiting. "You must sleep with me," she informed him with all the subtlety that Potiphar's wife had used on Joseph. "I have hired you with my son's mandrakes" (30:16).

It's a pathetic story, isn't it? Two women bargaining and bartering for the sexual favors of one man. And who, more than any of the other children, was watching? Who was probably just old enough to be aware of what was really going on? Who'd become an accessory to Leah's plan simply by bringing in some fruit from the field? Reuben. It's no wonder that he grew into young adulthood with a warped sense of sexual propriety. He had watched the Rachel-Leah-Bilhah-Zilpah soap opera for much of his life. It's not surprising that, at around fifteen to eighteen years of age, possessing all the natural drives of any young man, he allowed himself to have an affair with his father's concubine.

There's a lesson in all of this for us today. How carefully do we monitor the influences affecting our children? Do they finish their homework every night only to turn on the TV and watch some middle-aged siren seduce a younger man on an evening soap? Do they run across questionable magazines we've stashed in the nightstand? Do they frequently listen to talk shows where movie stars dish out sugar-coated comments about the virtues of sleeping around or living with a member of the opposite sex? If we give our children free rein in their own moral development, we can too easily end up with a Reuben on our hands. Our responsibility as parents is to guide our youngsters, to prepare them for the enjoyment of sex as God intended: within the marriage relationship.

There's an old saying that it takes two to tango. I've often wondered why Reuben and Bilhah wound up together on the dance floor. Why did Bilhah even seem desirable to Reuben? She was some years older than he. And why did Reuben interest Bilhah? He was barely more than a boy—certainly not the experienced, worldly man his father was. What explains the attraction? I believe there were two causes. First, Bilhah was incredibly lonely. Second, Reuben felt sorry for her.

I imagine that after Rachel's death, Bilhah, who had been her handmaid, figured she'd step right into her mistress's role. She'd been a faithful servant of Rachel, so naturally Jacob would begin desiring her now that the queen of the roost was gone. But it wasn't so. Leah stepped onto center stage as Jacob's number one woman. Bilhah was even more neglected than before—used, abused, unloved, and depressed. And Reuben? He must have had a tender heart. Perhaps he tried to comfort her. Emotional involvement led to physical desire and giving in to the temptation cost him much of his future.

Unstable as Water—A National Heritage

The rashness and instability that mark Reuben's character extend to his descendants. It is interesting to read about the future history of the tribe of Reuben and to see the impetuosity, the uncertainty, the irresponsibility, characterizing it. When General Joshua apportioned the land of Canaan among the twelve tribes, the tribe of Reuben elected to stay on the east side of the Jordan River (Joshua 13:15-23). They lacked the moral fiber to fight for the land God had promised them, so they took the easy way out and remained across the river and away from the challenge of God's choicest and best.

Unstable as water—that describes Reuben in a nutshell. Unfortunately, it also describes the United States. We don't like to take a stand. We've become inured to pornography, immune to moral shock, used to cheating on our taxes, expense accounts, and spouses. We extol individual "freedoms" and agree that everyone has the inalienable right to establish his own value systems. We cry that we can't legislate morality, and we support every splinter group claiming the right to practice its credo. There are no absolutes. We've become so much like the rebellious children of Israel, of whom Judges 21:25 says, "Everyone did as he saw fit." How I fear that we, like Reuben, will "no longer excel."

Simeon and Levi: the Consequences of Cruelty

Having spoken his piece with Reuben who, I imagine, is staring blankly at the floor, too numb for either tears or anger, Jacob next turns to sons number two and three, Simeon and Levi. Like Reuben, whose moral instability has traced a groove of sin in his character that mars the whole man, Simeon and Levi possess fatal flaws. They are hot-tempered and cruel. Says Jacob, "Simeon and Levi are brothers—their swords are weapons of violence. Let me not enter their council, for they have killed men in their anger and hamstrung oxen as they pleased" (49:5,6).

We read these words and remember that Simeon and Levi engineered the massacre at Shechem, detailed in Genesis 34. The viciousness of the attack on the unsuspecting men of Shechem appalled Jacob. That Simeon and Levi could be capable of such premeditated cruelty alarmed him, and caused him to back away from seeking their opinions. They cannot be trusted, and there is a penalty attached to their sheer meanness.

"Cursed be their anger, so fierce, and their fury, so cruel!" exclaims Jacob. "I will scatter them in Jacob and disperse them in Israel" (49:7). Examining the subsequent biblical accounts of these two tribes explains Jacob's statements. The tribe of Simeon was eventually absorbed into the tribe of Judah (Joshua 19:1,9). The Simeonites thus were scattered, dispersed, just as Jacob had said.

The tribe of Levi fared somewhat better. The Levites actually redeemed themselves in a sense by properly responding when Moses came down from Mount Sinai to find God's people worshiping a golden calf. In Exodus 32:26, Moses, glaring at the thousands of disobedient Israelites, demanded to know, "Whoever is for the Lord, come to me." And we read that "all the Levites rallied to him." They responded correctly, making the choice for God instead of for man. But even so, they were awarded a specific region when the inheritance of the land was apportioned. As the priestly or religious tribe, they were assigned to forty-eight cities scattered throughout the nation (Joshua 21). In a very real sense, although they did not lose their identity as a tribe, they were dispersed throughout Israel, as Jacob predicts upon his deathbed.

Judah: the Tribe of Kings

In the early part of their marriage, Leah presented Jacob with one more son: Judah. It is now his turn to receive his father's final words of prophetic blessing. And prophecy it is indeed, for much of what Jacob says about Judah concerns not only the future of the tribe itself, but also predicts the coming of Judah's descendant, Jesus Christ.

"Judah," begins the ailing patriarch, "your brothers will praise you; your hand will be on the neck of your enemies; your father's sons will bow down to you" (49:8). We recall that Judah's name means "praise," and so the promise of his name is fulfilled in that the members of the other tribes will praise him and his descendants.

"You are a lion's cub, O Judah; you return from the prey, my son," continues Jacob. "Like a lion he crouches and lies down, like a lioness—who dares to rouse him?" (49:9). Judah and those after him will be powerful, lion-like in their dominance over their enemies.

They will also be regal. In fact, Judah will become the tribe of kings. Says Jacob, "The scepter will not depart from Judah, nor the ruler's staff from between his feet, until he comes to whom it belongs and the obedience of the nations is his" (49:10). Judah's tribe will be praised; his descendants will be strong and mighty, and the scepter and ruler's staff—symbols of royal authority—"will not depart" from the tribe until a significant event happens. What is that important happening? It is the occasion when "he comes to whom it belongs and the obedience of the nations is his" (49:10).

Let me explain. The descendant of Judah, referred to in verse 10 by the pronoun *he,* is none other than Jesus Christ himself. The New American Standard Bible refers to him as *Shiloh,* meaning "rest or tranquility" (49:10 NASB). It is Jesus who is our rest, who is the bringer of inner tranquility, who will one day rule a world that is completely at peace. Judah is the forerunner of the tribe of kings. David and Solomon number among his earthly descendants. And from this tribe of kings would eventually issue Shiloh, the king of kings, the messiah. Jacob refers to Judah as a "lion's cub," and the messiah, his greatest descendant, will be known as the lion of the tribe of Judah.

According to Jacob, in a future day, "the obedience of the nations" will belong to this king of kings. Isaiah 9:6-7 speaks of this time. In the words of Isaiah, writing seven hundred years before the birth of Christ in Bethlehem:

> For to us a child is born,
> to us a son is given,
> and the government will be on his shoulders.
> And he will be called
> Wonderful Counselor, Mighty God,
> Everlasting Father, Prince of Peace.
> Of the increase of his government and peace
> there will be no end.
> He will reign on David's throne
> and over his kingdom,
> establishing it and upholding it
> with justice and righteousness
> from that time on and forever.
> The zeal of the Lord Almighty
> will accomplish this.

Most of Isaiah's prophecy concerning Christ remains yet to be fulfilled in our time. Today, we're waiting somewhere between the cross and the kingdom. Jesus was born and died, was buried and arose. After spending a short time on the earth following the resurrection, he ascended into heaven. Currently he is calling unto himself the church, his bride, from every tongue, tribe, and nation. There will come a day, however, when he will return, ushering in his eternal reign. His will be an everlasting throne and, with complete righteousness and justice, he'll rule a perfect earth, a world in which there is no hunger, horror of war, or hopelessness.

As he continues his dying words to a special son, a son who has not disappointed him, a son whose heirs will be leaders among their brothers, Jacob reveals more about the future of Judah's tribe and also the coming messiah. "He will tether his donkey to a vine, his colt to the choicest branch," says Jacob (49:11). Partly this speaks of Judah's tribe, who eventually occupied a lush, fertile area of Canaan where grapevines were plentiful and branches grew in abundance. Partly Jacob's remark foreshadows the entry of Christ into Jerusalem during the Passover. We recall that he rode into the city gates astride a colt, the foal of a donkey (Matthew 21:1-11).

Jacob goes on: "He will wash his garments in wine, his robes in the blood of grapes. His eyes will be darker than wine, his teeth whiter than milk" (49:11,12). Judah's tribal territory would be rich—a land with grapes as abundant as water, a fertile region of milk and wine. But the mention of the garments drenched in "the blood of grapes" also suggests the sufferings that Jesus Christ would endure upon the cross, spilling his own blood as a sacrifice in payment for the sin of humankind.

Thus Jacob's message to his fourth-born son is full of double meanings. It is a promise of the good life for Judah's heirs, and it contains the promise of the abundant life everlasting for all of us who are called the children of God because of our faith in Christ Jesus.

Zebulun and Issachar: Prosperity and Procrastination

With Jacob's comments about Judah finished, he turns his attention to the two remaining sons of Leah. He's been dealing with the boys in chronological order, from oldest to youngest, but he shifts gears in verse 13, considering Zebulun before the older son, Issachar.

"Zebulun will live by the seashore and become a haven for ships," predicts Jacob, "his border will extend toward Sidon" (49:13). The portion of land the tribe of Zebulun eventually possessed was not on the shore, but it was relatively close to the great Mediterranean seaport of Haifa. Zebulun's descendants benefited economically from the trade route emerging from Haifa and proceeding into the land. They did "become a haven for ships" in that sense.

His brief comments to Zebulun finished, Jacob moves on to the remaining son of Leah, Issachar. "Issachar is a rawboned donkey lying down between two saddlebags," says the patriarch. "When he sees how good is his resting place and how pleasant is his land, he will bend his shoulder to the burden and submit to forced labor" (49:14-15).

1 Chronicles 12:32 contains this statement about the tribe of Issachar: "Men of Issachar, who understood the times and knew what Israel should do." It sounds like the men of Issachar were on the cutting edge of things. They knew what policies the nation of Israel should follow. They were leaders, men who could get the job done. But, if that's true, why does Jacob call Issachar "a rawboned donkey lying down between two saddlebags," who enjoys his pleasant surroundings so much that he even submits to "forced labor" in order to preserve the status quo?

Combining 1 Chronicles 12:32 with Jacob's comments in verses 14 and 15, we realize that the men of Issachar did not become the movers and shakers of Israel. Instead, they were men who knew what they ought to do, but were either too comfortable or too lazy to do it. They were like the lethargic donkey who plants his hooves in the ground and refuses to budge.

The portrait of Issachar and his descendants is also a rather accurate picture of many of us, isn't it? I'm reminded of a poster one of my children had that read, "When I get the urge to study, I lie down until it goes away." We can be so lazy, can't we? We can be so apathetic and complacent, perfectly content to put our heads in the sand and hope the bad things will just go away by themselves. We know what we ought to do in a situation, but we really don't care.

I recall a story told me by a friend who recently attended a sales meeting in Phoenix, Arizona. The speaker came up to the podium and announced, "It's a waste of your time and mine that I'm here this evening, because you're not going to do what I say anyway." Imagine stunned silence in a roomful of salesmen! The mute audience looked on as the speaker descended from the platform and walked over to the first table in the dining room. He picked up a pack of cigarettes lying on the table, and read the label aloud: "Warning, the Surgeon General has determined that smoking is hazardous to your health." Looking at the man seated there who owned the cigarettes, the speaker asked, "Do you believe that?"

"Yeah," came the reply.

"Are you going to quit smoking?"

"No."

"See, what did I tell you," exclaimed the speaker, again facing the crowd. "You know what's right and you still don't do it. You refuse to respond!" He might as well have been talking about the tribe of Issachar. The potential was there; the knowledge of right and wrong was there. But there was no motivation and only tremendous human waste.

THE SONS OF THE HANDMAIDS—GENESIS 49:16-21

> "Dan will provide justice for his people
> as one of the tribes of Israel.
> Dan will be a serpent by the roadside,
> a viper along the path,
> that bites the horse's heels
> so that its rider tumbles backward.
>
> "I look for your deliverance, O Lord.
>
> "Gad will be attacked by a band of raiders,
> but he will attack them at their heels.
>
> "Asher's food will be rich;
> he will provide delicacies fit for a king.
>
> "Naphtali is a doe set free
> that bears beautiful fawns."

His predictions about the sons of Leah complete, Jacob begins to speak to the four sons of the handmaids, Bilhah and Zilpah.

DAN: A SERPENT

Bilhah's oldest son Dan is addressed first. "Dan will provide justice for his people as one of the tribes of Israel," proclaims Jacob (49:16). Then he makes a curious remark, "Dan will be a serpent by the roadside, a viper along the path, that bites the horse's heels so that its rider tumbles backward" (49:17). We know little about the subsequent history of the descendants of Dan. We do know that in the promised land the tribe possessed an area at the northernmost border of Israel. We also know the identity of a famous judge who emerged from the tribe of Dan during the period of the judges. That judge was Samson.

Jacob depicts the descendants of Dan as bringers-of-justice who practice treachery—serpents by the roadside, sneakily nipping the heels of a horse so that its rider would fall. They would be unscrupulous, unsteady, violent, untrustworthy men. If Samson was a representative of the tribe, then the predictions came true. Samson single-handedly brought havoc to the Philistines, but never marshaled an army. He ruled in compromise and finally became a flamboyant playboy who wasted his potential. Ironically, he ultimately succumbed to the treachery of Delilah and died, blind but vengefully victorious, taking thousands of Philistines with him in a shocking, thoroughly unsuspected show of strength (Judges 14-16).

AN OUTBURST OF PRAISE

After foretelling the fate of the tribe of Dan, Jacob pauses in his dealings with his sons. He cannot help himself—an outburst of praise slips from his lips. "I look for your deliverance, O Lord," he exclaims. What a gem it is in the midst of a farewell address.

God's word is like that. Read a few of those long passages nobody wants to read, where generation after generation of foreign names are listed, and you might be pleasantly surprised. 1 Chronicles chapter 4 contains just such a long register of the descendants of Judah and Simeon. We read about Perez, Hezron, Carmi, Hur, Shobal, their sons, grandsons, granddaughters, and so on. At first glance the chapter appears only to be a family tree whose branches blossom with strange-sounding names. Then we come to verse 9.

There, nestled in among Judah's grandsons and great-grandsons, is a brief statement about a fellow named Jabez. It seems this man was "more honorable than his brothers" (4:9). Besides that, he prayed. We read that Jabez cried out to God, "Oh, that you would bless me and enlarge my territory! Let your hand be with me, and keep me from harm so that I will be free from pain" (4:10). And we also read that God granted his request (4:10). What a special little jewel—the account of an answered prayer—right in the middle of a family charter! Get to know God's word—it will surprise and delight you!

Jacob has been pronouncing serious prophecies to his boys. He's had to be especially harsh with Reuben, Simeon, Levi, and Dan. With his remarks to Dan, the worst is over. The comments directed toward the remaining sons won't have to be so cutting, so pointed, so reproachful. It's almost as if Jacob breathes a sigh of relief.

Maybe he begins to look forward to his journey to be with the Lord, the deliverance that will come with his death. It could be that he catches a glimpse of the finish line, much as Sheldon Vanauken's dying wife Davy evidently did in her final moments. "Oh dearling, look," were the last words she uttered before lapsing into unconsciousness and finally slipping away (Vanauken 176).

Maybe Jacob is treated to a peek at the grand finale, or perhaps he starts thinking about what he has said to

Judah. His excitement bubbles over at the thought of Israel's messiah, Shiloh, the coming king of kings, the deliverer of his people. It thrills him so that he cannot help but cry, "I look for your deliverance, O Lord"! An old man named Simeon and an old woman named Anna would centuries later echo his sentiments as they cradled the infant Jesus in their arms when he was presented at the temple in Jerusalem (Luke 2:25-36). They'd waited all their lives to see the savior, and God had granted their heartfelt desires.

Gad, Asher, and Naphtali: Valor, Richness, and Freedom

Jacob resumes his messages to his sons, rapidly addressing the remaining children of the handmaids. Zilpah's son Gad is described next.

"Gad will be attacked by a band of raiders," says Jacob, "but he will attack them at their heels" (49:19). The men of Gad settled east of the Jordan River, and often had to fend off border raids from hostile groups. The Bible characterizes them as mighty warriors, men of valor, men of courage and strength. As Moses blesses the tribe of Gad in Deuteronomy 33, he proclaims, "Blessed is he who enlarges Gad's domain! Gad lives there like a lion, tearing at arm or head" (33:20; see also 33:21). They were brave, persistent, possessive men.

"Asher's food will be rich," continues Jacob, speaking of the younger son of Zilpah, "he will provide delicacies fit for a king" (49:20). Foreshadowed is the fact that the tribe of Asher would settle in a fertile and productive area, the lush northern coast of Canaan (Joshua 19:24-31). Asher's name means "happy," and so his descendants were destined to be.

Jacob concludes his prophecies concerning the sons of the handmaids with this statement about Bilhah's younger son Naphtali: "Naphtali is a doe set free that bears beautiful fawns" (49:21). The tribe of Naphtali would settle in the mountains northwest of the sea of Galilee, and there would experience the relative isolation and freedom of mountain peoples. They'd be fruitful as well, producing many children. It was to be a thoroughly agreeable future.

THE SONS OF RACHEL—GENESIS 49:22-28

"Joseph is a fruitful vine,
  a fruitful vine near a spring,
  whose branches climb over a wall.
With bitterness archers attacked him;
  they shot at him with hostility.
But his bow remained steady,
  his strong arms stayed limber,
because of the hand of the Mighty One of Jacob,
  because of the Shepherd, the Rock of Israel,
because of your father's God, who helps you,
  because of the Almighty, who blesses you
with blessings of the heavens above,
  blessings of the deep that lies below,
  blessings of the breast and womb.
Your father's blessings are greater
  than the blessings of the ancient mountains,
  than the bounty of the age-old hills.
Let all these rest on the head of Joseph,
  on the brow of the prince among his brothers.

"Benjamin is a ravenous wolf;
  in the morning he devours the prey,
  in the evening he divides the plunder."

All these are the twelve tribes of Israel, and this is what their father said to them when he blessed them, giving each the blessing appropriate to him.

Finally we come to the last two of Jacob's boys, his special sons, the offspring of Rachel. Justifiably, Jacob reserves his most impressive praise for Joseph.

"Joseph is a fruitful vine," he begins, "a fruitful vine near a spring, whose branches climb over a wall" (49:22). As we have mentioned, Joseph has borne much fruit in his life. He epitomizes the words revealed by God to the prophet Jeremiah, who writes in Jeremiah 17:7-8:

> But blessed is the man who trusts in the Lord,
> whose confidence is in him.
> He will be like a tree planted by the water
> that sends out its roots by the stream.
> It does not fear when heat comes;
> its leaves are always green.
> It has no worries in a year of drought
> and never fails to bear fruit.

Contrast Reuben's instability with Joseph's well-rooted constancy, and you see why Jacob chooses the latter to receivethe blessings of the firstborn. He is firmly grounded, strong, stable, fruitful—not impetuous or irresolute like his oldest brother.

"With bitterness the archers attacked him; they shot at him with hostility," Jacob continues, describing Joseph. "But his bow remained steady, his strong arms stayed limber" (49:23-24). Who were these "archers"? They were Joseph's brothers, the slave traders, Potiphar, Mrs. Potiphar. They shot at him with hostility and bitterness, but he did not fall. His "bow remained steady," his strong arms "limber." He remained constant despite the pit, the caravan, the slavery, the prison sentence, the misunderstanding, the temptation.

Why was Joseph able to persevere? Jacob reveals the answer as he continues. As he tells Joseph, it was "because of the hand of the Mighty One of Jacob, because of the Shepherd, the Rock of Israel, because of your father's God, who helps you, because of the Almighty, who blesses you" (49:24-25). His relationship with God has been Joseph's key throughout. It has been his ticket to spiritual freedom, even in the midst of physical captivity.

And God, in turn, has blessed Joseph abundantly, according to Jacob. He's given Joseph "blessings of the heavens above" and "blessings of the deep that lies below"—a plethora of gifts such as an obedient heart, spiritual insight, the ability to interpret dreams, the wisdom to run a kingdom, the desire to serve, a consistent character, an ability to remain faithful to God's purpose. God has also granted Joseph children—"blessings of the breast and womb." Ephraim and Manasseh are special joys in Joseph's life, gifts from the Lord.

And Jacob ends his record of the blessings of Joseph's life by expressing this deep desire: "Let all these rest on the head of Joseph, on the brow of the prince among his brothers" (49:26). Joseph is like royalty among his siblings; he is the one who has saved their lives. Intelligent, strong, reliable, unwavering, he deserves their allegiance and is, as much as is humanly possible, worthy of the tremendous blessings of God which he has received.

Benjamin: A Ravenous Wolf

His praise of Joseph finished, Jacob at last turns to his youngest boy, Benjamin. "Benjamin is a ravenous wolf; in the morning he devours the prey, in the evening he divides the plunder," the patriarch reveals (49:27). The tribe of Benjamin would become a tribe of warriors—tough, rugged individuals. Judges 20:16 describes some of the soldiers of Benjamin this way: "Among all these soldiers there were seven hundred chosen men who were left-handed, each of whom could sling a stone at a hair and not miss." These Benjamites were left-handed slingshot artists. It's out of the tribe of Benjamin that Saul, the great military genius, comes. So warlike was the entire tribe that its members did not fear taking on the rest of the nation of Israel. Indeed, the Benjamites were nearly wiped out in the bloody civil war that is recorded in the book of Judges (Judges 20–21).

Wrapping It Up

It's interesting to note how many references to animals Jacob makes while blessing his sons. He calls Judah a lion, Issachar a strong ass, Dan a serpent, Naphtali a deer, and Benjamin a ravenous wolf. His metaphors hit home; he accurately describes each son and the character of that son's descendants.

With his message to Benjamin, Jacob's farewell address nears its close. Verse 28 reveals that each blessing bestowed upon each son has been "appropriate to him." Jacob has chosen his words wisely. Some have been painful to utter; others have spilled forth in joy. The effort spent in communicating with his twelve boys has surely demanded the last shred of Jacob's strength, leaving him exhausted. There are but a few items left on his agenda . . . then it will be time to pull up his tent stakes and head for his heavenly home.

Last-Minute Instructions—Genesis 49:29-33

> Then he gave them these instructions: "I am about to be gathered to my people. Bury me with my fathers in the cave in the field of Ephron the Hittite, the cave in the field of Machpelah, near Mamre in Canaan, which Abraham bought as a burial place from Ephron the Hittite, along with the field. There Abraham and his wife Sarah were buried, there Isaac and his wife Rebekah were buried, and there I buried Leah. The field and the cave in it were bought from the Hittites."
>
> When Jacob had finished giving instructions to his sons, he drew his feet up into the bed, breathed his last and was gathered to his people.

"I am about to be gathered to my people," Jacob advises his sons, sensing that death draws ever nearer. "Bury me with my fathers in the cave in the field of Ephron the Hittite," he continues, giving them instructions for the funeral (49:29). Jacob wishes to be laid to rest in the cave purchased by his grandfather Abraham. Abraham bought the cave from the Hittite in order to bury his beloved Sarah when she breathed her last. Isaac and Rebekah lie there in death, as does Leah. Ironically, Rachel, her remains lying in an obscure grave, will not rest beside Jacob. In death, it is the less-loved Leah who occupies the place of honor as his wife.

His funeral arrangements made, Jacob reiterates the fact that the cave and field had already been purchased from the Hittites long ago. Shrewd businessman that he is, he doesn't want the boys paying for property the family already owns.

A well-ordered death is the final act of a well-ordered life. Edith Schaeffer, knowing that it would be his wish, brought her husband Francis home from the hospital to die. In familiar surroundings, the music he loved playing in the background, his favorite things surrounding his bed, theologian Francis Schaeffer succumbed to the cancer from which he had suffered, and crossed over to his eternal home (Graham 147). Surrounded by the sons he holds so dear, Jacob likewise dies with dignity. He draws his feet up into the bed and breathes his last. He is gathered unto his people, those who have preceded him into the hereafter (49:33).

It's time to go. Jacob has discharged his stewardship; he has said the things that needed to be said; he has bound up the loose ends of family life and national policy. Leadership of the young nation will rest with the tribe of Judah. Joseph will retain the rights of the first-born, replacing Reuben and receiving all that which is due. Surely the brothers will never forget watching their father, faithful to the finish, go out a winner. He has shown them how to die.

LESSONS

What lessons can we learn from Jacob's final hours? There are several worthy of our review.

Lesson one: *how much we need the stability of God in these unstable times!* God, grant us the strength to be Josephs, not Reubens—unwavering in our convictions, firmly grounded in our faith, fully rooted in your righteousness.

Lesson two: *Simeon and Levi are judged because of their unreasoning viciousness.* May the Lord deliver us from such anger and cruelty.

Lesson three: *Jesus Christ is the lion of the tribe of Judah who is going to come again to rule and reign.* On his deathbed, Jacob reveals a glimpse of the future glory that we shall witness.

Lesson four: *we can miss God's best by failing to do his will today.* Like the men of Issachar, how easy it is for us to lapse into apathy, sitting down between the saddlebags instead of standing on the promises!

Lesson five: *our lives should be characterized by freedom and fruit.* If we know Jesus Christ as savior, he is able to free us from the domination of sin, and to work in our lives so that we, like Joseph, are fruitful. In turn, our heavenly father is glorified with much fruit.

Lesson six: *Jacob teaches us how to die.* He leaves no stone unturned, no word unsaid, no matter unsettled. Then he journeys to his heavenly home, ready to depart and eager to see his Lord.

Ready to Go

Two years ago this January, a good friend and member of the ministry's executive board, Don Guion, went in for a routine check-up. He was sixty-three years old, and had hardly been sick a day in his life. He wasn't a pound overweight, jogged several miles a day, had never touched a cigarette. But during the medical exam, an Xray revealed a spot on Donnie's lung. The biopsy showed it to be cancer. By April of that same year, Donnie was gone.

As we buried my friend on that warm, windy, spring day, I cried. Yet what a comfort it was to hear so many of the mourners reflect on the kind of person he had been. "He was the epitome of the successful man." "Don had it all—success in his family life, with his wife, in his career." "He was such a good man. We're going to miss him." "He had things together spiritually like no one I've ever known." These are the kinds of things I want people to say about me at my funeral. I want them to have seen that my priorities were straight, that I valued my wife and family, and, most of all, that I treasured my relationship with God. I want them to reflect on the fact that I fought the good fight, and went out a winner. Don't you?

Although it was only three months from the time his illness was diagnosed to the day he went home to be with the Lord, Donnie Guion was ready to die. You see, his preparations to leave didn't begin with a dismal medical report in that dreary January. His whole life had been a process of preparing to go. He had maintained close relationships with his children and with his dear wife Pat. The loose ends had been tied up along the way. Donnie had grown to know the Lord intimately, so I'm sure that his death was merely a homecoming for him, as he was greeted by his very best friend, Jesus Christ, on the other side.

The question is, can *you* honestly say that you are ready to follow Don and Jacob? Are you prepared to die? If you knew that you had only thirty minutes left in this world, could you exclaim with the patriarch himself, "I look for your deliverance, O Lord"? I believe I could. I pray that you could, as well.

Questions for Study

1. Why does Jacob remove Reuben from the position of firstborn in the family? What are some principles we can apply to our own family lives from the example of Reuben and Bilhah?

2. Jacob's final blessing to Judah promises the good life for Judah's descendants. What promises concerning Israel's messiah do Jacob's words also contain?

3. Describe the men of Issachar as Jacob depicts them. In what ways are we like them today?

4. Jacob calls Joseph "a fruitful vine." In your own words, explain how Joseph fits this description.

5. Jacob shows us, in Genesis 49, how to die. Think about your own death. Will you be bothered by the might have beens and the what ifs? What can you do now to avoid these?

12

Rites of Passage

Genesis 50

I have mentioned that my father recently passed away from cancer. The months of waiting hung over the entire family like a shroud. Mom's own cancer and surgery made Dad's terminal situation all the more traumatic. The experience of his death has affected me like nothing else ever has. It has made me all the more conscious of my own mortality. With Dad's death, the three Ps—pain, preparation, priorities—that I so often have shared with others dealing with grief have finally become personal.

First, there is the pain of the experience. When a dearly loved one dies, the sense of separation spawns an ache that doesn't go away. The finality of it all descends like a dense, heavy fog, the sensation of permanent loss sinking in with leaden heaviness.

Besides provoking intense pain, the death of another engenders in us a desire to prepare. Death is no longer deniable. The inevitable must be faced, and accepted. After Dad's funeral, I found myself sorting the strings of my own life, beginning to bind up the loose ends, starting to prepare my wife, my children, and myself for what will be.

Part of preparing for our own final hours involves examining our priorities. With Dad's passing I find myself striving to spend the time I have left where it is most productive. I now say no when necessary. My fervent prayer has become that of Psalm 90:12, where Moses asks the Lord, "So teach us to number our days, that we may apply our hearts unto wisdom" (KJV).

As many a flight attendant has said, our ground time will be brief. Our parents' deaths are followed all too closely, it seems, by our own. The pain of watching our folks conclude their earthly lives should cause us to consider our own priorities and our own plans of preparation. This is what we see happening in Genesis 50, as we first watch fifty-six-year-old Joseph and his brothers bid goodbye to their father, and then later witness Joseph's own final moments. Funerals—unavoidable rites of passage—frame this final chapter of the Bible's first book.

Realizing the imminence of his own death, the apostle Paul writes in 2 Timothy 4:7, "I have fought the good fight, I have finished the course, I have kept the faith" (NASB). His statement rings true of Jacob and Joseph, too. They have fought the good fight; they have finished the course; they have kept the faith. They've shown us how to live. Now Joseph, like Jacob in Genesis 49, will show us how to die.

Burying Jacob—Genesis 50:1-14

> Joseph threw himself upon his father and wept over him and kissed him. Then Joseph directed the physicians in his service to embalm his father Israel. So the physicians embalmed him, taking a full forty days, for that was the time required for embalming. And the Egyptians mourned for him seventy days.
>
> When the days of mourning had passed, Joseph said to Pharaoh's court, "If I have found favor in your eyes, speak to Pharaoh for me. Tell him, 'My father made me swear an oath and said, "I am about to die; bury me in the tomb I dug for myself in the land of Canaan." Now let me go up and bury my father; then I will return.' "

> Pharaoh said, "Go up and bury your father, as he made you swear to do."
>
> So Joseph went up to bury his father. All Pharaoh's officials accompanied him—the dignitaries of his court and all the dignitaries of Egypt—besides all the members of Joseph's household and his brothers and those belonging to his father's household. Only their children and their flocks and herds were left in Goshen. Chariots and horsemen also went up with him. It was a very large company.
>
> When they reached the threshing floor of Atad, near the Jordan, they lamented loudly and bitterly; and there Joseph observed a seven-day period of mourning for his father. When the Canaanites who lived there saw the mourning at the threshing floor of Atad, they said, "The Egyptians are holding a solemn ceremony of mourning." That is why that place near the Jordan is called Abel Mizraim.
>
> So Jacob's sons did as he had commanded them: They carried him to the land of Canaan and buried him in the cave in the field of Machpelah, near Mamre, which Abraham had bought as a burial place from Ephron the Hittite, along with the field. After burying his father, Joseph returned to Egypt, together with his brothers and all the others who had gone with him to bury his father.

Our last vision of Jacob saw him revealing prophecies and imparting final blessings to his sons. After leaving them clear-cut instructions concerning his funeral arrangements, the 147-year-old man draws his knees up into the bed, perhaps curling up like a newborn infant, and breathes his last. The great patriarch of the clan is gone. His sons, gathered around his deathbed, view his final, fleeting breaths in stunned silence. They haven't had time fully to comprehend all that he has said to them in these last few moments; now they must accept the reality of his death also.

Joseph is the first graphically to express compassion

and grief. Verse 1 tells us that he throws himself across his father's lifeless body. Tears spill from his eyes as he kisses Jacob for the last time, his lips chilled by the coldness of death. The sorrow of Jacob's passing pierces him to the marrow, and he shatters the silence with sobs and cries.

It is not surprising that Joseph is the first to show his emotion at Jacob's demise. In Jacob, he is losing more than a father. He is also losing his guide and his best friend. There has been nobody like Jacob in Joseph's life.

Death often has an amazing effect on the survivors of the deceased. Suddenly, negative memories of the dearly departed are wiped out. The slate is clean, and only good things come to mind. I've attended hundreds of funerals. Once in awhile, after the service is over, I think about looking into the casket just to make sure that the deceased really was the same man I knew in life. Such marvelous things had been said about him in the eulogy! Such primrose accolades were poured out from the pulpit in his memory! The fellow I knew didn't deserve all that praise. But of course, funerals aren't the place for the negative. And death really does have a way of erasing the bad.

I imagine Jacob's passing awakens every pleasant memory of him that Joseph possesses. While sobbing over his father's lifeless frame, Joseph probably recalls a few of these. I think he remembers the beautiful coat Jacob had given him as an expression of a father's love; surely he thinks of their joyous reunion in Egypt, when Jacob finally comes; certainly he blesses God for the seventeen good years he has had to care for his father. It is an intensely painful time of mourning, and Joseph's mind is filled with warm and poignant recollections of the past.

Funeral Preparations

When tragedy strikes, we find ourselves forced to numbly go about the ordeal of making preparations. The funeral parlor is visited, the undertaker consulted, the gravesite selected, the casket chosen, the service planned, the flowers ordered, the relatives and friends notified. Each movement is necessary, and the business of busyness momentarily dulls the sharpness of our grief.

His expression of initial sorrow over, Joseph, too, turns to the business of arranging his father's funeral. He first directs his physicians to embalm Jacob, a process requiring forty days (50:2-3). This seems like a long time, but the length is understandable. The Egyptian method of mummification was a very sophisticated, time-consuming practice of literally pickling a corpse—removing the organs, preserving the shell, and wrapping the body with yards and yards of gauze. Embalmed corpses remained intact for centuries. Jacob's body receives the full forty-day treatment.

With the embalming process complete, a period of official mourning begins. For seventy days, Joseph, his brothers, and the people of Egypt express their sorrow over Jacob's death. The time spent grieving over Jacob is only two days fewer than the seventy-two day period reserved for mourning the death of a pharaoh. What royal honor is accorded a lowly shepherd in a strange land! The Egyptians grieve over Jacob out of respect for his son Joseph, the savior of their country. Yet I also wonder if perhaps Jacob, godly old man that he was, had made enough of an impact during the seventeen years he resided in Egypt to merit some grieving on his own.

When the days of mourning are ended, Joseph asks members of pharaoh's court to represent him to the ruler. "If I have found favor in your eyes, speak to Pharaoh for me," requests Joseph. "Tell him, 'My father made me swear an oath and said, "I am about to die; bury me in the tomb I dug for myself in the land of Canaan." Now let me go up and bury my father; then I will return' " (50:4-5). We remember that Jacob, after blessing Joseph's two sons, Ephraim and Manasseh, commanded Joseph to place a hand upon his thigh and promise that he would bury his father in Canaan (47:29-31). Later, after he bestowed his blessings, Jacob repeated these directions in front of all his sons. Being laid to rest in the promised land was of paramount importance to the patriarch.

Why doesn't Joseph approach pharaoh himself with the request that he be allowed to transport his father's body to Canaan? Surely the king and his second-in-command are on speaking terms. Certainly Joseph has no reason to fear the ruler for whom he has done so much.

It isn't out of fear or because of a broken relationship that Joseph sends a delegate to pharaoh to voice his request. During periods of mourning, those in deep grief did not attend to personal needs. They didn't bathe or shave or change their clothes. Everything virtually came to a standstill. Joseph and family have been mourning the passing of Jacob for seventy days, remember. In his present condition, Joseph doesn't dare appear before pharaoh. It is a matter of respect and consideration.

Pharaoh's response to Joseph's request is an unequivocal yes. The ruler's message is relayed to Joseph: "Go up and bury your father, as he made you swear to do" (50:6).

The Funeral Procession

From the heart of Egypt an immense procession goes forth. Pharaoh's officials, court dignitaries, VIPS from across the land, accompany Joseph, the members of his own household, his brothers, and the members of Jacob's household on a march of mourning into Canaan (50:7-8). Chariots and horsemen add to the vast numbers (50:9). It is an enormous company—an ancient funeral train rambling along the 250 miles to Hebron, bearing the body of the patriarch. It is an elaborate display, one which Jacob would never have imagined possible or believed he deserved.

When the throng reaches the threshing floor of Atad, near the Jordan River, the travelers pause. Great weeping and loud cries of lamentation burst forth as Joseph and the entourage begin to observe the traditional Hebrew period of mourning, a time of grieving lasting seven days. People of today might consider this additional period of mourning to be excessive—even unnecessary. After all, they spent over two months in Egypt shedding tears and not taking showers. Surely they've shown sufficient respect for the memory of Jacob!

But it is important to remember that the lengthy period of mourning in Egypt was part of that culture. Joseph and his family are of Hebrew descent, and now they are in the land of the Hebrews. It's time to follow the customs of their own culture, and this is the place to do it. Besides, Jacob would want it that way. He'd approve of his sons remaining a distinct people, respecting Egyptian tradition but not adopting it as their own. They are the forerunners of God's chosen nation, and separation, not assimilation, is the appropriate choice when faced with the customs of another land.

Evidently the Egyptians accompanying Joseph and his family join in on the expression of grief at the threshing floor of Atad. At the very least they remain respectfully subdued, because the onlooking Canaanites make this comment: "The Egyptians are holding a solemn ceremony of mourning" (50:11). Apparently none of the natives recognizes any of the Hebrews, for all are assumed to be Egyptians. Jacob's sons have only been gone from the land of Canaan for seventeen years, and yet they've been virtually forgotten. It's a sobering, humbling thought. We think we're indispensable, but the truth is that the void we leave is filled nearly as soon as we shut the door on our way out. The Hebrews haven't been missed in Canaan. They're not even remembered.

The Service

Once the seven-day period of mourning ends, Jacob's sons do as he had commanded them. They carry their father's body to the cave of Machpelah in the field that, like the cave, had once belonged to the Hittites (50:12-13). And there they lay Jacob to rest, beside the remains of Leah, in the company of his father, mother, grandfather, and grandmother.

What a joy it must be for Joseph, Judah, Benjamin, and the rest to be able to bury their father according to his final wishes. They must be thankful that they can do one last thing for Jacob by fulfilling his desires. As a minister, I know that feeling well. How great it is to speak at a funeral service and be able to preach precisely the words the deceased would want to hear. It's essentially a fulfillment of final wishes, even though they might have been unexpressed.

A year or so ago I was privileged to conduct the funeral of a dear elderly Christian lady, and it was the easiest sermon I've ever prepared. You see, I used her Bible. Taking the passages she had boldly underlined and scribbled most of her notes beside, I allowed her to preach her own message, in a sense. Her Bible was the means of communication with her grieving friends and family. I was merely the mouthpiece and the organizer. The content was all hers, and the Lord's.

It is special to be able to fulfill the dying wishes of another. A member of the congregation at that funeral whispered to me on the way out of the church, "Don, when I go, be sure to tell my husband that the poems I want you to use in my funeral are in my wallet." Of course I promised her I would.

Return to Egypt

The burial of Jacob complete, Joseph, his brothers, and the vast entourage which had accompanied them return to the land of Egypt. Surely it is emotionally difficult for Joseph to leave. The occasion of Jacob's funeral marks the first time Joseph has been back in the land of Canaan in at least thirty-nine years. He left at age seventeen, spent thirteen years in Potiphar's house and prison, experienced seven years of plenty and seven years of famine. Two years into the famine, Jacob and family arrive in Egypt. We know they've been there for seventeen years. Add it all up, and you get thirty-nine. That's a long time to be away from home! And now, as Joseph prepares to return to Egypt, he has to leave his father behind.

What about the brothers? Do they, too, find it difficult to depart the promised land? Their families are still in Egypt, so that might make the going back easier. Yet it would be surprising if there weren't at least some twinges of regret at the departure from Canaan. They hadn't been anxious to leave home back in the days when hardship forced them to journey to Egypt in the first place. Surely leaving the place where they'd grown up is painful for them now. But the marvelous thing is that all twelve of Jacob's sons accept the fact that they are going back. They don't try to resist God's sovereign purpose. They know it's his plan for them to be residents of Egypt—strangers in a strange land—for four hundred years, just as they know their descendants will one day return to the land of promise.

High Anxiety—Genesis 50:15-21

> When Joseph's brothers saw that their father was dead, they said, "What if Joseph holds a grudge against us and pays us back for all the wrongs we did to him?" So they sent word to Joseph, saying, "Your father left these instructions before he died. 'This is what you are to say to Joseph: I ask you to forgive your brothers the sins and the wrongs they committed in treating you so badly.' Now please forgive the sins of the servants of the God of your father." When their message came to him, Joseph wept.
>
> His brothers then came and threw themselves down before him. "We are your slaves," they said.
>
> But Joseph said to them, "Don't be afraid. Am I in the place of God? You intended to harm me, but God

> intended it for good to accomplish what is now being done, the saving of many lives. So then, don't be afraid. I will provide for you and your children." And he reassured them and spoke kindly to them.

Asking "What If?"

We've already mentioned that Jacob, after stealing the blessing from Esau by deceiving Isaac, fled to Paddan-Aram in fear of his life. Actually, Esau did threaten to kill Jacob, but only after his father's death (Genesis 27:41). Out of respect for Isaac, Esau planned to restrain himself while his father lived. Once the funeral was held, he intended to strike. It was the tradition of the day to wait for revenge until after the mourning.

Understanding the custom of the culture helps us comprehend what happens next in Genesis 50. With Jacob dead and buried, Joseph's older brothers naturally begin to get a little worried. Has Joseph really forgiven them, or has he just been waiting for Jacob to die so that he can get even with them? The brothers succumb to a classic case of the what ifs.

You know what I mean. We worry ourselves sick about what might happen, and most of the time our fears are groundless. We at the Ministries are no exception; we're no strangers to the what ifs. I can't count the number of mornings we've spent worrying about the what ifs before the beginning of each week of camp. What if someone drowns? What if a child falls off the balcony? What if there's a riding accident? What if we have an epidemic of flu? When we allow the what ifs to get the better of us, the whole idea of going to camp becomes pretty discouraging. We've found it's better to hand the what ifs over to our all-powerful Lord.

"What if Joseph holds a grudge against us and pays us back for all the wrongs we did to him?" the brothers murmur among themselves (50:15). Jacob is dead, and they're scared. Obviously, they haven't truly fathomed the character of their brother. They really don't know him, or they wouldn't be worried. They'd realize that his forgiveness, like that of the Lord Jesus Christ, is total, unconditional, and free for the asking. Instead, their guilt over the long-forgiven past gets the better of them.

Just Following Instructions?

Walter Wangerin writes of guilt:

> The guilty live in dreadful uncertainty. Because of their own unworthiness, the good world may collapse around them—and they are helpless, they feel, to sustain it. They caused it, and they deserve the collapse. In despair they may do nothing at all to help your relationship. Or in abject shame, they may rush to and fro doing *everything*, trying to "make up" for their sin (Wangerin 103).

Joseph's brothers fall into the latter camp. Alarmed, they decide to act—rushing to and fro, striving to do everything they can to appease him. The first part of their scheme involves sending word to Joseph, a little message that wounds him because it so plainly shows that they do not understand him. Here is a copy of the communication:

> Your father left these instructions before he died: "This is what you are to say to Joseph: I ask you to forgive your brothers the sins and the wrongs they committed in treating you so badly." Now please forgive the sins of the servants of the God of your father (50:16-17).

Did Jacob really leave those instructions behind? I doubt it. His relationship with Joseph was so richly intense that he surely knew Joseph had forgiven his brothers. Even if Jacob were worried about the possibility of Joseph's seeking revenge, he would have confronted his favorite son directly. The old man never was one to mince words!

Actually, what the brothers' message reminds me of is what some of us did in grade school. When we wanted to skip a day in the classroom, we'd forge our parents' signature on a phony note excusing us from school. Mom and Dad had no idea—most of the time—that they were being grossly misrepresented.

Of course, there's always the possibility that the content of the brothers' note is genuine. Maybe Jacob did reassure them at some time. Perhaps, sensing their tremendous anxiety, he did give them directions to follow in dealing with Joseph after his own death. But knowing what they've been capable of in years gone by, I wouldn't put it past the brothers to have concocted the whole thing themselves.

The Tears of the Misunderstood

What is Joseph's response to his brothers' message? Verse 16 reveals that he weeps. He is hurt—hurt because his brothers obviously mistrust him, hurt because of their unbelief. The brothers are begging for a forgiveness that has been theirs for over seventeen years!

With his weeping, Joseph mirrors the Lord Jesus Christ. Perhaps you are making tears run down the face of Christ at this very minute because you will not believe that he is able and willing to forgive you. You figure that there's too much water under the bridge, that it's too late, that you've sinned too deeply. You've sunk below the reach of his exceeding great grace. But it isn't so.

Christ is always ready for you to receive him as savior. After that, you'll be totally free, eternally reconciled to God. How often we preach about the cross of Jesus Christ and his ability to forgive, but we deny that his grace is continuous and his salvation is everlasting! The fact is that, as Christians, we are forgiven forever! Jesus himself, speaking in John 10:27-29, puts it this way:

> My sheep hear My voice, and I know them, and they follow Me; and I give eternal life to them, and they shall never perish; and no one shall snatch

> them out of My hand. My Father, who has given them to Me, is greater than all; and no one is able to snatch them out of the Father's hand (NASB).

Once we're born again, we'll never be unborn. We can't forfeit our positions as children of God. But how it must grieve the Lord when we forget that he has declared us righteous in his sight! Like Joseph, God holds no grudges.

REASSURANCE

After allowing enough time for Joseph to receive their message, the brothers make an appearance in Memphis. They come to their younger brother and throw themselves down before him, and we catch a final glimpse of the fulfillment of Joseph's dreams of long ago. "We are your slaves," the brothers exclaim (50:18). This is part two of their plan—what an extreme they went to in order to cover guilt and make up for the past!

Joseph looks at them. "Don't be afraid," he says reassuringly. "Am I in the place of God?" (50:19). God is the avenger . . . Joseph makes no claim to being his equal.

"You intended to harm me, but God intended it for good to accomplish what is now being done, the saving of many lives," Joseph continues (50:20). In other words, haven't you brothers caught on yet? Haven't you seen the Lord's involvement in all that has happened? Haven't I preached it? Haven't I demonstrated it?

Joseph is faithful and consistent. When he reveals himself to his brothers in Genesis 45, he explains that while they sold him into Egypt, God actually sent him there. Now, seventeen years later, he echoes his original remarks. The key to Joseph's victorious life, particularly his ability to forgive and forget, is that in every circumstance he is able to see God as the sovereign administrator over the events of his life. He can rise above the pettiness, the wrongs, the ruins.

"So then, don't be afraid. I will provide for you and

your children," concludes Joseph (50:21). And verse 21 tells us that he reassures his brothers and speaks kindly to them. I'm sure he is praying that they are convinced.

One of the poems of Ruth Harms Calkin, entitled "Personal Hurt," accurately conveys the outlook of Joseph as his brothers confront him in guiltridden fear:

> O God—
> In this personal hurt
> That pierces so deeply
> Give me, I pray
> The high and holy privilege
> Of proving to the one
> Who initiated the hurt
> That the love of Jesus
> Can withstand it.

That the brothers have hurt Joseph, there can be no doubt. Time and the Lord have erased the sting of thirty-nine years ago in the pit, but their recent display of mistrust has pierced him to the quick. It is a personal hurt, as Calkin would say. Yet Joseph responds to his brothers with kindness. He assures them of his continued provision for them. It's as if, like the poet, he is desiring to prove to those who have initiated the hurt that the love of God can withstand it. It is a high and holy privilege for him to consistently, faithfully, care for his brothers and their families, so that they will see reflected the love of God, and know that the forgiveness is real.

The Last Days of a Faithful Servant—Genesis 50:22-26

> Joseph stayed in Egypt, along with all his father's family. He lived a hundred and ten years and saw the third generation of Ephraim's children. Also the children of Makir son of Manasseh were placed at birth on Joseph's knees.
>
> Then Joseph said to his brothers, "I am about to

> die. But God will surely come to your aid and take you up out of this land to the land he promised on oath to Abraham, Isaac and Jacob." And Joseph made the sons of Israel swear an oath and said, "God will surely come to your aid, and then you must carry my bones up from this place."
>
> So Joseph died at the age of a hundred and ten. And after they embalmed him, he was placed in a coffin in Egypt.

At the time Joseph reassures his brothers of his continuing affection and loyalty, he is fifty-six years old. The next thing we learn about him in scripture is that he remains in Egypt, along with his father's family, and that he lives "a hundred and ten years" (50:22). The Bible so meticulously portrays Joseph from the age of seventeen until he reaches his mid-fifties, and now, in one verse consisting of a solitary sentence and a single phrase, skips over the final fifty-four years of his life. Oh, to be able to fill in the gaps! I'd like to know what Joseph did during those years about which scripture is largely silent.

We do know that the silent years have contained some pleasing and proud moments for Joseph. He's not only become a grandfather, but also a great-grandfather in that time. Verse 23 tells us that Joseph has been able to see the "third generation of Ephraim's children," and that at their births the children of Manasseh's son Makir were placed upon Joseph's knees, an act signifying that he claimed them as his own. It's been a happy, fruitful period for the patriarch, and the reward of his grandchildren and great-grandchildren has only made it even better. As any grandfather will tell you, it's more fun to have grandchildren than children of your own. There's a minimum of responsibility and a maximum of enjoyment. Just the other night, my grandsons Ian and Andrew and I were wrestling and playing on the floor. The pure, uninhibited laughter of a little child is a pleasing tonic to an old man's heart. Roughhousing with grandchildren is a great way to grow old.

We also know that during these fifty-four years, Joseph has kept his word. He has cared for his brothers and their families, just as he promised. He has not grown bitter with the passage of time; he has not reneged on his commitment.

I really believe it would be safe to say that Joseph has consistently lived a godly life during his last five decades. The Bible is faithful to record the failures of its men and women, regardless of whom they are or how glorious their records may have been to date. Scripture produces no plastic saints or phony heroes; God's word presents the bad as well as the good. The fact that there is no mention of a moral or spiritual downslide in Joseph's later life suggests that one never happened. He probably just faithfully plugged along, pulling his load, keeping his promises. The way he played in the first half is the way he played in the second. And I'm confident that when time ran out, Joseph heard the Lord himself exclaim, "Well done!"

A Time to Die

Inevitably the day comes for Joseph, as it will for each of us, when he becomes fully aware of his frailty and mortality. His step grows slower, his muscles weaker, his joints stiffer, his breathing more labored. Sleep encroaches at unexpected moments. Vivid recollections of his childhood and young adulthood amuse him, while events of yesterday are impossible to remember. He is old, but aware enough to realize that death is approaching.

Joseph calls his brothers together. "I am about to die," he tells them. "But God will surely come to your aid and take you up out of this land to the land he promised on oath to Abraham, Isaac and Jacob" (50:24). When Jacob dies, he's looking back, desiring to return to Canaan and be buried beside Leah. As Joseph prepares to depart, he isn't looking back, but forward—to the fulfillment of God's promises to Abraham. He firmly and fully believes that the time is coming when the descendants of his brothers will leave Egypt to occupy the promised land. And when that happens, Joseph wants to be present!

"God will surely come to your aid, and then you must carry my bones up from this place," continues Joseph in speaking to his brothers (50:25). He wishes his remains eventually to be transported to the land of God's blessing, and he makes each son of Jacob swear an oath that it will be so (50:25). Great is his faith, even as he faces eternity. This tangible act of trust earns Joseph a place in the book of Hebrews, where we read, "By faith Joseph, when he was dying, made mention of the exodus of the sons of Israel, and gave orders concerning his bones" (Hebrews 11:22 NASB). And as we have mentioned previously, Joseph's descendants, under the leadership of Moses, eventually keep the promise their forebears make in Genesis 50 (Exodus 13:19-21).

The final verse of the book of Genesis contains these words, "So Joseph died at the age of a hundred and ten. And after they embalmed him, he was placed in a coffin in Egypt" (50:26). There his body was to remain for four hundred years, awaiting the day when Moses would lead the people out.

Final Words about a Man of God

With Joseph's demise, we say goodbye to a good man, a great man. Joseph feared God and respected his sovereignty all of his life. He deeply desired to please the Lord, and ordered his life with that intention in mind. He possessed a heart open to God, flexible, pliable, teachable. The Lord was ever with him, guiding, directing, blessing. And Joseph's entire life provides an object lesson for us all: that things do work together for good for those who love the Lord, and who are called according to his plan and purpose.

Had I been able to preach at Joseph's funeral, I'd have

centered my sermon on two words: fellowship and faithfulness. Consistently, he maintained fellowship with the father. Faithfully, he did the will of his God. Having every reason to be bitter toward those who wronged him, Joseph dies a peaceful, joyous, gracious, and grateful man. I want to grow old just as he did.

LESSONS

Let's look at a few of the lessons from the final chapter of Joseph's biography. His last years, like all the others, suggest some solid principles for us to follow.

Lesson one: *death for the person who walks with God is just a simple conclusion to a well-ordered life.* It's the time when the Lord is calling, "Come on home. I've got some new assignments for you!" That's all death is, for the man or woman who loves the Lord.

Lesson two: *one of the best things we can do for those who depart this life is to fulfill their final wishes.* We can do what they wanted done.

Lesson three: often, as it did to the brothers, the guilt from past sins comes back to haunt us. If we're Christians, we're forgiven. *God expects us to forget those things that are behind and press on toward that which is ahead.*

Lesson four: *as Christians, we grieve our savior when we are unable or unwilling to believe that his forgiveness is legitimate and eternal.* God doesn't hold grudges. He doesn't try to get even with us. He offers us his forgiveness freely.

Lesson five: *Joseph's forgiveness of his brothers is valid and unconditional.* We know this because his attitude is consistent toward them. He keeps his word, even after Jacob's death.

Lesson six: *when it comes time for him to die, Joseph is looking to the future with confidence.* He firmly believes that what God has promised will happen: the children of Israel will return to claim the promised land as their own.

Lesson seven: the final lesson is simply a verse of scripture, Romans 8:28: *"And we know that God causes all things to work together for good to those who love God, to those who are called according to His purpose"* (NASB).

At the End

We begin and conclude our final chapter in the life of Joseph with funerals—rites of passage. I cannot help but think once again of my own father's going home. Dad chose to die with dignity. All the life support systems were removed and he was kind, coherent, and cooperative to the very last. He fell asleep and slipped away, and one knew that he, like the apostle Paul in Philippians 1:23, had "the desire to depart and be with Christ, for that is very much better" (NASB).

Preaching at my father's funeral was one of the most difficult things I have ever done, but it helped immensely that I knew he was free from pain and in the presence of the Lord Jesus Christ. The soloist accepted our invitation to sing at the funeral with these words, "It would be a joy to sing at Mr. Anderson's graduation service." And in a sense, the funeral really was a celebration of Dad's graduation—his transition from the flawed temporary to the flawless everlasting.

We've witnessed Jacob's and Joseph's graduation services, too. The words of the psalmist sum up their final journeys more eloquently than I ever could, and I close with his lyrics:

> Precious in the sight of the Lord
> Is the death of His godly ones
> (Psalm 116:15 NASB).

Precious, indeed, is the going home of a believer.

QUESTIONS FOR STUDY

1. Think about the preparations for Jacob's funeral. In what way(s) do we see the Hebrews maintaining their position as a separate people from the Egyptians?

2. Are Judah, Joseph, and the brothers recognized by anyone in Canaan when they return to bury their dad? What does this tell us about our own "indispensability"?

3. Why do the brothers become fearful of Joseph once Jacob is dead? Are their fears justified? What kinds of fears are plaguing you today? What can you do about them?

4. What can we learn about God's forgiveness from Joseph's example in Genesis 50:16-21? (See also John 10:27-29.)

5. When Joseph dies, he is looking forward to the future. How do his final wishes suggest this? What are some of the things God has promised that we, as Christians, can also eagerly anticipate?

Reflections

From birth to death, life is like a marathon: crowds of people see you start, and crowds of people watch you finish. It's the long, lonely miles in between that determine what we are made of. Thank God that he himself has said, "I will never desert you, nor will I ever forsake you" (Hebrews 13:5 NASB).

As we've looked at the life of Joseph, we've seen the marathon in which he has raced, and we've caught portions of the race his father Jacob has run. The finish line for each has been beautiful to behold. These verses from Genesis and Hebrews depict a scene with which we're now familiar.

> "Swear to me," he said. Then Joseph swore to him, and Israel worshiped as he leaned on the top of his staff" (Genesis 47:31).

> "By faith Jacob, as he was dying, blessed each of the sons of Joseph, and worshiped, leaning on the top of his staff" (Hebrews 11:21 NASB).

Jacob is 147; Joseph, fifty-six. The son has been a national figure for twenty-six years. Not time, success, popularity, nor power have eroded his confidence in God's eternal purpose. The father's race has been somewhat different—long and rough because of his resistance. He has lost the use of a hip in one conflict, and nearly starved to death in another standoff with God's perfect plan. Joseph's submissive spirit and obedient heart have made it possible for him to avoid much of the trauma that has characterized Jacob's life. But, as Jacob leans upon his staff, all this doesn't seem so important.

What is important is the worship that is going on as Jacob nears the end of the line. I'm sure that both father and son raise their voices in praise. Their lives have been richer than either could ever have dreamed, and there is much they must want to tell God together. Can't you hear their prayers?

I imagine Jacob lifts his weakening voice to God with words such as these:

> Lord,
>
> I bear on my body the marks of service and the evidence of my resistance. Thank you for letting me live long enough to see some of the glorious unfolding of your purpose and plan, and the faithful fulfillment of many of your promises. You have been a good shepherd, and I have learned what you wanted to teach me in the times I went astray.

Then Joseph surely begins to pray. Emotions well up inside that almost overwhelm him. Tears sparkle on his cheeks as the words flow forth:

> Lord God,
>
> I am doubly blessed to have had the love of both a heavenly and an earthly father. My life has been enriched beyond anything I could have imagined. Not only have those teenage dreams all come true, but you've given me so much more. Lord, I see all the hard times now in the light of your purpose,

> and I have to say that your way was the best way. Thank you for your presence, power, and peace which sustained me in the tough years. Thank you for the wisdom you gave me to lead this great nation. Thank you for my beautiful wife and those two boys, our gifts from you.

Faithful, Fruitful, Fighters, Finishers

Jacob and Joseph remind me of the four Fs which I would like to have characterize my life when I'm leaning upon my staff, worshiping God, and preparing to go home to be with him. Both father and son have been faithful and fruitful. They've been fighters, and they are finishers.

The Faithful

Lamentations 3:22-26 is a classic passage about God's faithfulness to us and about how we, in turn, should faithfully respond to him. Here are the words of the prophet Jeremiah:

> Because of the Lord's great love we are not
> consumed, for his compassions never fail.
> They are new every morning;
> great is your faithfulness.
> I say to myself, "The Lord is my portion;
> therefore I will wait for him."
> The Lord is good to those whose hope is in him,
> to the one who seeks him;
> it is good to wait quietly
> for the salvation of the Lord.
>
> (Lamentations 3:22-26).

God's compassions are new every morning; he is dependable; he is trustworthy. Just as he is faithful, so he longs for us to demonstrate this quality in our lives. He particularly desires us to be faithful servants. I can think of no greater joy at the end of the race than to hear from the lips of the savior, "Well done, thou good and faithful servant. Enter in to the joys I have prepared for you." I'm sure the Lord greeted Jacob and Joseph with very much the same words as they came unto the place he had prepared for them.

The Fruitful

In speaking to his disciples, Jesus says this about fruit in the life of a Christian:

> You did not choose Me, but I chose you, and appointed you, that you should go and bear fruit, and that your fruit should remain, that whatever you ask of the Father in My name, He may give to you (John 15:16 NASB).

As believers, we are appointed by God to bear fruit through our actions, our activities, and, most of all, our ever-deepening relationship with him. He desires that love, joy, kindness, and peace reign in our hearts and be made manifest in our lives. We have a choice: to reap sparingly or bountifully, as the apostle Paul teaches us in 2 Corinthians 9:6. The quality of the harvest is ours to determine by how much we are willing to let the Lord work in our lives. As for me, like Joseph and Jacob, I want to bear fruit for eternity. How about you?

The Fighters

When I am gone, I'd also like to be remembered as one of God's fighters. I don't mean someone who constantly fought against his will, but a person who stood strong in the Lord, battled to uphold the reputation of his word, grasped the darts of Satan in mid-flight and dashed them to the ground. Paul puts it this way in Ephesians 6:10-12:

> Finally, be strong in the Lord, and in the strength of His might. Put on the full armor of God, that you

> may be able to stand firm against the schemes of the devil. For our struggle is not against flesh and blood, but against the rulers, against the powers, against the world forces of this darkness, against the spiritual forces of wickedness in the heavenly places (NASB).

Certainly Jacob and Joseph were fighters. At times they—particularly Jacob—struggled against God's purpose. But ultimately they learned the lesson that fighting for the Lord is far more fulfilling than struggling to thwart him. Cooperation with God beats competition against him every time.

The Finishers

I've asked the Lord to make me faithful, fruitful, a fighter, and, finally, a finisher. As the writer of the book of Hebrews, depicting the way to finish well, exhorts us:

> Let us also lay aside every encumbrance, and the sin which so easily entangles us, and let us run with endurance the race that is set before us, fixing our eyes on Jesus, the author and perfecter of faith, who for the joy set before Him endured the cross, despising the shame, and has sat down at the right hand of the throne of God (Hebrews 12:1-2 NASB).

Jesus is the epitome of one who finished his earthly race magnificently. Just prior to his crucifixion, he prayed to his heavenly father the prayer that is recorded in John 17:4, "I glorified Thee on the earth, having accomplished the work which Thou hast given Me to do" (NASB). And from the cross itself he cried, "*Tetelestai!*" or "It is finished!" (John 19:30 NASB), meaning that his work on earth—that of providing a means of salvation for sinful man—was completely accomplished, once and forevermore.

Singing His Praises

Jacob finished his earthly chores at age 147. Following his father's death, Joseph spent fifty-four years of faithful, uneventful service before crossing his own finish line. They've been in eternity for thousands of years now, together. And I can only imagine that, like Paul and Silas in the depths of a dungeon in Philippi, they're singing praises to the king:

> Praise God, from whom all blessings flow;
> Praise Him all creatures here below;
> Praise Him above, ye heavenly host;
> Praise Father, Son, and Holy Ghost!

Suggested Readings

Barnhouse, Donald Grey. 1971. *Genesis*. Vol. 2. Grand Rapids, MI: Zondervan Publishing House.

Bush, George. 1976. *Notes on Genesis*. Vol. 2. New York: Ivison, Phinney and Co., 1860. Reprint. Minneapolis, MN: James and Klock Publishing Co.

Delitzsch, Franz. 1978. *A New Commentary on Genesis*. Sophia Taylor, trans. Vol. 2. Edinburgh: T. and T. Clark, 1899. Reprint. Minneapolis, MN: Klock and Klock Christian Publishers.

Flynn, Leslie B. 1979. *Joseph: God's Man in Egypt*. Wheaton, IL: Victor Books.

Kidner, Derek. 1975. *Genesis*. The Tyndale Old Testament Commentaries. Downers Grove, IL: Inter-Varsity Press.

Kunz, Marilyn and Catherine Schell. 1969. *Four Men of God: Abraham—Joseph—Moses—David*. Neighborhood Bible Studies. Revised ed. Wheaton, IL: Tyndale House Publishers.

Leupold, H.C. 1942. *Exposition of Genesis*. Vol. 2. Grand Rapids, MI: Baker Book House.

Mackintosh, C.H. 1972. *Genesis to Deuteronomy: Notes on the Pentateuch*. Neptune, NJ: Loizeaux Brothers, Inc.

McGee, J. Vernon. n.d. *Going through Genesis*. Los Angeles: Church of the Open Door.

Meyer, F.B. 1975. *Joseph.* Fort Washington, PA: Christian Literature Crusade.

Palau, Luis, 1976. *The Schemer and the Dreamer.* Portland, OR: Multnomah Press.

Phillips, John. 1980. *Exploring Genesis.* Chicago: Moody Press.

Pink, Arthur W. 1922. *Gleanings in Genesis.* Vol. 2. Chicago: Moody Press.

Ross, Allen P. 1985. *Genesis.* In *The Bible Knowledge Commentary,* edited by John F. Walvoord and Roy B. Zuck, vol. 1. Wheaton, IL: Victor Books.

Scroggie, W. Graham. 1923. *Tested by Temptation.* London: Pickering and Inglis, Ltd.; distributed in U.S. by Christian Literature Crusade, Fort Washington, PA.

Stigers, Harold G. 1976. *A Commentary on Genesis.* Grand Rapids, MI: Zondervan Publishing House.

Swindoll, Charles R. 1982. *Joseph: From Pit to Pinnacle.* Fullerton, CA: Insight for Living.

Thomas, W.H. Griffith. 1946. *Genesis.* Grand Rapids, MI: Wm. B. Eerdmans Publishing Company.

Unger, Merrill. 1966. *Unger's Bible Dictionary.* Third edition. Chicago: Moody Press.

Wood, Leon J. 1975. *Genesis: A Study Guide Commentary.* Grand Rapids, MI: Zondervan Publishing House.

Acknowledgments

Bennett, S.F., and J.P. Webster. "Sweet By and By."
Breck, Carrie E., and Grant Colfax Tullar. "Face to Face."
Brown, Joan Winmill. 1979. *Corrie: The Lives She's Touched.* Minneapolis, MN: World Wide Pictures by special arrangement with Fleming H. Revell Company.
Calkin, Ruth Harms. 1976. *Lord, You Love to Say Yes.* Elgin, IL: David C. Cook Publishing Co. Used by permission.
Carlson, Carole C. 1983. *Corrie ten Boom: Her Life, Her Faith.* Old Tappan, NJ: Fleming H. Revell Company. Used by permission.
DeMoss, Arthur, and Nancy DeMoss, eds. 1972. *The Family Album.* Valley Forge, PA: The Family Album.
Dobson, James. 1970. *Dare to Discipline.* Wheaton, IL: Tyndale House Publishers. Reprint. New York: Bantam Books, Inc.
Elliott, Charlotte, and William B. Bradbury. "Just As I Am, Without One Plea."
Foster, Robert D. 1978. *Has Life Given You a Lemon . . . Make Lemonade.* Colorado Springs, CO: Challenge Books, Ltd.
———. 1973. *When the Ceiling Is Zero.* Chicago: Moody Press.
Gehring, W. Robert. 1985. *Rx for Addiction.* Grand Rapids, MI: Zondervan Books.
Graham, Billy. 1987. *Facing Death and the Life After.* Waco, TX: Word Books. Used by permission.
Gunther, Peter F. comp. 1984. *A Frank Boreham Treasury.* Chicago: Moody Press.
Guest, Edgar A. 1917. *Just Folks.* Chicago: The Reilly and Lee Co.

Iacocca, Lee, and William Novak. 1984. *Iacocca: An Autobiography.* New York: Bantam Books.

Ken, Thomas, and Louis Bourgeois. "Praise God, from Whom All Blessings Flow."

Kipling, Rudyard. "If."

Norman, Larry. 1969. "I Wish We'd All Been Ready." Beechwood Music Corp., J.C. Love Publishing Co.

Powell, Paul W. 1986. *When the Hurt Won't Go Away.* Wheaton, IL: Victor Books.

Rambo, Dottie. 1980. "We Shall Behold Him." Nashville, TN: The John T. Benson Publishing Co./ASCAP.

Sammis, John H. and Daniel B. Towner. "Trust and Obey."

Sterner, John. 1985. *Growing through Mid-Life Crises.* St. Louis, MO: Concordia Publishing House.

Swindoll, Charles R. 1980. *Three Steps Forward, Two Steps Back.* Nashville, TN: Thomas Nelson Publishers.

Unger, Merrill F. 1966. *Unger's Bible Dictionary.* Third edition. Chicago: Moody Press.

Vanauken, Sheldon. 1981. *A Severe Mercy.* New York: Harper and Row, Publishers, Inc., 1977. Reprint. New York: Bantam Books.

Wangerin, Walter. 1987. *As for Me and My House.* Nashville, TN: Thomas Nelson Publishers.